D0710336

CP 1st 10^y

Inside
the Philippine
Revolution

Inside
the Philippine
Revolution

★★★

WILLIAM CHAPMAN

W · W · NORTON & COMPANY
New York London

Copyright © 1987 By William Chapman
All rights reserved.
Published simultaneously in Canada by Penguin Books Canada Ltd., 2801 John
Street, Markham, Ontario L3R 1B4.
Printed in the United States of America.
The text of this book is composed in Cheltenham Book, with display type set
in Cheltenham Outline Shadow. Composition and manufacturing by The Had-
don Craftsmen, Inc.
Book design by Jacques Chazaud.

First Edition

ISBN 0-393-02461-X

W. W. Norton & Company, Inc., 500 Fifth Avenue, New York, N. Y. 10110
W. W. Norton & Company Ltd., 37 Great Russell Street, London WC1B 3NU

1 2 3 4 5 6 7 8 9 0

For my wife, Christine,
and my sons, Peter and Daniel

Inside
the Philippine
Revolution

1

★★★

On December 26, 1968, the anniversary of the birth of Mao Zedong, eleven young Filipino radicals met secretly at a remote spot in Pangasinan Province in Northern Luzon to found a new communist party, the goal of which was to transform the Philippines through armed revolution into a socialist state. They labored for two weeks to produce the Communist Party of the Philippines—Marxist-Leninist (Mao Zedong Thought) and to adopt the revolutionary master plan, which, following the Maoist formula, prescribed a protracted peasant war in the countryside. The semblance of an armed force was formed through a pact with a small, rag-tag band of agrarian rebels loosely affiliated with the nearly defunct Huk guerilla army. When the New People's Army (NPA) was formally chartered in March 1969, its armory consisted of some seventy weapons. From mountain hideouts in central and northern Luzon, it began the people's war to conquer the countryside.

The new cadres established a central base in northern Luzon. Some called it their "Yenan Phase" after Mao's model of an impregnable headquarters in the caves of Shensi. From this base the NPA would advance in wave after wave until the countryside was theirs and the cities encircled. In fact, the new army was hounded from camp to camp by government soldiers. "We were so busy running," one of them recalled years later, "that we had no time to fight." Several were killed and some defected. Most of their documents describing the party program and military strategy were uncovered by troops in a shallow tunnel where a fleeing cadre had tried to hide them. Within weeks, the New People's Army was forced into more remote hideouts in northern Luzon.

In Manila, the communist cause was taken up noisily by thousands of students from the city's best colleges: the University of the Philippines, and the Lyceum. The sons and daughters of elite families demonstrated in the streets by day and met in small cells by night to study Mao's works and to grope for the meaning of the three great evils, "feudalism, imperialism, and bureaucrat capitalism." Sometimes they took field trips to the farms north of the capital where, wearing Mao caps and Mao medallions, they mingled earnestly with the farm workers and their families. Always there were lessons from the *Little Red Book* to be memorized and then shouted, like religious chants, at the bewildered farmers. Friends who did not share their commitment thought their behavior bizarre. They were forever giving one another angry quizzes to determine whether one held the "correct line" or had drifted into "leftist adventurism" or some other deviation.

Sixteen years later, high on a volcanic mountain in the province of Negros Occidental, I met a product of those improbable beginnings. He had been caught up in the anti-American demonstrations of 1969 that swept Manila, where he attended college, and, although never much attracted to Marxist ideology, had become convinced of the necessity for armed revolution to "free" his country from foreign domination. Gradually, he had drifted into the underground movement. In November 1985, Francisco (his party name) was the commander of a guerilla company which had become the terror of the NPA's central front in Negros Occidental. By then in his late thirties, he had spent his adult life in the hills and he spoke casually and without emotion of his unit's successes. They had killed a local mayor suspected of ordering the deaths of nine farmers loyal to the NPA. A few months earlier, they had organized a raid on a maritime academy and seized more than 400 precious weapons without a fight. Then had come the bloody assault in the small town of Isabela, far down the coastal plain. Francisco had led the force which entered the town square late one afternoon and, in a furious gun battle, killed fourteen of the government's elite Scout Rangers.

Francisco led me to the fringe of his camp where a small knoll offered a sweeping view down the mountainside to the plain that stretched away to the Panay Gulf. Beyond a few small farms on the lower slopes extended miles and miles of sugar cane, the crop which provides most Negrenses with a minimal livelihood. The landscape was flecked with small palm-covered shacks where the farmers lived. There, Francisco said, waving a hand toward the lowlands, was the real success of his company's endeavors. The military actions were important, he went on, but what mattered was organizing the people in those hunts to support the cause. From a handful of supporters four years earlier, the popular base in the central front had grown rapidly. Sixty percent of the people living in his front's fourteen towns and cities favored the NPA and sheltered them from the Philippine military. His fighters could walk among them unmolested, assured of safety because townsmen would warn of any military movement in the neighborhood. The people there fed the soldiers, sending bags of rice up the mountain to the base camp, and let them gather in the huts overnight as they planned ambushes of government soldiers. It would not be long, Francisco thought, before every family in this central front would be educated supporters of the NPA, their sons and daughters volunteers in the "armed struggle." There was nothing the military could do about it any longer, he thought, although it was likely the fighting might continue another ten years. "We are growing every day and we know it will come."

The distance Francisco has traveled—from student activist to hardened guerilla commander—is an appropriate measure of one of the world's most unusual and least recognized insurgencies. It began as an amateurish exercise taken from textbook histories of other Third World conflicts and fought by neophytes who scarcely knew one end of an automatic rifle from another. It became a wholly indigenous war waged by

13

seasoned fighters skilled in the arts of ambush, assassination, and armed propaganda. Scattered through the sprawling Philippine archipelago in 1985 were hundreds of Franciscos leading second-generation revolutionaries drawn from peasant and lower-class families. Like him, they were stoic professionals, veterans of hiding and fighting and seemingly prepared to continue for another generation. Their war had cost thousands of lives—their own, government soldiers', and those of the uncommitted innocent caught in crossfires. It was a war of great bravery and much savagery on both sides, one which had taken on a life of its own during nearly two decades, and which appeared to have no end in sight.

By 1986, many large areas of the Philippines, like Negros, were affected by the communist guerillas and their converted citizen allies. Begun in the mountains of northeastern Luzon, the insurgency had edged down the archipelago's eastern provinces and had become deeply rooted in many places. It grew most swiftly in the Bicol region south of Manila; in Samar, an impoverished island in the eastern Visayas; in northern and eastern Mindanao, and in some islands of the western Visayas, such as Negros, and Panay. By the time President Ferdinand E. Marcos was deposed, in February 1986, it was known that the NPA was active in sixty-two of the country's seventy-three provinces and that it controlled or influenced at least twenty percent of the *barangays,* the basic local political units of the Philippines. It had approximately 20,000 full-time armed guerillas in the field and perhaps half that number in armed militia units formed for local protection. Communist party leaders claimed a nationwide "mass base" of a million people, most of them farmers and workers. Although largely inactive in major cities, the movement had achieved remarkable influence in the country's largest southern urban center, Davao City, where huge slum areas and the rural approaches were under party control and NPA "sparrow units," or assassination squads, roamed at will.

As in most guerilla wars, the statistics on troop strength and territory controlled were largely meaningless. On paper, the Armed Forces of the Philippines far outnumbered the rebels, with some 250,000 men under arms and access to an armory of the most modern American-supplied weapons. In a strict military sense, the communists controlled not one square mile of Philippine soil. There was no corner of the archipelago into which the government troops could not enter if they cared to mass sufficient force. The insurgents' *military* war was one of ambushes, raids, and assassinations mounted for one of two purposes: to gather arms or to show their peasant allies that they could be protected and the government forces punished. They followed the cardinal rule of attacking in superior strength and fading back into the forests and fields, giving the government's reenforcements nothing to pursue. Militarily, no terrain was taken, no strongpoints occupied, and the impression was left that neither side had won or lost.

This was classic guerilla war and, despite its growing numbers, the NPA in mid-1986 was not winning it. What it was winning, it seemed to me, was the political war that received far less public attention. For nearly two decades, the cadres had worked in thousands of *barangays* and had won the allegiance of thousands of peasants, farm workers, fishermen, and those who lacked any livelihood. Their successes were uneven, and much of the Philippines, especially the cities, remained outside their grasp. But in village after village, I found the extent of their penetration astonishing. In many, the NPA and its Communist party affiliates were virtually uncontested and in some they were the de facto government, their underground organizations engaged in levying taxes, meeting out punishment, instructing in communal work, and even performing the mundane municipal services of health, sanitation, and medicine.

My trail led me to a fishing village on the southern island of Mindanao, a fitting place from which to reflect on the struggle so ludicrously launched in 1968. Punta Dumalag was a communist showplace, a village so completely dominated by the party that it hardly seemed a Filipino community any longer. A revolutionary underground committee was in total control. It financed the electricity and water systems from extorted "taxes" on businessmen. Its militia policed the streets. Local justice was a party matter, the revolutionary committee determining guilt or innocence in "people's courts." The fishing economy was under communal control. Children from eight to ten years of age formed spy patrols to keep watch on outsiders. Punta Dumalag was no longer part of the battle, for government

15

troops no longer came there and even the NPA, its protection no longer needed, had moved on.

The story of the Philippine insurgency in many ways resembled the other Third World upheavals of the twentieth century, especially those in China, Latin America, and Indochina. The pattern was familiar: Intellectuals and middle-class radicals provide the revolutionary spark, the organizing skills, and the dogma. The poor provide the armed mass. The combination is explosive, for what was before the unfocused resentment of society's poorest members becomes a fighting and educational force with clear goals, a military-political strategy, and the ideological conviction that sustains years of combat. In the early days, Filipino Marxists took their cues from Mao's conquest of China and the revolutions in Cuba and Indochina. Later, the Sandinistan experience in Nicaragua became the admired model. In each, the conditions that transformed peasants into rebels were superficially similar—an impoverished rural class, a repressive military force supporting rich landlords, vestiges of colonialism. When the architect of the Philippine revolution, José Ma. Sison, first read Mao, he was startled by the descriptions of reactionary China in the 1920s and '30s. "I thought," he has said, "that's the Philippines, now."

But most of the world and, indeed, most Filipinos would consider that analogy preposterous. The whole notion of the Philippines as an impoverished Third World nation governed by an irresponsible elite and ripe for Marxist revolution does not fit with our perception of that sprawling island-nation on the Pacific rim. Its major regions—Luzon in the north, the Visayan Islands in the center, and Mindanao in the south—are rich in farmland and amply endowed with almost all of the resources needed by a modern industrial state. Its people are literate and talented, their drive for educational attainments as powerful as those of other Asians. Visitors to Manila find a cosmopolitan capital that blends an energetic modern bustle with a relaxing tropical cadence. The elements of prosperity are everywhere. Indeed, in the 1960s, when the young radicals were plotting their revolt against a society which to them resembled backward China, the Philippines seemed a bright chapter in modernization. They were most often compared not to the economic basket cases of Latin America or Indochina but to the coming colossus seventeen hundred miles north, Japan. Nor was the Philippine republic politically backward. When the United States granted the islands independence in 1946, it left a legacy of democratic practice and popular rule that made the Philippines a model state, or so it seemed. Elections were regularly held, power changed hands peacefully, and the military establishment stayed out of politics. It was the Americans' purpose, devoutly believed in by most thinking Filipinos, that this former colonial nation should remain a "showcase for democracy," an example of political maturity that all developing Asian nations could emulate. And so in 1968, when the young communists declared war on a "fascist" state ruled by corrupt warlords, their behavior seemed not so much threatening as ludicrous. How could one plot a "national-democratic" revolution, as Sison styled it, against a functioning democracy which had governed itself for two decades?

It all seemed ridiculously inappropriate, and for that reason alone the Philippine insurgency was for years not taken seriously. Even as the reports of disturbances and battles mounted in the 1970s, it seemed somehow a made-up affair, a revolution invented by young hotheads who wanted an excuse to fight. Disengaged Manilans looked upon the New People's Army as yet another group of romantic bandits of a type common in Philippine history. There was something un-Filipino about the ideology of class struggle and a war on imperialism. These were foolish, alien concepts much too serious for the Filipino mentality, and the notion that peasants and fishermen might be induced to believe in them seemed absurd. As late as 1984, a Manila intellectual acknowledged the guerillas' appeal to poor farmers in the remote hills, then quickly added: "But of course they *are* Filipinos, after all"—as though their very nationality precluded any serious revolutionary undertaking.

But this view of the Philippine government as a developing democracy moving confidently toward prosperity and egalitarianism was simply not accurate. It was and still is a predominantly poor, rural nation of haves and have-nots, a majority of

17

whose people—perhaps three out of four—live in poverty. There are glittering enclaves in Manila, but seventy percent of Filipinos live in the country: tenant farmers who own nothing more valuable than a carabao, or water buffalo, day laborers for whom $1.50 a day is the standard wage, and the totally unemployed living on handouts and a diet of root crops. In one of Asia's most fertile countries, one that is technically self-sufficient in food, at least seventy percent suffer from malnutrition. Behind the exterior charm of Manila's modernity are more than 200 communities of squatters, landless immigrants living in hovels and searching garbage dumps for food. Nowhere in Asia is the contrast between rich and poor more vivid.

There is a comforting and widespread notion that this poverty and inquality is a legacy of Ferdinand E. Marcos's twenty-year presidency. That also is untrue. The conditions preceded his depredations and unfortunately will remain for many more years. It was in the pre-Marcos years that the Philippine land problem became severe and that the specter of a huge landless underclass first appeared, along with the first arrival of urban squatters. That alarming, widening gap between rich and poor, a gap which conventional economics assumes will narrow with the first signs of development, predated the Marcos era. The 1960s are remembered now as a kind of Philippine Golden Age when a suddenly unleashed entrepreneurial spirit created jobs and the first taste of middle-class prosperity. The statistics show, however, that during the decade, the poorest Filipinos' share of national income sharply declined.

Nor was the pre-Marcos Philippines the leveling democratic society it was pictured to be by political analysts in the Philippines and abroad. To be sure, the democratic forms existed. Poor people did vote. But real politics was an affair of the elite, the rich landlords, and newly arrived business leaders who controlled the selection of candidates. No political party represented the landless. Labor unions were weak, farmers' organizations helpless. Twice, in the 1950s and '60s, pressures from the farm workers forced governments to enact land-reform programs to transfer farms to the peasants. Twice they were whittled to meaningless statements of intent, never to be enforced. Philippine politics was a plaything of the gentry and the commercial classes who catered to the poor at times, because the poor liked to vote and looked upon election days as fiestas, but who never allowed the peasants near the real levers of power.

The Philippines I traveled displayed one more enduring reality, one which made the country vulnerable to a communist appeal as much as its poverty and political powerlessness. This was its utter lawlessness and its remoteness from the normal workings of government. The rural Philippines existed in a kind of civic vacuum where the government's writ did not run and public services were minimal. Armed bandit gangs moved about the hills unhampered, stealing cattle, household goods, and crops. If a farmer had protection, it was because he and his friends provided it in vigilante patrols. Agencies of law enforcement either could not or did not bother to help, and indeed in many places I visited were themselves knee-deep in banditry of a sort. Welfare and other services came rarely and if they came at all they were manipulated for partisan uses by local politicians. Much of the Philippines—especially Mindanao, which has its own peculiar remoteness and Wild West character—simply seemed not a part of a functioning social system.

And so it was not into a model democracy blessed with portents of prosperity that the young communists moved. It was into an impoverished countryside cursed with an almost anarchic criminality and regarded indifferently by the government in Manila. They were the conditions of third-world revolution. The only real mystery is why revolution had not come to the Philippines much earlier.

Until at least late 1986, when this book was completed, the Philippine rebellion seemed to occupy no place in the international scene. It had not become a chapter in the Cold War, largely because the great communist powers, China and Russia, had for years taken no interest in it. The United States government was alarmed by its sudden growth in the 1980s, but recognized it as a local insurgency unsupported by foreign communist parties. With the exception of one purchase of weapons on the international black market, reportedly through the Palestine Liberation Organization, the New People's Army supplied itself with arms. Its nearly exclusive source was the Armed Forces of the Philippines. Automatic rifles, machine guns, and a few mortars were obtained by looting, confiscation on the battlefield, and black-market deals with Philippine soldiers. Almost all of them were of American manufacture because the United States, through arms sales agreements established years earlier, was the major supplier of arms to the Armed Forces of the Philippines. Thus, the American military found itself in the peculiar, perhaps unprecedented, position of arming both combatants.

In the early days, the new Communist Party of the Philippines had received both moral encouragement and a modest amount of material aid from China. Its founders looked to Mao's China as the model for a successful people's war and a few of them had received training there in the 1960s. It was a period in which China, wrestling with the Soviet Union for leadership in Third World revolutions, was eagerly abetting communist movements throughout Southeast Asia and was willing to place a small wager on the unlikely amateurs then clustered on the northern island of Luzon. By the mid-1970s, however, Beijing had made its opening to the West and was seeking better relations with the governments of its Asian neighbors (with the exception of Indochina governments), one price of which was the cessation of support for communist insurgents. The Communist Party of the Philippines (CPP) was left to forge alone.

Because of their ties with China, the Filipino communists naturally had had no connection with the Soviet Union. Their propaganda broad-sheets had slavishly followed Beijing's line in the great Sino-Soviet ideological conflict and referred to Moscow as the fount of "social imperialism," a scourge every bit as dangerous as America's "capitalist imperialism." Nikita Khrushchev, by intermittently seeking peace with the West, was the evil agent of a great sell-out, and the country of the much admired Lenin was no longer entitled to lead Third World insurgencies. Moreover, the Philippine Communist party was itself born of a fierce internecine conflict within an older, Stalinist party that had been founded in Manila in the 1930s, one which had withered to a state of impotence when the young Maoist firebrands came along. Moscow had continued to support, on

20

paper at least, that older party, even though its aging leaders' radicalism had decayed to the point that they found nothing wrong with embracing Ferdinand E. Marcos.

But sometime in the 1980s this equation began to change. Labels such as "social imperialism" disappeared from the CPP's tracts, and although certain Soviet actions, like the invasion of Afghanistan, were censured, a warming trend toward Moscow could be discerned. The suspicion grew that the Philippine party, desperate to build its under-armed NPA, was willing to bury old theoretical disputes and do business at last with the Soviets. It was clear in my early interviews with middle-level party cadres that some change was in the wind. They routinely spoke of accepting aid from foreign sources so long as no strings were attached. Even the Soviet Union? So long as no strings were attached.

It was Satur Ocampo who first made this revisionism explicit. Ocampo, a former newspaperman who had gone underground after martial law was proclaimed, was, in mid-1986, a top leader of the National Democratic Front, the party-controlled popular front organization, and the single party official in those days who spoke confidently and publicly about CPP policies. He had become especially prominent after President Marcos was deposed in February 1986, and when I met him was preparing to open negotiations with the government of President Corazon Aquino, negotiations which, incidentally, he did not expect to succeed. We met in the home of a party member's relative in suburban Manila for dinner one evening and he talked at length of the party's new opening to the world.

In the past, our lack of ties to foreign governments was a kind of moral point with us. It made us independent. It also demolished any notion of the government prosecuting us under the anti-subversion act if we were caught, because the act specifies foreign subversion.

We are now reviewing this party line, the international line. Some of us think the line is too fuzzy. We are proud that we got this far through our own efforts, but we need to establish links with other revolutionary movements, like Salvador, for example.

21

The sticking point for us with the Soviets was always its support for the PKP [the older, nearly defunct Philippine Communist party]. But it is almost irrelevant now and so we no longer find this to be a big issue.

Would the CPP accept arms from the Russians?

We are not actively seeking aid from the Soviets, but we would accept all forms of aid if there were no strings attached. If the USSR offered it, we would accept.

Had contact been made with the Soviets to discuss this?

There have been indications before that they were interested in political relations with us, but nothing has come of it yet. This new development [the fall of Marcos] changes things and we do not know what to expect.

The Pentagon had spoken forcefully of giving more military aid to the Philippines to combat the communist insurgency. Ocampo said it was in this context of a greater Philippine military dependence on the United States that the CPP was reexamining its old policy toward the Soviet Union. New, more sophisticated weapons for the Armed Forces of the Philippines would seem to justify the communists' reliance for the first time on their own foreign sources:

Getting more sophisticated arms is now a real question for us. With the [growth] of the NPA, we must face the question of new sources of sophisticated guns. We are now in a new context, of fighting against the American arms given to the AFP. There is this threat not only of more American arms but also, we think, the possibility of American intervention. So, although we had no links to foreign powers in the past, we could do so now, because of the new context of American arms and intervention.

For a dozen years after the new communist adventure was launched, the government of the United States regarded it as a trifling affair. It generally accepted the Philippine military's version of events, which was that the New People's Army was an unthreatening assortment of poorly armed mavericks roaming the hills. President Marcos, who had used the NPA as an excuse to declare martial law, routinely pronounced the rebellion crushed. The large American embassy on Roxas Boulevard, with its splendid view of Manila Bay, hardly kept track at all. One summer day in 1979, I asked a military attaché in the embassy to assess the insurgency. He drew from a shelf above his desk a scrapbook of yellowing newspaper clippings describing the occasional encounters in the hills. He handed it to me, explaining that his information on the NPA was mostly contained in its pages.

Gradually, however, indifference gave way to alarm and finally to something near panic. In 1981, embassy cables to Washington began describing an insurgency spreading throughout the archipelago, from Luzon, its birthplace, to the central Visayan Islands of Samar, Panay, Negros, and then to the large southern island of Mindanao. Estimates of NPA armed strength soared, and in February 1984, a new embassy expert on insurgencies put the total at about 12,500 and growing fast. A year later, the Pentagon was using estimates nearly twice as high. The picture presented in Washington briefings on the Philippines changed to one of a friendly Asian nation nearly engulfed in communist revolution. Shades of Vietnam. In October 1984, the assistant secretary of defense Richard L. Armitage informed Congress that the NPA was expanding swiftly and "could tip the balance of military power within the next several years."[1] One year later, the Senate Committee on Intelligence distributed a staff report predicting that unless something was done the insurgency would force a fundamental change in government within three years.[2]

There was nothing mysterious about the reasons for Washington's alarm; there were two of them: Subic Naval Base, on the western coast of Luzon, and Clark Air Base not far away. They are the two most important American bases in the Pacific and had become, after the fall of South Vietnam and the removal of air bases in Thailand, the only significant military installations in that part of the world. Always viewed, at least by the United States Navy and Air Force, as the twin pillars of American military power in the Pacific, they had by the mid-1980s been ascribed even more importance in the global con-

23

test with the Soviet Union. Subic and Clark became the bases from which the United States could extend its power into the Indian Ocean and the Persian Gulf, where for a time it seemed the two superpowers were most likely to collide. And then came a sudden change in the regional balance. For years, Subic and Clark had given the United States a near monopoly of power there. The USSR had nothing to compare. But the rapid expansion of Soviet air and naval bases in Vietnam, especially at the former American enclave on Cam Ranh Bay, ended that era of dominance. In the Pentagon's strategic planning, the bases in the Philippines became not merely important but priceless, and their loss catastrophic.

Preserving the bases had been the overriding principle of American policy in the Philippines since World War II and with the loss of Vietnam this became a fixation. But a minority of Filipinos, composed of several distinguished political and business leaders, felt the presence of Subic and Clark was an infringement on national sovereignty. Many also believed they made the Philippines a pawn in the Cold War, a "magnet" for Soviet attack. In the 1960s, a great nationalist tide swept the country, demanding an end to American influence in general and the removal of the bases in particular. The new Communist party born in 1968 was one manifestation of that challenge.

Ferdinand E. Marcos was in many ways an embarrassment to the American interests. He was corrupt; he dismantled the democratic structures Americans prided themselves in having bequeathed the country; he ran a venal government and an abusive military and his tenure reduced an already poor country to near insolvency. But he was a safe bet on the only issue which really mattered: the bases at Subic and Clark. From time to time, Washington would try to prod Marcos to reform, at least to stop the military's torture of civilians and other human rights abuses. A skillful blackmailer, Marcos would remind them of the bases, remind them that he stood foursquare for their preservation, and suggest that without his steady support their leases might not be renewed. The United States might toy with lending encouragement to opposition politicians, those out-of-power former senators who despised Marcos. They were good democrats who believed in civil liberties. But many were not sound on the bases issue. Indeed, several had built early careers by demanding that they go. And so the United States and Marcos were locked into an arrangement that endured, an uncomfortable arrangement in many ways from the American point of view, but one which served the interests of both. As late as March 1985, when the house of cards began to tremble, the State Department did not want to see the basic alliance disturbed, did not want Marcos out. "While President Marcos at this stage is part of the problem," said a State memorandum outlining reforms that were needed, "he is also necessarily part of the solution."[3] The communist insurgency intruded on this arrangement, faintly at first and then alarmingly. The educated cadres who led the peasant rebellion were veterans of that nationalist crusade of the 1960s. Most had been ardent nationalists before they became convinced Marxists and their political initiation had come from the street protests which demanded that the bases be removed along with other vestiges of what they called American "neo-colonialism." They spent years politicizing remote Philippine villages with the idea that American imperialists were as much responsible for rural poverty as feudal landlords. And their national-front propaganda dwelled endlessly on this theme. In Vietnam, the communists had succeeded in part by capturing control of the nationalist movement, had come to be perceived as the only meaningful agent of anticolonialism. Replicating that achievement in the Philippines was the principal strategy of the CPP's National Democratic Front.

The United States officials with whom I talked never feared an outright *military* victory by the communist NPA. At least, not so long as it lacked a foreign supply of weapons. What they did fear was a *political* victory, some set of events in which the Communist party would become organizationally strong enough to impose an anti-American orientation on any government which succeeded Marcos's. During the 1980s, American embassy public information surveys detected a sharp change in the level of popular support for the bases; in Manila, the proportion favoring renewal of the base leases declined from a comfortable to a bare majority. This was not thought to be a result of communist proselytism; rather, it seemed to reflect the increasing conviction of ordinary citizens that the United States kept Marcos in power only to maintain the leases on Subic and

Clark. If allied with the communists' growing control of the countryside, this shift in attitudes could spell doom for American interests under future governments. The analysis by the staff of the Senate Select Committee on Intelligence in October 1985, put the point starkly:

In the increasingly confrontational political climate, even a democratic successor regime would find it difficult to accept continued U.S. use of the bases under present terms. To protect its nationalist credentials, a new government would demand that Washington renegotiate the lease or leave.[4]

In other words, a moderate post-Marcos government might have to make a deal with the communists. "What we fear most," said an American diplomat, "is an accommodation." That remark was made in August 1986, six months after Marcos was deposed and a new government was struggling to take over.

The American reader will see in the foregoing synopsis a drearily familiar pattern. A friendly country of considerable value to the United States in global politics is threatened by a communist guerilla army. The revolutionaries, led by educated radicals skilled in propaganda and grassroots organization, enlist wide support among a landless underclass whose poverty is the result of feudal exploitation and indifference. The armed rebels are strong in some places, weak in others, and conclude that a military victory will be ever out of reach without stustained support from abroad. Warily, but with diminishing reluctance, they turn to that foreign force, the Soviet Union, which has the most to gain from their success. This is a prescription for transforming a local Third World rebellion into another ugly chapter in the Cold War, with the Philippines becoming one more marker in the game played by the superpowers. As this book was being completed, there was no reliable evidence that the Soviet Union would enter the game overtly, although intelligence reports described its apparent growing interest in the Philippine radicals.

Many believed that this scary equation had been lastingly altered by the coming to power, in February 1986, of Corazon

Aquino. A bright and determined woman, she seemed honestly devoted to the cause of reconciliation and peace. Her public statements suggested that she understood the roots of the rebellion were imbedded in generations of poverty and injustice. She had deposed a corrupt and impotent regime that had made the communists' task of politicization easier, and that had enabled communism to appear as the only means of deliverance. She promised elections, economic growth, and a more equitable distribution of the good things in life for all Filipinos.

Aquino's accession seemed to some Americans a validation of an old idea. During part of the cold war, the United States had sought to foster in former colonial countries what was known as a "third force." An idea now largely discredited by events, it presumed that America could help to erect progressive, democratic governments with western values and through them provide an alternative to communism. Marxism would lose its appeal to those rising nationalist forces seeking to erase the vestiges of colonialism. The concept failed in Vietnam. The place where it once seemed a success was the Philippines where, in the 1950s, a forceful American intervention helped a popular president, Ramon Magsaysay, defeat a local communist movement. Some saw in the victory of Corazon Aquino the opportunity to replay those events and they believed that a revival of American intervention could recreate the success of the 1950s.

But the Philippines has changed much in three decades and not the least of the changes is the diminished ability of the United States to influence events there. Its influence was already declining in the late 1960s amid the nationalist resurgence of which the then tiny communist movement was a part. It was further reduced in the Marcos years when a great many Filipinos, only a minority of them communists, came to judge the United States as unreliable and hypocritical, a nation preaching democracy but bound by its narrow interests to support a tyrant. That feeling was strong among many in the Aquino government. One of the healthier aspects of her victory was a resurfacing nationalism which insisted that for better or worse the new era demands that Filipinos work out their own destiny and decide for themselves what part the communist movement will have in it. That was the real meaning of her administration's patient efforts to negotiate a truce with the communist party's front, the National Democratic Front. In the drama still unfolding in late 1986, it is difficult to imagine what, if any, role remains for the United States to profitably play.

2

★★★

On a steamy day in the summer of 1946, with the rubble of Manila still visible, the Republic of the Philippines celebrated independence with the inauguration of its first president. It was an event unlike most separations from a colonial past in the fact that the former colonial power was letting go willingly and with pride in its benefactions, which were honored that day with as much fervor as the new nation's birth. Looking proudly on the inaugural ceremony near Manila Bay were Gen. Douglas MacArthur, American proconsul of the prewar dependency who for most Filipinos was a national hero, and Paul V. McNutt, the last in a chain of governors and high commissioners which stretched back to the conquest of 1898. General MacArthur was at his hyperbolic peak as the American flag was hauled down and the Philippine flag raised. "Let history record this event in flaming letters as depicting a new height of nobility in the relationship between two separate and distinct peoples of the earth, peoples of the East and peoples of the West," he declared.[1] Sirens blared and church bells pealed and the country's new president responded in kind. "In the hearts and minds of Filipinos," said Manuel A. Roxas, "the stars and stripes flies more triumphantly than ever before." Even the date bespoke an unusual fondness between the two countries. It was July 4 and it had been deliberately selected as Philippine Independence Day to emphasize the shared history, ideals, and aspirations of the former colony and one-time ruler.[2]

The new president had good reason to celebrate the past in a spirit of friendship. A prewar patrician, Roxas had been an aide and confidant to General MacArthur and, like other native oligarchs, had prospered under the stability of the colonial period. He also had been a collaborator with the Japanese during the occupation and might well have been put in a prison cell, rather than the presidential box. Instead of punishment, he had received only help and encouragement from his old friend MacArthur whose influence spared him from arrest and assisted his presidential campaign. Roxas that day repaid his American benefactors handsomely. "The world cannot but have faith in America," he said. "For our part, we cannot but place our trust in the good intentions of the nation which has been our friend and protector for forty-eight years. To do otherwise would be to foreswear all faith in democracy, in our future and in ourselves."[3]

Millions of Filipinos shared in the euphoria, for reasons both heartfelt and pragmatic. The obvious reason was that MacArthur and American soldiers had fulfilled their promise to return to the islands and drive away the Japanese invaders, so the war had ended with the two countries allied in victory. It might have been otherwise. Many Filipinos had been dismayed and angered in 1942 when the United States had abandoned them to Japanese conquest and had chosen to fight first for Europe. Their freedom had been relegated to a lower priority and the awareness of that hard fact stung. But tens of thousands of them had believed in MacArthur's promise of deliverance with sufficient conviction to fight the Japanese from mountain camps, often accepting instructions that he radioed from Australia. Thousands had been killed or cruelly tortured. But the survivors had fought well and it had been Philippine guerillas who guided American forces the last miles from Lingayen Gulf to the outskirts of Manila. The war had ended in a spirit of jubilant unity that was still present on Independence Day.

The more practical reason was that impoverished Filipinos

desperately needed American aid and financial assistance. The war had left the country a basket case. Millions were hungry to the point of starvation and the price of rice had soared out of reach. Railways, electric power stations and factories had been destroyed by the Japanese, and the country's always modest manufacturing base was in ruins. A final, suicidal effort by the Japanese air force and navy to hold Manila had provoked days of furious house-to-house fighting and American bombing. Manila suffered more wartime damage than any world capital except Warsaw. Hundreds of millions of American dollars would be needed to fight off starvation and disease and to make the first tentative advances toward economic recovery. Filipinos hoped Uncle Sam would be generous. Had not President Roosevelt, in the early days of the war, promised to compensate them for every loss, down to the last water buffalo? The new government expected the United States both to grant large amounts of direct assistance and to compel the defeated Japanese to contribute millions more in reparations.

The cheerful optimism of that Fourth of July did not endure, largely because of certain demands the United States chose to impose on its former colony and wartime ally. For nearly a half-century, the United States had had certain uses, economic and strategic, for this nicely placed Pacific archipelago and had enjoyed certain benefits from its colonial status. These, it turned out, were not destined to expire with the grant of independence. Two forces acted to retain them. One was composed of American businessmen who wished to recapture advantages they had enjoyed in the colonial period and who had the friends in Congress to see that this would be done. The second was Washington's new concern with international communism, a concern that almost overnight transformed the Philippines into a front in the Cold War. Specifically, these pressures required the fragile new nation to grant its former sovereign both extraordinary economic privilege and military bases on its soil. Sometimes grudgingly, sometimes willingly, Philippine leaders accepted almost all of these impositions, believing acquiescence necessary to keep the friendship of the strongest Pacific power. Officially, the two countries would remain close friends despite the evident domination of Washington. But the events of the late 1940s produced strains and an underlying bitterness—a feeling of many Filipinos that they had been forced, while weak, to bow too low—that would be sources of trouble for years to come.

For those who like to read history as a series of grand designs logically conceived and systematically carried out, the American conquest of the Philippine Islands in 1898 is not a glorious chapter. Americans never quite understood why they conquered some seven million non-English-speaking natives halfway around the globe and lacked a consistent plan for dealing with them afterward. We were reluctant imperialists in those days, despite all of the comforting blather about Manifest Destiny and bearing the white man's burden. Most Americans—including, initially, President McKinley, who called them those "darned islands"—scarcely knew where the Philippines were. In Washington, dusty old maps and coastal surveys were unrolled to discover just what it was that our military forces had annexed. Mr. Dooley, Finley Peter Dunne's barroom philosopher, caught the confusion of the times precisely: "I've been r-readin' about th' country," he explained. "'Tis over beyant ye'er left shoulder whin ye're facin' east. Jus' throw ye'er thumb back, an' ye have it as ac'rate as anny man in town."[4]

Many noble motives were asserted to explain this colonial adventure, but none withstood examination for even a few years. Some Americans wanted to Christianize the heathen, but that hardly made sense for a people who had been Christianized by the Spanish more than three centuries before. Or was the purpose to defeat the Spanish fleet as part of the global war to free Cuba? It had taken Admiral Dewey but a few hours to dismantle Spain's wretched little Pacific Navy in Manila Bay. Or to bring independence to an oppressed victim of colonialism? Filipinos themselves had all but accomplished that with Gen. Emilio Aguinaldo's insurrection by the time Dewey arrived in May 1898. Even the base and pragmatic motives did not stand up very long after annexation was complete. Theodore Roosevelt had envisioned the islands as the site of a great Pacific naval base extending the United States' power into Asia. He soon had second thoughts. By 1907, as president, Roosevelt had decided that the Philippines were an "Achilles heel" which might draw this country into a war with Japan. Even those whose eyes glistened with dreams of great profits to be wrung from the islands were proved wrong. Except for a few who persevered, American businessmen rather quickly lost interest in the Philippines and the predicted deluge of American investments never materialized.

For Filipinos who had watched Asia's first war of national liberation brutally crushed, the shock and bitterness were at first great. Gradually, they came to terms with the new imperialists who were, on the whole, more congenial than the old ones. Gone was the power of the hated Spanish friars who through the centuries had taken the choicest lands. The old rulers had belittled the natives' desire to speak Spanish; the Americans sent teachers of English by the boatload. Reconciliation was easiest for the colony's native elite, the *ilustrados* and the *mestizo,* owners of great *haciendas,* who found their lot not greatly changed and who moved quickly to accommodate the interests of the newcomers. They had been uncomfortable all along with the plebian insurrectionists who had begun the revolution against Spain. The flame of nationalism was lowered as Filipinos of all classes found ways of accepting the new colonial master. But the desire for independence remained a strong emotional force and endured as virtually the only political issue, one which no aspiring colonial politician could ignore until the American flag was hauled down in 1946.

This persistent nationalism might have created a deep hostility between Filipinos and their new sovereign, provoking a prolonged resistance. That did not happen largely because of the commendable restraint and considerable hypocrisy exhibited by leaders on both sides. William Howard Taft, who was appointed president of a civilian commission to administer the colony, became quickly popular when he announced a policy of "Philippines for the Filipinos" and encouraged the belief that the United States favored eventual independence. But Taft, spelling out the fine print, stated that colonial control should ultimately end "unless it shall seem wise to the American and Filipino peoples, on account of mutually beneficial trade relations, that the bond shall not be completely severed."[5] Taft seems to have recognized that Americans would not tolerate forever an exercise in imperialism and so he conceived the policy of "attraction." By this he meant that Philippine leaders could be led to appreciate, through a sensitive commercial policy, that their country's interests and hopes for prosperity would be best served by continued American sovereignty. In plain terms, the islands' elite was to be co-opted.

On the Philippine side, Manuel L. Quezon and Sergio Osmena, two *mestizo* politicians who were to dominate the nation's affairs for nearly four decades, skillfully did their part to bridge the independence issue. They were among the loudest in demanding immediate independence, having led their new *Nacionalista* party to victory in 1907 assembly elections by whipping a more moderate party which supported only eventual sovereignty. By doing so, they captured the issue of nationalism and manipulated it to their advantage by publicly clamoring for Washington to pronounce a specific schedule for the grant of independence. Privately, however, Quezon intimated that this was a matter of no great urgency. He seems to have changed his own mind several times and one American scholar of the period doubted that this masterful tactician really desired early independence. Quezon could never admit to his vacillation publicly. To do so would have outraged more militant nationalists and spoiled a brilliant career.[6]

With such polished dissembling by both parties, the ruler and the ruled settled down to what in many ways was a rewarding co-existence. There were visible gains for the islands. Americans built schools, roads, bridges and harbors and raised the levels of health services and education. English came close to becoming a national language, although Spanish remained the preferred tongue of the intelligentsia. Americans insisted on separation of church and state, thus moving the reactionary Catholic hierarchy to the fringes of politics, and retrieved thousands of acres of prime farm land owned by the friars. Washington retained essential political control through a governor-general and the higher civil service, but in 1916, with an anti-imperialist in the White House, a Democratic appointee turned over many senior positions to Filipinos. The Americans were condescending masters, often treating their wards as mere children, but by the standards of older imperial powers, were gentle. They fended off the more gross forms of commercial exploitation. Most important of all, they brought democratic politics to the Filipinos who embraced it with exhilaration. Election day became a kind of fiesta, full of excitement. It was also, already, a day of corruption, bombast and hypocrisy, but the play of politics suited the Filipino. Sometimes Americans thought they played at it too much. When Quezon proposed a national referendum on the independence issue, in April 1927, a grouchy President Coolidge enjoined Filipinos to think less of politics and more of stable government.

One purpose of these American beneficences was to win the hearts of Filipinos so that they would be inclined to accept a more or less permanent colonial status—the policy of "attraction" laid down by Taft and other Republicans. The core of that policy was aimed at the conservative elite which was encouraged to recognize that its interest lay in becoming a fixed part of the American economic system. The key to that system was reciprocal free trade; the products of each country were accepted into the other with few tariffs or other restrictions. In the bluntest terms, Philippine landlords and their business associates would discover a free-market system profitable, their resistance to the arguments of ardent nationalists would be stiffened, and they would direct the country along the Taftian line of permanent retention by the United States. Years later, Filipino communists would cite this strategy as a sample of colonialism at its most devious. Taft considered it just and wise. "If we bring them behind the tariff wall, if they see that association with the United States is beneficial to them . . . it is unlikely they will desire full independence," he explained candidly in 1904.[7] Naturally, it would be good economic policy for Americans as well. The Philippines would become valuable both as a market for goods manufactured in the United States and as a home for the investment of surplus American capital.

Quezon and other *Nacionalistas* immediately saw the dangers of reciprocal free trade to the cause of eventual independence. One of Quezon's more prophetic acts was to oppose the offer of free tariffs, picturing it as a threat to the cause his party espoused. Free trade would open up his country to monopolistic control by powerful American corporations against which domestic business could not compete. Philippine business interests, in turn, would become totally dependent on U.S. markets and, in time, would be so eager to preserve those markets that they would oppose independence. "I fought the measure [in the Philippine Assembly] upon the ground that free trade relations between our countries would result in making the Philippines absolutely dependent upon the markets of the United States," Quezon wrote in his autobiography. "This, I contended, would create a most serious situation in Philippine economic life, especially when the time came for the granting of independence."[8]

The American Congress ignored this opposition and in 1909 enacted the Payne-Aldrich Tariff Act and the accompanying Philippine Tariff Act. They were probably the most important actions of the entire colonial period because they shaped the islands' economic structure for decades to come. American consumer goods flowed untaxed into the Philippines while Philippine agricultural commodities and raw materials flowed into the U.S. As anticipated, U.S. manufacturers obtained virtual monopolies in the Philippines, stifling local attempts to establish an industrial base. Philippine growers of sugar, tobacco, coconuts, and hemp benefitted greatly from the assured markets and they converted large tracts of land to the production of those crops. The acts of 1909 tied the Philippines to the American economy just as Taft had foreseen and as Quezon had feared. Moreover, they strongly reenforced the economic pattern that already had been developing in the colony—the pattern of large farms dependent on the export of commodities to a single market and a non-existent base for manufacturing finished goods.

With this economic relationship settled, the Philippines ceased to be a significant issue in the United States for at least two decades. Americans simply lost interest. Congressional debate on the colony tended to revolve around minor tariff revisions and featured undignified squabbles among competing farm interests. Not a single congressional visit was made to the islands between the time of annexation and passage of the independence legislation in the mid-1930s. American business, which had been expected to make large investments there, generally ignored the Philippines. The argument over independence churned on and on. Democrats, under President Wilson, finally reached a consensus that the country was capable of governing itself, only to be reversed by Republican administrations who fended off independence for more than a decade. Throughout this period, Filipinos waited with official impatience and private apprehension for the day of deliverance.

When it came at last, the cutting of the colonial tie was accomplished in a tawdry assertion of American economic self-interest. The United States did not so much grant independence to the Philippines as cast her away like an unwanted fish plucked from the Pacific. The Great Depression had brought together an alliance of interest groups who deemed themselves harmed by the colonial relationship and who were determined to get rid of the economic competition that relationship had sponsored. American sugar beet growers objected to Philippine sugar imports. Dairymen feared coconut oil would damage their oleomargarine market. Tobacco growers, cottonseed crushers and domestic cordage producers joined the throng and by 1929 the American Farm Bureau Federation was demanding immediate independence. American labor organizations, claiming that free immigration of Filipinos endangered scarce American jobs, added their voice, and so did a few patriotic societies. As the depression became more severe, this alliance encountered little opposition in Congress where its spokesmen turned on the Philippines as if they were some hostile power. The Philippines, said Senator Heflin of Alabama, were a "millstone" weighing down American agriculture. Senator Long of Louisiana called on Congress to grant immediate independence to get the colony "out of the way."[9] Independence, when it came, was not the noble act of a generous power. It was granted in the same haste and callous spirit with which the American adventure in colonialism had begun.[10]

The postwar troubles began in the spring of 1946 in Washington where Congress passed two interlocking pieces of legislation which were signed by President Truman two months before Manual Roxas was sworn in. The Philippine Rehabilitation Act provided compensation for those who had suffered damage as a result of the Japanese invasion and occupation and it was intended as a reward for those who had remained loyal to the United States. To Filipinos it was objectionable on several counts. It provided for a total compensation of $620 million, far less than they had expected (damage claims submitted amounted to twice that amount). From that sum, moreover, payments would be made to foreign nationals as well as to Filipinos, so that American business interests which had suffered damages in the Philippines would siphon off a large share. Worst of all, no payment exceeding $500 would be made until the Philippine government acceded to the terms of an executive agreement. That agreement was to cover trade and economic relations between the two countries as spelled out in a separate piece of legislation.

This second law, the Philippine Trade Act, went far toward restoring the trade and investment benefits which American companies had enjoyed during the colonial era. It permitted the unlimited importation into the Philippines of American goods, duty-free, for eight years, after which time those goods would be subject to only partial tariffs for two decades. The Philippines were thus secured as a free trade zone for American goods while those from other countries were subject to tariffs and other restrictions. Similar U.S. tariff benefits were conferred on some products exported from the Philippines. These principally assisted the islands' sugar industry, some of which was also owned by American companies. A second and more onerous feature tied the value of the Philippine peso to that of the American dollar indefinitely. This, of course, was intended to assure American firms that they would be able to remit profits from investments in that country without fear of currency exchange losses. The linking of the peso and the dollar was so grossly unfair to a struggling undeveloped country and so contrary to the American policy being preached elsewhere in the world that the U.S. Treasury Department strongly objected, to no avail. Congressional supporters explained the linkage was necessary to encourage investment. The effect of both these measures was to deprive the Philippines of import and currency exchange controls, the essential elements of economic planning in a developing country, then and now.

The most humiliating feature of the trade act, however, was a provision that became known as "parity." It declared that American entrepreneurs would enjoy the same rights as Filipinos in developing and exploiting all timber, mineral and agricultural lands and would be similarly entitled to own and operate public utilities. The effect would be to provide American companies, with their large pools of capital and great expertise, an easy opportunity to dominate the few sectors of the Philippine economy that might become profitable. They could log and mine and grow plantation crops with cheap local labor just as they had in the prewar colony. The parity clause was so blatant a give-away to American interests that even the U.S. Chamber of Commerce opposed it and lawmakers who witnessed the skillful lobbying that produced it were shocked. "Their whole philosophy," said Senator Millard Tydings of Maryland, "is to keep the Philippines economically even though we lose them politically."[11]

The two statutes, taken together, amounted to a cunning piece of legislative blackmail. If Filipinos wanted the sweet meats of the Rehabilitation Act, small as they were, they had to first swallow the bitter fruit of the Trade Act. The price of obtaining war-damage compensation, which an American president had called their just reward, was acceptance of vestiges of economic colonialism they thought had disappeared with independence. Moreover, the parity clause of the Trade Act clashed with provisions of the 1935 Philippine constitution which required native Filipino control of at least sixty percent of any enterprise. To comply with the Trade Act and become entitled to the compensation money, then, the Philippines had to rewrite its constitution. Ever obliging, President Roxas initiated a constitutional amendment that would eliminate the sixty percent rule and legitimize the parity clause. There was of course much opposition. When it appeared that the final vote in the Philippine congress on a resolution proposing the amendment would be close, Roxas managed to refuse seats in the lower house to six leftists and two *Nacionalistas* on flimsy charges of election fraud.

The second post-independence event which was to haunt both countries was the establishment of permanent American military bases. For most of the colonial era the United States had been ambivalent about the utility of the Philippines as a military outpost, a major concern being that it might draw America into an unwanted Asian war. In 1933, Quezon's government had rejected the first independence bill enacted by Congress in part because it permitted permanent retention of military bases. The United States willingly modified that section in the Tydings-McDuffie Act of 1934, agreeing to settle the question of naval facilities through later negotiations. By 1943, however, U.S. military leaders had decided that future bases would be absolutely necessary to support a postwar military presence in Asia. Quezon and Sergio Osmena, then in exile in the United States, both agreed. After the war, President Roxas, too, was of course amenable.

The Military Bases Agreement, signed in March 1947, provided virtually all that the War Department wanted. It granted ninety-nine years unhampered jurisdiction over sixteen base facilities, including a huge naval reservation at Subic Bay and the one hundred thirty thousand-acre Clark Air Base in central Luzon. By that time, the Cold War had begun and Washington had determined that the Philippines must be a Far East bastion against international communism. The bases, together with those in occupied Japan, would be the forward wall of defense against aggression by the Soviet Union. At no time was it asserted that the bases were for the protection of the Philippines; all agreed there was no perceptible military threat to that country from any source. The former high commissioner for the Philippines, McNutt, even acknowledged that the bases were not for the defense of the United States either—they were merely to be supply and staging facilities for the support of American Far East forces.[12] The agreement was reached with very little public fuss at the time and not for several years were Filipinos to take note of the fact that sovereignty over a considerable portion of their soil had been ceded without their advice or consent.

Although the economic arrangements, particularly the one granting parity rights to American businessmen, had occasioned some opposition, the postwar agreements and treaties with the United States were in the main passively received. The Filipinos' silence was explained by their desperate economic condition. They were literally too weak to protest. There was also still a strong inclination to trust the American people and to believe in that supposed mutuality of national interests of which Roxas preached. Some Philippine historians would later look back on the half-decade after the war's end as evidence

40

of the Filipinos' peculiar pliancy—their chronic "virus of capitulationism," as one called it—which had led them to accept American colonialism and justified collaboration with the Japanese.

The Filipinos [historian Teodoro A. Agoncillo wrote], childlike as they have always been, with an innocence that is at once touching and exasperating, trusted the American sense of justice and fair play too much and found themselves victims of their own delusion which still afflicts many of them to this day. It was thus that [for] approximately five years after the painful liberation of 1945, they swallowed their pride and self-respect and with misgivings accepted American impositions in order to survive.[13]

Acquiescence soon faded, however, and those "American impositions" became the objects of sharp debate. At first, it took the form of almost scholarly dissection of the postwar Trade Act, the Military Bases Agreement, and the Philippine-American Mutual Defense Treaty which was signed in 1951. The new nationalist criticism held that all of these had compromised Philippine independence and had been inflicted on a weak and helpless country still accustomed to taking orders from Washington. Gradually the debate was broadened and was taken up in political campaigns and in the lively press, where the objects of derision often were Filipino leaders who had done Americans' bidding in the crucial years after the war. Lawyers, professors, journalists and a number of businessmen joined in. The new nationalists were men of prominence in the professions and political figures of importance. Although they never achieved direct political power they were able, as the 1950s wore on, to direct the course of political debate along nationalist lines, and their impact on the first post-independence generation of Filipinos was immense.

The most brilliant polemicist of the lot was Sen. Claro M. Recto, an attorney with sharp analytical talents and great oratorical flair. His pre-independence political career had included many high positions, including leadership of the 1935 convention which drafted the Philippine constitution. It also displayed a chameleonlike adaptibility to whomever wielded power, domestic or foreign. When Washington was still calling the shots in 1935, Senator Recto welcomed a visiting American delegation with this obsequious message: "You who have been our conquerors could have become ruthless and followed a policy of imperialism. However, everyone knows that the policy of the United States towards the Philippines has always been one of benevolence and disinterestedness."[14] The Japanese occupation found Recto a compliant collaborator. Appointed foreign minister in the puppet cabinet, he praised Japan's "benign policy" and its "unselfish guidance and leadership."[15] Arrested on twenty-six counts of treason after the war, he won eventual dismissal of the charges by claiming that he had secretly cooperated with the Philippine resistance and had collaborated only to lessen Japanese cruelty. His postwar anti-Americanism, some believed, stemmed from his imprisonment by U.S. military forces while other collaborators, like Roxas, had gone free. Whatever the cause, Recto emerged in the 1950s as the leading nationalist critic and turned his considerable wit and sarcasm on all of the postwar agreements.

Recto launched his crusade in April, 1949, in a university commencement address lamenting his government's acceptance of both the parity clause of the Trade Act and the military bases agreement.

To secure the continued enjoyment of the American market and those marvelous American assembly lines, without whose preferences and advantages it seemed that we might perish, or at least suffer, we granted Americans the right of citizens in our own country for the exploitation and enjoyment of the national patrimony. We sacrificed our sovereignty over strategic bases within our frontiers. . . . The world was thus presented with the admirable phenomenon of a new nation more dependent, and more willingly dependent, on its former sovereign after independence than before.[16]

Two years later, Recto delivered his most memorable critique on both American bullying and Philippine subservience. "Our Mendicant Foreign Policy," an address given at the University of the Philippines where many of his admirers taught and studied, denounced his government for slavishly adhering to Washington's policies in Asian affairs. The government's most fundamental mistake, he said, was an assumption that

American and Philippine interests were identical and that Filipinos had simply to sustain their trust in American good will.

The tragedy of our foreign policy is that being an Asian people ten thousand miles away from the effective center of American power, our behavior has been that of a banana Republic in the Caribbean. We have fed upon the fancy that we are somehow the favorite children of America and that she, driven by some strange predilection for our people, will never forsake us nor sacrifice our interests to her own or to those of others for her own sake.[17]

In fact, Recto observed, Washington had been more generous in giving postwar aid to India, Yugoslavia, and even the old enemy Japan than to her former ward. "And because beggars cannot be choosers we can be safely ignored, taken for granted, dictated to, and made to wait at the door, hat in hand, to go in only when invited."[17]

Recto's major targets were the Military Bases Agreement and the Philippine-American Mutual Defense Treaty. The first had granted foreign control of Philippine soil, a humiliating loss of sovereignty. In a practical sense, the foreign bases would make the country a "magnet" for attack by any power that chose to challenge the United States in Asia. Most objectionable was the aspect of "extraterritoriality" inherent in the agreement, which conferred on American forces jurisdiction over all crimes committed by American servicemen on the bases. Americans were thus exempt from Philippine justice when they committed crimes against Filipinos, a feature which recalled those "unequal treaties" imposed on Asians by Western powers through the centuries. One clause, Recto noted, exempted American offenders anywhere in the country during time of war. "In other words," he said, "in time of war the Philippines becomes ipso facto a territory of the United States. It will be nothing more than a country militarily occupied by an enemy army."[18]

The Mutual Defense Treaty was a devious American imposition, Recto asserted, because it did not, as supposed, actually bind the United States to come to the aid of the Philippines if the latter were attacked by a foreign power. It required America only to "meet the common dangers in accordance with its constitutional processes," which meant the Philippines would be defended only if the American Congress chose to defend it. Recto pointed out that American mutual defense treaties with European allies provided an automatic response without congressional approval. The disparity revealed, he said, the lesser value which the United States placed on Philippine survival and exposed the falseness of the assumption that American and Philippine interests were inevitably identical.[19]

Recto's arguments were reenforced by a number of nationalist economists and businessmen who found their voices in the 1940s and '50s. Their attention was focused on features of the Philippine Trade Act which had restored the opportunities for foreign exploitation common in the colonial period. Many of the American firms which had prospered before the war returned with new investments when the Trade Act was passed, enjoying most of the rights and privileges of the past. Official Philippine policy encouraged their return because it was dogmatically believed that American investment would spark an economic revival by generating jobs for Filipinos and a rising standard of living. The nationalist economists regarded this as naive. The parity clause, which gave American entrepreneurs equal commercial rights to develop natural resources of the Philippines, would guarantee large profits for the foreigners but provide few jobs with decent wages for the natives. Tying the peso to the dollar and permitting foreign companies to remit their earnings without limit gave American firms even greater advantages. Such devices, argued one authority, Vicente G. Sinco, would "enable the American capitalist to remove the meat of the Philippine oyster for himself, leaving only the empty shell to the Filipinos."[20]

The nationalist critique went beyond the obvious inequities of the Trade Act to assert a more sweeping allegation that, by deliberate design, the United States intended to preserve the Philippines in a state of colonial helplessness. The islands were intended to remain forever an agricultural society with little industrial development of its own. The Philippines would serve American economic interests as a supplier of cheap labor and raw materials in the classic colonial manner while at the same time assuring American manufacturers a reliable, duty-free market for finished goods. The American intent, then, was to

44

prevent Philippine industrial development and stifle its efforts to become a modern self-supporting and prosperous nation. American companies and the government in Washington worked together to devise policies to pastoralize the Philippines, and their work, wrote the economist Alejandro Lichauco, was the "principle barrier to economic reforms."

Such a policy and business practices suppress efforts of the Philippines, and other developing countries of Asia, toward full economic development. To be specific, the primary interest of American policy and American business here evidently is to maintain a source of cheap raw materials for the American manufactured products. And where . . . America is unable to prevent Filipino industrialization, then the alternative strategy is to control it.[21]

The conclusion that American intrusion meant Philippine poverty was pounded home relentlessly. "Foreign imperialism," Recto said, inevitably constrained growth and bled the native enterprise. "The imperialist needs spheres of influence as sources of raw materials and as markets for finished products. A nation that falls into an imperialist sphere of influence loses its freedom and remains poor because it is forced to remain agricultural. Thus, without complete independence, a nation is forever condemned to poverty . . ."[22]

American arrogance and insensitivity during the 1950s added to the growing din. Not content with the onesided ninety-nine-year lease on American bases, the Eisenhower Administration pressed a legal claim insisting that the large tracts actually had never reverted to Philippine ownership with the grant of independence and remained American property. It backed down after furious criticism from Recto and others. The Central Intelligence Agency attempted to manipulate every presidential and senate election during the decade. Led by an ambitious station chief later to gain renown in Vietnam, Col. Edward G. Lansdale, the CIA created, financed, and managed the 1953 campaign of President Ramón Magsaysay. Secret agency money and a $250,000 slush fund compiled by American business interests in Manila paid for the "Magsaysay For President Movement," produced a Madison Avenue–style campaign with "Magsaysay's My Guy" buttons, and financed a national organization to supervise polling and minimize cheating. The CIA's grand scheme envisioned the Philippines becoming a Southeast Asia surrogate power for the United States, carrying out operations that would alienate Asians if performed by white Westerners. Filipino agents were recruited to popularize the Diem regime in South Vietnam. One of them even wrote the constitution designed to legitimize that regime as a new democracy. Much of the agency's time and money was spent arranging slates of Filipino candidates acceptable to the United States and disparaging those of nationalists. Although supposedly clandestine, the money and manipulation were widely acknowledged in political circles. Among the CIA's more unseemly enterprises was the 1957 assault on Recto, who was then running for president on a minor-party ticket. A local dirty-tricks specialist distributed pro-Recto literature in envelopes containing condoms punctured with tiny holes, a stratagem apparently intended to make the nationalist appear untrustworthy.[23]

Such intervention into routine Philippine affairs naturally fed the nationalist crusade and increased its popularity. As the 1950s faded, the devious American hand was seen in virtually every development and an exaggerated anti-Americanism laced with hyperbole was in vogue. It was tinged with resentment of American racism. House Speaker José P. Laurel, Jr. pressed this theme:

It is claimed in platitudes now tired and empty that as the prodigious child of American enlightenment we are the living example in Asia of democracy in action. Nonsense. We are under the heel of a new oppression that shatters not our bodies but our illusions and subjects us to a great disenchantment because it takes the form of discrimination, prejudice and ingratitude, and comes with a profession of friendship.[24]

A popular columnist described Americans as "impatient with Asian claims to dignity and self-respect, imperious, condescending, crafty and above all violently outraged by anything less than a yard boy's servility."[25] The litany of American misdeeds and treachery was so widely repeated and so frequently believed that an American college instructor noted an eager-

46

ness to reject all traces of American influence. One of his students said, only partly in jest, that "American blood has done nothing for us but increase the height of our basketball players and improve the figures of our movie stars."[26]

Their inability to channel this resentment into a formal, unified movement was the nationalist leaders' great failure. They tried periodically to launch political parties and pressure groups devoted to cleansing the Philippines of foreign influence, but little came of their efforts. Recto formed the Nationalist Citizens party for the 1957 presidential campaign. It failed miserably and the futile exercise revealed a disappointing truth: The nationalist crusade was an elitist undertaking, popular in the press and in some business and political circles but largely ignored by the Filipino masses with their more pressing need of getting enough food. Recto and others strongly resembled their *ilustrado* ancestors in their class instincts. They rarely spoke of land reform and never seem to have considered a broad democratic party concerned with helping the *tao,* or common man. The businessman's nationalism was also self-serving. It was obviously in his interest to fend off American competition and to create a tariff wall to protect infant industry. Their pressure was not totally unsuccessful. By the late 1950s the government had enunciated a "Filipino First" policy which was designed to favor domestic producers over foreign ones.

But if it had small immediate political impact, the nationalist movement exerted a powerful appeal on the generation of Filipino students who, in the first wave of postwar prosperity, began filling up university classrooms. They had come of age during the ferment and a number of their professors, especially at the University of the Philippines, had themselves been *Rectistas,* as Senator Recto's followers were known. Many had become politically involved as high school and college students in Recto's 1957 campaign and were more susceptible to his anti-American preachings than their parents. They lacked their parents' instinctive appreciation of things American and did not share their parents' emotional attachment to Americans as liberators. Their heroes were polemicists and historians like Renato Constantino and Teodoro A. Agoncillo, both of whom deplored American cultural influences. Ironically, it was an

American's book that left the deepest impression on many, Shirley Jenkins's *American Economic Policy toward the Philippines,* a scholarly dissection of the Trade Act and the shabby parity agreement. "This group represented a new generation of Filipinos who had no recollection of the harrowing days of the Japanese occupation, who did not share in their parents' postwar euphoria," one scholar later wrote. "For them, U.S. imperialism was the scourge of the nation."[27] One student activist of that period recalled years later:

We came to understand the truth of the U.S.–Philippine relationship. Growing up, we had thought it had been one of equality and then we felt that we had been sold down the river and that our elders had not negotiated (with Americans) as well as they should have. It was heady stuff, reading those speeches by Recto and we were also greatly influenced by the Shirley Jenkins book—there it was, all written down and documented by an American and published by Stanford University Press. Because she was an American, she made the whole thing convincing.

But the bases were our issue and that was mainly, I think now, because our pride was hurt. There was a piece of our country under American control. Filipinos were being killed there for scavenging for metal and then the United States spirited the killers out of the country—it was very open in its callousness. Also, Recto showed us that the bases were not there to protect us but only to protect American interests and that they would become a magnet for attack on the Philippines. We were not as sentimental [about the United States] as our parents. There was a strong feeling by all of us that we were treated as inferior by Americans.[28]

While Recto's ideas remained holy writ for the young generation, the political style followed by him and his colleagues did not impress them. Recto and the others were men of the political center. They had achieved prominence by playing the Philippine political game, which encouraged incessant compromise and shifting alliances. They believed in elections. The young faithful were profoundly disappointed with electoral politics—especially when Recto himself was soundly trounced in 1957—and believed, with considerable evidence, that any politician's honor was for sale. Many were eager to move on to other means of change.

Those of us who became radical had become disenchanted with Recto and the others, especially when he lost so badly in 1957. That was a great disenchantment. We felt we could not rely on the election process. It was controlled by the United States and rich Filipinos, we felt, and elections merely legitimized the power of the elite. We believed that all of these liberal processes just sanctified the existing system. We needed a new political force.[29]

One who was at first enamored of and then repelled by Recto was a bright, bookish student at the University of the Philippines whose nationalism was inherited. José Ma. Sison was the child of a well-to-do landed family in Ilocos Sur, a northwestern Luzon province noted for its historic resistance to imperialists, both Spanish and American. A wealthy great grandfather and his son had been interrogated harshly by Spanish friars and soldiers on suspicions, which were correct, that they supported the *Katipunan,* the secret society plotting rebellion against Spain. Later, Sison's great uncle was killed by the American cavalry on grounds, which were also correct, that he abetted the underground resistance. The great-grandfather and three sons were charged by Americans with murder, although no victim was ever produced; their real crime had been to siphon off their tenant farmers' grain into the hands of *insurrectos* fighting the new conquerors. Young Sison grew up in Ilocos Sur hearing tales of how America's abusive soldiers forced peasants to leave their homes for days while suspects were hunted down in the barrios (Sison recalls it now as "the first American 'strategic hamletting' in Southeast Asia").

In high school at Ateneo de Manila and then the University, Sison compiled a brilliant academic record and was swept up in the nationalist fervor. He was expelled from the strict Jesuit-run Ateneo, in part because he had objected to one priest's description of Andres Bonifacio, the lower-class hero of the 1896 insurrection, as a "thug." The university, then filled with nationalist crusaders, was more to his liking and he read Agoncillo's history, Cesar Adip Majul's work on Apolinario Mabini, the intellectual of the revolution, and Hernando Abaya's *Betrayal of the Philippines,* a journalistic account, tinged with anti-Americanism, of the postwar years. He also read the works of Karl Marx. In the late fifties, Sison was an avid *Rectista,*

49

revelling in the master's skillful assaults on latter-day imperialism. Rather quickly, however, he became disillusioned with Recto, especially the senator's habit of taking care not to offend rich audiences.

"I once heard Recto tell a crowd, 'You should not be the clerks of the Americans,'" Sison later recalled. "Then in a little aside he very quickly said, 'Of course, there is nothing wrong with being clerks, clerks are always needed.' I decided Recto was a very limited man."[30]

3

☆☆☆

I t began unthreateningly as a series of isolated and un-coordinated protests by the usually docile farmers in the central plains of Luzon. In one barrio, a group of tenants awkwardly handed a list of modest demands to their landlord and patiently awaited a response. In another, the more adventurous marched shouting and singing to the public square where some gifted orator among them belligerently baited the authorities. In still another, the entrance to a sugarcane estate was ringed with pickets. Gradually the militance grew and the violence began. Granaries and entire cane fields were put to the torch. On some great hacienda, the morning sun exposed the bloody, disfigured body of a *katiwala,* the overseer hired by an absentee landlord to govern troublesome workers. Or a dark night would explode in flames which consumed a municipal hall and the stored land records that proved landlords' titles. Unfrightened and unyielding, the *hacenderos* fought back ruthlessly, first with their own private armies and then with the might of the Philippine Constabulary. Shootouts and pitched battles became common, the farmers firing back with antique rifles and shotguns or rushing at soldiers with the most primitive of weapons, the bolo. Throughout the late 1920s and early 1930s, the plain which stretches more than a hundred miles from Manila north to Lingayen Gulf echoed with the sounds of rebellion.

Rural revolts have been common in Philippine history. Most were short-lived uprisings characterized by mystical, supernatural beliefs and led by charismatic quacks who promised followers everything from riches to deliverance from earthquakes. One such rebel, a former fish merchant who styled himself "Emperor" and claimed to speak with God, amassed 10,000 peasant disciples and terrorized the Visayan provinces in 1927 before being captured and certified as insane. A far more serious movement, the *Sakdalistas,* motivated by nationalistic yearnings and a desire for social reforms, mustered tens of thousands of farmers in uprisings in Southern Luzon in 1935 before being crushed by the Constabulary.

The revolt which gripped central Luzon between the two world wars was different from any that had gone before. It embraced peasants and farm workers in six provinces in what became coordinated organizations of great complexity. It produced its own talented leadership and became allied with intellectuals of considerable sophistication. Over the course of two decades, during which it faced three distinct enemies, it developed a remarkable capacity for prolonged guerilla warfare and for a brief time threatened to paralyze the Republic. The mini-rebellions which dotted the central plains grew and became woven together in a great agrarian and nationalist movement, molded by the turns of events and its own momentum into what the world came to know as the revolt of the Huks.

The life of the Luzon peasant had never been an enviable one and his lot had changed little from Spanish days. Tenant farming was a brutally simple arrangement. The landowner provided the land, the peasant the labor. The latter cleared away the forests, diked the rice fields, tended the crop during growing seasons, harvested the grain by hand, and divided the product with the landlord, usually by a fifty-fifty formula. It was a form of permanent peonage because, unlike tenancy in some countries, the Philippine version rarely provided a first step upward to eventual ownership of land. Rich *hacenderos* gobbled up the loose parcels as they became available and planted thousands of hectares with cash crops like sugar, which the wondrous American market made profitable. Tenancy in the Philippines actually increased during the American period. So, inevitably, did the tenants' debts. The system was made tolerable only by the enduring paternalism which bound landlord and tenant in a relationship of mutual trust and friendship. The old *hacenderos* were required by custom to grant loans, both in rice and cash, in those inevitable times when the crop was short. The tenant could also fish in the master's pond and grow vegetables on unused plots. The two lived in familial closeness, despite the great gulf in classes, and it was common for the landlord to be godfather of his tenants' children. For the peasant, accustomed to poverty and expecting little else, it was a bearable existence. He could rarely advance, but neither did he fall further behind, and there was comfort in knowing that, unlike less fortunate Filipinos in other regions, the safety net of paternalism was there to save him when disaster threatened.

But by the 1920s and '30s, a great economic and social change had swept over central Luzon, one which radically undermined the tenant's security. Today it would be called farm capitalism or agribusiness. The demand for rice at home and sugar abroad soared and a new generation of planters recognized an opportunity for wealth unimagined by their fathers and grandfathers. That wealth would depend on a more efficient use of ancestral resources, the acquisition of more hectarage, and, most of all, a more productive labor force. The result was a loosening of the paternal bonds that had governed *hacienda* life for generations and the substitution of a kind of cash-crop mentality that had little time for old-fashioned benevolence. Landlords rewrote all the rules under which tenants labored. Instead of loose verbal agreements backed by personal honor there were written contracts binding tenants strictly in their daily work. The all-important loans of rice or cash were either denied or were granted at exorbitant interest rates, sometimes as high as 150 percent. Peasants found themselves charged even for fish caught in plantation ponds. Their contracts, which few understood anyway, levied fees for medical services, irrigation rights, and even the use of religious chapels, all of which had before been part of the owners' patrimony. Moreover, the landlord often moved away to Manila, where his new riches could be better enjoyed and displayed, and his absence effectively destroyed a once cozy relationship. Peasants were left to deal with a hired foreman, or *katiwala,* whose duty it was to extract a maximum output of rice or sugar at a minimum cost. The objecting tenant was simply moved off his share, by force if necessary. The harsh changes were altogether frightening to the central Luzon peasant and the new conditions of his servitude produced an unexpected response. He began to fight back.[1]

The early rebellions were sporadic, crudely organized, spur-of-the-moment incidents involving small numbers of peasants. A typical one followed this pattern: The landlord demanded a larger share of the harvest. Tenants retaliated by refusing to harvest or by holding out a secret share. A confrontation led to gunplay by the estate's private army and next day the *katiwala* was found slain in retaliation. Farmers marched in protest to the public square. One scholar discovered from news clippings that more than 600 such incidents were reported in the central Luzon provinces during the '30s.[2] As the decade wore on the scale of protests expanded, the peasants in one province discovering their grievances shared by those in an adjoining one. Alliances were formed that transcended municipal and then provincial boundaries and the revolt took on the proportions and complexity of a mass movement with permanent organizations. The most formidable of these was the *Kalipunang Pambansa ng mga Magsasaka sa Pilipinas* (KPMP), or National Society of Philippine Peasants, with chapters throughout the plains. Like earlier, more primitive movements, KPMP had its mystical trappings. Members joined by signing their names in blood pricked from fingers and its symbol, tatooed on many an arm, was the yoke of the carabao. Another new organization, *Aguman ding Malding Talapagobra* (AMT), or General Workers' Union, embraced thousands of field hands. When they merged in 1939, KPMP and AMT formed the largest amalgamation of farmers in Philippine history.

For all the tumult that accompanied these movements, the peasants' demands were strikingly unrevolutionary. Essentially they were in search of a fairer distribution of the harvests and other modest gains. The growing number of cane workers on daily wages sought higher earnings. Neither the KPMP nor the AMT advocated radical innovations and their protest rallies, though raucous, did not ring with appeals for redistribution of the land. Only much later was the cry of "land for the landless" heard and even then it came from urban radicals with little experience in rural uprisings. One list of proposed reforms included a larger share of the rice harvest, free rations to sustain families through hard times, an end to usurious interest rates, and medical assistance for tenants "who meet with accidents, fall sick, are bitten by snakes, are struck by lightning, or suffer injury in the performance of their duty."[3] For the most part, these were requests for conditions which had been common during the old days of benevolent paternalism. More than anything else about the period, they reveal the fundamental conservatism of that rebellious decade. What the peasants wanted was a return to the good old days.

That inherent conservatism is worth remembering in the light of what was to happen over the next two decades and, indeed, of what is still taking place in the rural Philippines. What became a full-fledged agrarian revolt claiming thousands of lives had had conservative origins and most likely could have been deflected by the authorities with minimal concessions. Instead it was met by unrelenting resistance on the part of landlords and only tepid reforms by the Philippine government. The mighty *hacenderos* responded with hired guns and the Philippine Constabulary, which hunted down and arrested the peasant ringleaders and placed whole territories under a form of martial law. In the legislature in Manila, the landed interests held a balance of power and either rejected or watered down the feeble efforts at reform. Toward the end of the 1930s, Manuel Quezon, by then the commonwealth president, was sufficiently shocked by the uprisings to propose a well-intended program of land reform. It was diluted by the legislature and further weakened by provincial administrators and by the time its modest palliatives reached the barrio level it was all but meaningless. It was a pattern to be repeated several times in the coming decades.

The early leaders of the central Luzon movement had been home-grown heroes of peasant background whose concern was for local, immediate issues. They were not men of philosophical inclination and for the most part were ignorant of radical ideologies. But as the movement grew in size and complexity, a different kind of leadership with broader horizons began to emerge. The most prominent among them was a frail and gentle idealist, Pedro Abad Santos, the son of a well-to-do Pampanga family who had severed his ties with the provincial elite to help workers in the AMT with money and legal advice. Well read in Marxist literature, Santos almost single-handedly founded the Philippine Socialist Party, although he was never a dogmatist (he once said he could be satisfied with American-style capitalism if it produced benefits for Philippine workers). Perhaps his major contribution was the recruitment, in 1935, of a determined young man, Luis Taruc, as secretary general of the party. A brilliant organizer who had helped to spread AMT locals throughout central Luzon, Taruc established a network of Socialist Party chapters. Another rising star in the movement was Juan Feleo, one of the few peasant-born leaders of the *Partido Komunista ng Pilipinas* (PKP), or Communist Party of the Philippines. Largely because of his militance in defending evicted peasants, Feleo was elevated to the presidency of KPMP.

In 1938, Santos, although hostile to Soviet-style communism, led his Socialist Party into a merger with the PKP, an alliance which has left the impression that the peasant movements were very early brought under communist control. The event was of less practical importance than it might seem. The PKP was a small, urban-based collection of intellectuals and union activists who, except for Feleo, had little interest in or knowledge of the peasant struggle. Neither the Socialist nor the Communist parties exerted any significant ideological influence over the rank and file. Their main service to the movement was in providing legal and organizational assistance, for as the 1930s came to an end peasants were turning increasingly from armed militance to legal and political activities. Litigation and local elections came more and more to be the arenas of combat and as a result the movement needed lawyers and leaders with language and political skills. These the communists and socialists could supply. This approach also happened to fit the PKP's strategy, which had been fashioned as part of the Comintern's worldwide Popular Front war against fascism. The initial success of this peculiar new alliance was encouraging. A Popular Front ticket supported by the Socialist Party in 1940 swept a number of local offices in Pampanga Province. It is tantalizing to speculate that, given a bit more time, the agrarian revolt of the 1930s might have transformed itself into a respectable left-of-center political party representing peasant interests. The Japanese invasion in 1942 ended any chance of that.

As the Japanese armies marched through central Luzon toward a defenseless Manila, looting and burning barrios on the way, the first signs of Philippine resistance appeared. Small bands of farmers formed in the mountains, armed with a few rifles looted from municipal buildings or taken from dead Japanese soldiers. Their initial forays were sporadic and disorganized. Gradually, as contacts were made among them, a resistance network took shape and along with it an extensive intelligence apparatus. It happened that many of these early guerilla bands were composed of men and women who had become active in the peasant rebellions, veterans of the AMT and KPMP. They had a history of shared goals and united action and they rather naturally formed themselves into underground fighting units. By some accounts, their raids and ambushes against Japanese forces in central Luzon were the fiercest resistance of the occupation. Luis Taruc, who led many of them into battle, later wrote:

The resistance movement that sprang up in Central Luzon was unique among all the groups that fought . . . against the Japanese. The decisive element of difference lay in the strong peasant unions and organizations of the people that existed there before the war. It gave the movement a mass base, and made the armed forces indistinguishable from the people, a feeling shared both by the people and the fighters.[4]

In March 1942, in Tarlac Province at the foot of Mount Arayat, representatives of these bands met and formed, along with communist leaders from Manila, the *Hukbong Bayan Laban sa Hapon,* or People's Army Against Japan, a title shortened first to *Hukbalahap,* then to *Huk.* The PKP, obedient to Comintern instructions, had planned an anti-fascist united front during meetings in Manila even before the invasion. Many of its top leaders, including the aging Santos, had been captured by Japanese soldiers as soon as Manila fell, but several escaped and led in forming what was to be the united front's armed wing, the Huk army. Among those at Mount Arayat was the new PKP chairman, Vicente Lava, the first of three unusual brothers who were to guide the party's destiny for years to come. Among the 200 or so armed guerillas, too, were many veterans of the peasant revolt. From the first the Huks were a hybrid army of party members and non-communist peasant leaders allied for the purpose of fighting the Japanese. Few of the latter were ideologically committed. Even Luis Taruc, who was both a PKP official and the first Huk military commander, never counted himself a committed communist. Scholars still dispute the extent of PKP control over the Huks throughout the war and the postwar rebellion. Certainly the PKP, from behind the united front curtain, issued orders and battle plans. The Huk guerillas obeyed some of them and ignored others. In general, the fighting units were too dispersed to receive many orders and there is evidence that they ignored many which were handed down from the party's central committee. Benedict J. Kerkvliet, who interviewed many Huk veterans, concluded that "The Communist Party lacked deep roots in central Luzon and could add little to the resistance. Consequently, the PKP did not control the Hukbalahap, although individual communists participated actively in it."[5]

Huk military operations became legends. Patrols ambushed Japanese units, raided municipal offices, seized stocks of rice to distribute to peasants, sabotaged enemy installations, and collected intelligence throughout the central provinces. By the end of the occupation period, it was estimated that the Huk army included more than 10,000 guerillas in 76 fighting squadrons. Many hid in mountain base camps, full-time soldiers summoned to battle by a blast on the *tambuli,* the carved horn of a carabao, while others lived in the barrios, farmers by day and guerillas by night. By some accounts, they killed between 20,-000 and 25,000 people, but probably a majority of those victims were Filipinos—suspected spies, collaborators, or members of the Philippine Constabulary incorporated into Japanese forces as native police. The Huks were more than a fighting army. They had broad support among citizens who could not risk

58

armed resistance and they became in many localities a sort of shadow government which doled out food, policed barrios against bandit gangs, and executed a crude form of justice. In some municipalities, Huk civilian organizations worked clandestinely with the Japanese-installed puppet governments. In more than one case, the invaders' authorized government was in reality composed of secret Huks.

Throughout the resistance struggle there were also traces of the class war which had begun in the 1930s. Many of the landed barons, weary of the devastation and unable to farm profitably, fled to Manila and collaborated willingly or passively with the occupation authorities. Some also were killed by Huks or other guerilla gangs who saw in the upheaval an opportunity to settle old scores. In some cases, peasants took advantage of the turmoil to occupy land formerly denied them and imposed impromptu land reform programs of their own making. There never existed any formal Huk plan to seize control of the estates on a broad scale or to deliberately destroy the landlord system, although the fear they might attempt to do so was widespread among elite families. But the Huks gained much popular support during the war as a nationalist, anti-Japanese army while sympathies for the old landowners declined. The old elite formed the basis of the collaborationist government constructed by Japan in Manila and its ally, the Constabulary, was incorporated into the Japanese effort to suppress the Huks. The puppet government repeatedly called for an end to resistance. The murdering of landlords, their overseers, and their political allies in the provinces, then, became justified as acts of patriotism, not, as before, the callous excesses of agrarian revolt. By the end of the war, the Huks were popular heroes in much of central Luzon.

The Postwar Rebellion began peacefully enough. With the invaders vanquished by the returning American soldiers, most Huks simply walked home to farm and family, finished with politics and war. Others talked of joining the new government's military. Almost all expected recognition, approval, and financial compensation, if not from their own government then from the United States. Although most Huk units retained the weapons assembled with much ingenuity during the war, there was at first no concerted plan for using them. The peasant groups and the PKP, however, did intend to use their new popularity and unity to pressure the postwar establishment for social reform. Casto Alejandrino, a party leader, recalled years later:

Perceiving that the Filipino people, already fatigued and suffering from four years of brutal Japanese occupation and pillage, preferred to continue the fight for freedom in ways other than violent, the party and its military arm, the Hukbalahap, and its mass organizations made plans for the organization of an alliance of all nationalists and progressive forces prepared to struggle the non-violent way.[6]

The PKP, eager to maintain its wartime United Front policy, took the lead in forming the Democratic Alliance, an amalgamation of liberals, communists, civil liberties advocates, farmers and labor leaders. Numerically, the Alliance was of influence only in central Luzon where the farmers' organizations offered a ready-built mass base, although its founders intended a national political force. Its platform was moderate, encompassing the type of rural reform popularized in the prewar period. The emphasis was on what the PKP called "parliamentary struggle" in the politics of the new republic and on amassing power through peaceful means.

Two series of events then unfolded to mar this generally peaceful demobilization and set the Philippines on a course toward civil war. The first was launched by American forces which were to remain the country's de facto government until independence in 1946. The U.S. Armed Forces in the Far East (USAFFE) had decided midway through the occupation that the Hukbalahap was a communist revolutionary army bent on establishing a socialist state. A young intelligence officer, Edward Lansdale, referred to them as "disciples of Karl Marx" and General MacArthur's Southwest Pacific Command concluded that "their policy is definitely communistic and . . . their plans include the establishment of a communistic government in the Philippines after the war, on the early Russian model. It is probable that there are also connections with communistic elements in China."[7] This conviction had prevented extensive cooperation between the USAFFE and Huk units during the occupation period, although Americans had worked closely with, and sometimes directed, other guerillas. In the immediate post-liberation period, the U.S. Army's Counter Intelligence Corps (CIC) met many Huk units with abrupt orders to turn in their weapons and disperse to their homes. Several Huk leaders were arrested on charges of subversion. In Bulacan province, 109 members of a Huk squadron heading home to Pampanga were arrested and then massacred by a Filipino force cooperating with Americans. In the most damaging encounter, Taruc, Alejandrino and other prominent Huks were jailed. Released after a mass demonstration protesting their treatment, they were then recaptured by the CIC in April 1945, and sent to prison. Many alarmed Huks fled into hiding in the Zambales and Sierra Madre mountains. Within a matter of months after liberation, the Huk heroes found themselves hunted as outlaws.

The second disruptive course was the work of central Luzon's landowners. Many had settled in Manila for the occupation and now returned to their estates, confidently determined to pick up where they had left off in 1942. They found the political situation in the provinces much changed. The agrarian rebels were stronger and better organized throughout the plains and, as the 1946 elections were to reveal, were positioned to force the landlord class to share power for the first time in Philippine history. They were also agitating for reforms in tenant treatment and wages, their major demand being a sixty-percent share of the harvest instead of the prewar standard of fifty percent. The landlords retaliated and were abetted by both Filipino and American forces. Philippine Military Police, armed and organized by Americans, broke up tenant meetings, arrested pickets, and hunted down Huk leaders using lists of names gathered by U.S. intelligence. Prominent agitators were dismissed or evicted from tenant plots their families had occupied for generations before the war. As the Republic's first presidential campaign began in late 1945, the repression became more severe because the agrarian rebels and the new Democratic Alliance were openly supporting Sergio Osmena, the *Nacionalista* candidate, who endorsed the sixty percent harvest-sharing formula. In one of the more brutal incidents, Philippine MPs in Bulacan Province raided Huk homes and machine-gunned several men and a woman.[8] The landlords' reassertion of their prewar rights and their determination to dismantle the new political force were the origin of a conflict that turned central Luzon into a new bloody battleground.

Two incidents in 1946 fed the fires. During the 1946 election, the Democratic Alliance scored its first—and final—victory, electing six congressional candidates and helping Osmena carry the plains in his losing struggle with Roxas. All six winners were denied their seats, in part to give the new president the majority of votes he needed to enact the "parity amendment" to the constitution. The second was the murder of Juan Feleo, the veteran rebel and member of the PKP central committee. In August, Roxas had launched a "pacification" campaign to induce the former Huks to surrender their weapons and discuss a permanent truce. Both Taruc and Feleo had agreed to act as emissaries. Armed men in Military Police uniforms kidnapped Feleo as he returned to Manila with information for the government and he was never seen again. His murder infuriated Feleo's admirers and it was quickly followed by the announcement of Roxas' "mailed fist" policy which he said would crush the dissidents in sixty days. Systematic repression of the old Huks began in earnest with attempts to eradicate the mountain bases hastily constructed earlier in the year. Philippine forces used armored cars, tanks, and even small aircraft to blast away. The civil war was on.

The initial counterattacks of the peasant-based fighting units were, as they had been against the Japanese in 1942, defensive and uncoordinated. Gradually, the embattled bands based in mountain camps began conferring among one another and in June 1946, a joint war council was held which resulted in the establishment of two main Luzon fronts. Almost all of those who attended that conference traced their activism to the prewar agrarian movements. Some were communists, like Taruc and Alejandrino; others were not. But there was one major difference from the anti-Japan front days: The official Communist party, the PKP, did not endorse a military rebellion. From the safer precincts of Manila, the PKP leadership cautioned the new Huks—they had adopted the title of *Hukbong Mapagpalaya ng Bayan* (HMB), or National Liberation Army—to avoid armed encounters, surrender their weapons if necessary, and wage only peaceful, or "parliamentary," struggle. The bewildered

62

Huks responded that they had been attacked first and were essentially defending themselves. The party refused to budge. The Lava brothers, José and Jesus, apparently thought the struggle hopeless and were interested in building an urban party. Labor members wanted no part of armed revolution. Since the party apparatus was then a mere paper structure, its involvement in the Luzon conflict probably would have made little difference. But its position firmly on the sidelines in the opening stages illustrates the shallowness of charges that the Huk rebellion was from the start a Moscow-directed communist plot to Sovietize the Philippines.

It was two years before the PKP reversed itself to endorse the HMB and attempted to control the rebellion. When it did, it produced a fiasco. By 1948, the HMB had expanded to a fighting force of some 11,000 members and seemed to be holding its own against government troops. Perhaps sensing that the revolution was leaving it behind, the PKP abruptly changed its approach. The Lava brothers produced an astonishing memorandum which declared that the Philippines was in a "revolutionary situation" demanding all-out battle and that the HMB was too undisciplined to be the revolutionary vanguard. To fill the gap and assume leadership, the PKP issued two instructions, both of them disastrous in their consequences. In the first, José Lava proclaimed a policy known as "geometric progression" under which all PKP and HMB members were to recruit three new members every three months. The party would then grow from 3,500 to 50,000 members by September 1951, and the HMB would be expanded to 172,000 soldiers. It was a preposterous notion which served only to bring into both organizations raw recruits, some of them government spies. Secondly, the party decreed a major change in military strategy. Instead of hit-and-run guerilla raids, the Huks were to launch large-scale coordinated assaults on government positions in preparation for conventional warfare and the ultimate insurrection. Taruc, the wily exponent of guerilla tactics, recognized the plan as absurd but, overruled by party theoreticians, he reluctantly accepted it. In the spring of 1950, Huk partisans launched a series of "dress rehearsals" with large raids on villages and regular army base camps. They were generally successful but before a new wave of assaults could be mounted in the fall, the suddenly aroused Philippine government unexpectedly intervened. It arrested nearly the entire PKP leadership in Manila.

It was the beginning of the end. By 1950, the Philippine government and its American military advisers were thoroughly alarmed. At American insistence, a young congressman named Ramón Magsaysay was appointed defense minister and the war plan against the Huks was sharply revised. A "psywar" program was worked out by him and Lansdale, who was by then CIA station chief in Manila, and it combined more aggressive military strikes with a highly publicized portfolio of reforms. Military assaults became larger and more sustained and the incompetent Philippine Constabulary was absorbed into the regular army. Military abuse of civilians, which had been a large factor in converting peasants to the Huk cause, decreased. The reforms, which promised better health care, resettlement of some tenants on land they could own, and cash credit for the perpetually strapped, never delivered much in substance, but the incessant publicity surrounding them swayed many peasant minds. Too, Magsaysay, who was elected president with American help in 1953, was a popular figure who convinced many that a new day was dawning for the common man. The combination of these fresh initiatives from the government and a deepening weariness among the Huk fighters gradually brought the rebellion sputtering to an end.

Why did the Huk revolt fail? Postmortems have advanced many reasons, all of them partly true. For one thing, the revolt never approached the scale of a national uprising. Although Huk units were dispatched to northern Luzon and some Visayan islands, they never ignited a mass revolt and the insurgency remained to the last a local affair in central Luzon where the Philippine military could mass its forces. American support and advice were important, possibly even crucial. Jesus Lava has said that his party's greatest error was in assuming that the United States would not become involved.[9] The Lavas' inept leadership was also to blame. Under them, the PKP at first ignored the Huks and then mismanaged them. There were arguments between the PKP in Manila and Taruc in the field and Taruc himself emerged bitterly critical of the absentee generalissimos at party headquarters. He later said:

64

Not enough party leaders understood peasants, what they wanted, how they wanted to work for it. . . . The Communist Party couldn't push people to revolution or propel people into a revolutionary crisis. The job of a revolutionary leader is only to guide the people's revolutionary anger, not try to create that anger. It can't do the latter. Lava and others figured the party not only could but should.[10]

An American who joined the Philippine communist movement echoed Taruc's sentiments on the party's failure to comprehend the peasant rebel's feelings and the indifference with which guerillas in the field received PKP manifestos:

We had thought that the people moved at our pace, to the rapid click of the mimeograph machine. We had thought that by the leaders' setting a high tempo we could set the tempo of the revolution. . . . We have been living in a fool's paradise.[11]

By the 1960s, the Huk army had disintegrated into a collection of gangs, most of them based in the province of Tarlac. Some were mere bandits, their military actions of such minor menace that government troops rarely bothered to hunt them down. Their dominant leader was a sinister and ruthless gangster, Faustino del Mundo, who went by the *nom de guerre* of Commander Sumulong. His base of operations was Angeles City, the sprawling, crime-ridden environs of Clark Air Base which was experiencing an economic boom as American forces expanded rapidly to support the war in Vietnam. Sumulong had settled comfortably into the Angeles rackets—real estate, gambling, bars and prostitution—and by some accounts used his former Huk fighters as enforcers. He seems to have arrived at a mutually satisfactory *detente* with U.S. authorities, who for a time employed the security firm owned by one of Sumulong's aides. His luxurious living style and his cooperation with the military outraged his old Huk allies in central Luzon. Once he was convicted by a party court martial of rape and "finance opportunism" but managed to be reinstated. His enemies within the scattered army were eliminated one by one, either by Sumulong's own gang or by Philippine soldiers acting on suspiciously well-timed information tips. The Sumulong reign reduced the already beaten Huks to a squalid state of quarrelsome renegades. Among his surviving underlings in the late 1960s only one seemed to retain any of the fierce idealism and willingness to take risks which had once been the sources of Huk pride. His name was Commander Dante.

Dante was literally born into the Huk movement and his youth mirrored the hard peasant life which gave rise to it. Born Bernabe Buscayno, he was one of eight children fathered in Capas, Tarlac, by an impoverished tenant who had been in the rebel armies fighting both the Japanese and the Philippine governments. The family farmed two hectares of sugar cane and rice for a landlord who took the customary half of each harvest. Buscayno's father regularly had to mortgage his own half to obtain fertilizers and the food needed to sustain the family each year between planting time and harvest. The debts mounted to an impossible sum, and when his wife was stricken with tuberculosis she could be treated only with herbal medicines, a hospital being out of the question. She died. So did a seven-year-old daughter afflicted with meningitis. Unable to support the remaining children, the father put them up for adoption one by one, a common custom, and the teenaged Bernabe was handed over to a landlord for day labor. He became a canecutter on a sugar plantation, earning 18 pesos (about two dollars) for a six-day week, and learned his first lesson in combatting landlordism. He led a brief uprising, extracting a small wage increase from the owner by daringly burning cane standing in his fields.

Still a teenager he was recruited by another ex-Huk farmer, who bestowed on him the code name of Dante. Buscayno very quickly demonstrated an unusual aptitude for the rebel's life. He was intelligent and intellectually curious and the party rewarded him with a course in Marxist ideology at a secret training school in the Zambales Mountains known colloquially as "Stalin University." For another, he was adept at killing people, often at close range. Dante was slim and wiry with boyish good looks and an innocent manner: His specialty was approaching his victims, usually police and Constabulary, before firing. The Philippine military had accused him of twenty-five murders while he was still a young man. Dante was a full-time revolutionary at age twenty-one, a district commander in Sumulong's outfit at twenty-three, and his intellectual achievements won him the position of education chairman. Yet he was also becoming an outcast. Sumulong's ducal ways and connivance with authorities in Angeles angered his young commander and by early 1969 Dante, the true believer, was searching for a new army.[12]

I n the 1960s, these two strains in Philippine history—
nationalism and agrarian revolt—came together and
produced the new revolutionary impulse which has been at
war in the nation for nearly twenty years. The combination is
familiar because a similar fusion brought about revolution in
China, Indochina, and Cuba, and is the stuff of several insurrections in Latin America. In most of those, the agent blending
those forces together was a strong leader of vision and personal force. Some have been charismatic figures, like Fidel
Castro. Others have been revered intellectual warriors, like
Mao and Ho Chi Minh. The new Philippine revolution produced
no hero of either type. It was propelled more by chance and
circumstance than by powerful personalities, and historical ac-
cident seems to have played a large role. If any single person
can lay claim to the leadership of this revolution, it is José Ma.
Sison.

I first met Sison in 1986, shortly after his release from nearly
nine years in a Marcos army prison. He is a slender man with
lively eyes and a thin, scraggly mustache. Gregarious and artic-

ulate, he loves conversation of all sorts and delights in the well-put aside and the *bon mot*. He was still testing the limits of his new freedom under the Aquino government (the military had been unhappy with his release) and kept his thoughts on the future of the insurgency carefully vague. The scene in his small two-story home in Santa Mesa Heights, Manila, was one of cluttered domesticity. A young son, conceived during a conjugal prison visit, climbed restlessly over his legs. Like any unemployed man in his mid-forties, Sison worried about money and he was counting on fees from a speaking tour of the United States to provide financial security. The thought of earning money in the land of the imperialists pleased his sense of irony and he was promptly carried away by recollections of other odd and whimsical turning points in his life. His favorite was an account of his first encounter with the works of Karl Marx. Marx was quoted extensively in a standard Catholic high school textbook written by a Fordham professor to expose the dangers of communism to impressionable young students. Sison said he instantly liked the sound of it, thought it made sense. Only once did the combativeness of which I had been warned flare to the surface. I had observed that after two decades of proselytism, the party he founded seemed to have produced rather few Marxist ideologues. "How many priests does the church have?" he shot back. "Only a few thousand, maybe. But it is enough."

In the 1960s, when Sison was plotting a Maoist revolution, he seemed to acquaintances anything but an *enfant terrible*. Those outside his tiny movement knew him as a frail intellectual whose writings appealed to a limited circle of leftist cranks and he was not personally an imposing figure. One recalled years later:

Sison always seemed to me a kind of fleeting figure in a crowd. One minute you'd be talking to him and the next he'd be gone. I was always loaning him bus fare to get him downtown [from the University of the Philippines campus in Diliman] and cigarettes. We never knew of him as a Marxist—either we were very naive or he was good at concealing it. I could not have imagined him taking up arms, and we always just laughed at the reports that he was a communist.[1]

But Sison had a visionary's talent for planning, organizing and educating. He spent much time designing grand political schemes, figuring out ways they might be made to work, and then selling them to the many small clandestine groups he formed or joined. His first great success was a national youth movement with chapters in every college and university, an achievement almost entirely his own. Awkward in public debate, Sison was poised and self-confident in small meetings and he could argue all night to win a point. Francisco Nemenzo, then a participant and now an analyst of the movement, was familiar with that style:

He was shy at times and not very articulate in big crowds. But in one-on-one debates and in small groups he was very persuasive. He had enormous patience with people and would spend hours trying to convert them to his side. He was something of a dreamer but he was a great organizer. He was always charting new organizations and drawing them in pictures, with boxes and all, to go with them. We would say, "But Joe, where are all of the people for this organization?" and he would laugh.[2]

Many of the people to fill Sison's organization charts would come from the vast and growing pool of college students. Their presence in large numbers was something unprecedented in Philippine history and without them recent history would undoubtedly have been much changed. They formed, as on Western campuses in that decade, a huge, volatile mass. The brightest and most politically aggressive attended the prestigious University of the Philippines, training ground for the elite. Others filled the classrooms at the Lyceum and in downtown Manila they overflowed the diploma mills of lesser institutions. A crucial reality was that a large majority were training for jobs that did not exist. One writer's research disclosed that of the 300,000 annual graduates of Philippine colleges only 17 percent secured jobs commensurate with the degrees they obtained.[3] Politicizing students was perhaps the real creative work of the 1960s. Most began as neophyte nationalists whose heroes were Recto and Renato Constantino, and whose villains were Americans. Their issues were the parity agreement imposed on the Philippines in 1946 and the establishment of American bases.

The installations at Subic and Clark became especially inflammatory causes. A number of Filipinos were shot there by American guards who spotted them scavenging for waste metal (one guard testified he thought he was shooting at a wild boar). Most of the guilty servicemen were quickly transferred out of the Philippines to avoid trial.

Sison's role began innocently enough in 1959 when he was a teaching assistant in English literature at University of Philippines, where his wife, Julie, was a librarian. Together they formed an innocuously titled study group, Students' Cultural Association of the University of the Philippines, or SCAUP. Initially it was devoted to discussions of Philippine nationalism and the preachings of Recto, although today Sison believes he was already a Marxist convert by that time. There were only about thirty members at first and Julie Sison remembers that adding new ones was difficult:

The problem then was that there was an anti-organization tendency among intellectuals. Everyone was reading Milovan Djilas' *The New Class* and Koestler's *The God That Failed.* People felt that organizations were stifling. But José said we could not do anything until we got organized. He had the idea of organizing an inter-university organization all over the Philippines.

SCAUP might have died quietly except for one of those chance interventions typical of the decade. In 1961, several witch-hunters in the Philippine Congress decided, with almost no evidence, that the UP was a den of communist professors, and a Committee on Anti-Filipino Activities began an investigation. Thousands of protesters massed at the Congress, among them legions enlisted by the Sisons and SCAUP. The committee backed down under pressure. SCAUP received much credit for the victory in student circles. Sison was jubilant and deeply impressed at the demonstration of power in the streets, of the role which thousands of properly organized students could play. SCAUP attracted many new faces and under Sison's guidance its studies moved on to what was for him a more important subject, Marxist revolution in poor Asian countries.

In those days, Marxist ideology and communism held little appeal for most young Philippine intellectuals. The country's

71

indigenous Communist party, the PKP, had been all but dismantled after the Huk defeat and the arrest of its leadership a decade earlier. Its popularity was at the lowest point since it was established in 1930 by a few labor leaders and intellectuals. The surviving apparatus in Manila had little contact with the remaining Huks in central Luzon. It was a brotherhood of tired old men who were almost afraid to talk with one another. The PKP secretariat had imposed the curious "single-file" policy under which a party member could know only two other members—one who brought him messages and one to whom he passed them on. The purpose of such caution was to preserve an underground leadership waiting for better days. In fact, it virtually dismembered the organization. Gradually, the cautious mandarins under Jesus Lava began to perceive a new public mood, especially in the exertions of young nationalists beginning to march in the streets against "U.S. imperialism." They sensed the possibility of infiltrating nationalist groups and annexing them to a new version of the united front. It was clear this could not be accomplished by party regulars who were known publicly and so the PKP began to search for new faces with good credentials in this strange new movement outside.

Sison was a natural choice and something of a plum when, in 1962, the PKP invited him in. He was by then a confirmed Marxist skilled in interpreting Lenin. He had a following among nationalist students at the UP and was also engaged in Marxist education among small radical labor groups. It appears that Lava first made contact with him through an Indonesian communist who was then studying at the UP and who had been befriended by Sison. The advantages of such a union for Sison are not obvious, for he must have been aware of the PKP's moribund condition. And he knew that these party bosses were bent on using him and his troops for their own purpose. He seems to have thought that joining the PKP would give him organizational stature and he undoubtedly dreamed of revitalizing an institution which had once played a noble role in leftist Philippine politics. When I asked Sison why he joined, he replied simply: "I wanted legitimacy." Their union, then, was one of mutual interest—each had something the other wanted. It began a five-year relationship that was often stormy. Sison concealed the fact of his membership from almost everyone, including his wife. Julie knew after a year that he was "vaguely with the Lavas" but not until 1967, when the relationship was broken with bitterness on both sides, did she become aware that he had been a party member.

They were hectic years in which Sison was at his peak as organizer, planner, and committee-room politico, fashioning new front groups and scheming to bend them to his and, at first, the party's purposes. He seemed to be everywhere. He was a vice president of the new party-sponsored *Lapiang Manggagawa* (LM), or Workers' Party. In 1967, he somehow turned up as secretary of the Movement for the Advancement of Nationalism, or MAN, a primarily middle-class organization of nationalists earnestly intent on purifying the Philippines by purging it of foreign influences. Sison also found time to launch and edit the *Progressive Review,* a popular left-wing journal devoted to Marxism and nationalism. Its editorials reflected the party's new enthusiasm for a popular front united for battle against the twin devils of "neo-colonialism" and "feudalism."

But the major achievement of Sison's party career was the founding in 1964 of *Kabataang Makabayan*, or Nationalist Youth, which became the national youth organization of his early visions. Sison was then the party's Youth Section director and was affiliated with the Lyceum, a quality university. KM from the first was more than a student organization. The PKP brought into it many sons and daughters of radical peasants, some of them allied with the Huks in central Luzon. Most of its members, according to Nemenzo, were in fact poor rural youth,[4] although the noisy student component received most of the publicity. KM was the first and most successful attempt to unite urban middle-class radicals with peasant groups and is the model for the much broader National Democratic Front, the communist front group which flourishes today. Its construction was vital to Sison's plan for revolutionary action. From KM came many of the educated cadres who spread Marxist ideology among poor recruits throughout the country and provided the first links with armed guerilla units in the countryside. Controlled at first by the PKP through Sison, it espoused a strident nationalism and tried to conceal its communist ties, although its leader attempted to infuse it with a Marxist's appreciation of the role of proletarian leadership. Sison had discovered in Andres Bonifacio, the slum-born hero of the 1896 insurrection against Spain, a prototype of the proletarian rebel he wished his followers to emulate. "If *Kabataang Makabayan* will ever succeed in its patriotic mission," he told KM members in an inaugural address, "one important requirement it shall have met is to be imbued with the proletarian-revolutionary courage of Andres Bonifacio, the only courage that gives life and force to the principles that we uphold in this epoch."[5]

In 1965, KM-led groups mounted the first major anti-American demonstrations on the streets of Manila. They were hugely successful and marked the opening of a long period of protests that grew in size and intensity until President Marcos imposed martial law in 1972. Their special target was the presence of American military bases, which had become even more controversial because they were used as staging and logistics centers for the growing U.S. operations in Vietnam. KM propaganda asserted that the United States was suppressing a nationalist revolt in Vietnam as it had crushed the Philippine independence insurrection in 1900. When President Lyndon B. Johnson visited Manila, he was met with the same cry—"Hey, hey, LBJ, how many kids did you kill today?"—that echoed in American streets. The great majority of protesters were non-communist nationalists and they attempted to steer clear of demonstrations organized by KM, which they suspected of being led by communists. "All of us wanted to separate the issue of nationalism from the communist underground," one of the leading UP demonstration organizers recalled. "We were anxious not to be tarred with that brush, as the government was trying to do." KM tried to tar them, too, with the brush of pro-Americanism, calling the reluctant ones "CIA agents." Led by communists and non-communists, sometimes separately but often intermixed, the protests intensified throughout the 1960s and culminated in huge and violent marches on Congress and Malacañang Palace. "I remember that in 1964 it had been hard for us to fill the buses to carry students to downtown Manila," the former UP organizer recalled. "But by 1969 there were thousands of us and the problem became one of how to find enough buses."

Meanwhile, within the small Marxist circles which Sison influenced, different kinds of winds were blowing. Communist successes in Third World countries were scrutinized in his study circles and they seemed to describe a new pattern of revolution. The guerilla wars in Cuba and Vietnam were being judged as models. The murdered Patrice Lumumba, the Congolese nationalist, became an imported martyr (Sison wrote an emotional "requiem" to honor him). The communist movement in Indonesia was winning support and it sent representatives to Manila to give instruction in the new doctrine. The intellectual force behind these advances originated not in the Soviet Union but in China. Gradually at first, with Sison leading the way, young Philippine Marxists began looking to Mao Zedong for guidance. Sison has said:

I was already a Marxist when I first read Mao. Then and now I consider him the greatest thinker on colonialism and imperialism and feudalism. Lenin was my pioneer, but Mao had made those extensive examinations of conditions in China and it seemed to me that they were similar to what I saw in the Philippines. And he was unbeatable on the subject of a people's war.

And then by 1964, the line between the USSR and Mao was very clear. Khrushchev to me meant cooperation with imperialism and China was the leader against him. China was a big force and was encouraging revolution of all colonial countries. China looked to me like the Philippines of today.[6]

The flowering of Maoism soon became fashionable among young radicals in KM, especially when accounts of the Great Cultural Revolution became popular. It was the custom then for KM members to spend short periods in the countryside where they mingled with farm families, imbibing peasant wisdom and also spreading the new faith. Middle-class college students from Manila began showing up in Luzon wearing Mao caps and Mao badges and declaiming whole passages from the *Little Red Book* to the bewildered peasants. They used the Cultural Revolution's techniques to purify one another. "We had the *Little Red Book* and studied it before falling asleep at night," one veteran remembers. "Then the next morning we would wake up and start checking on each other's attitudes. We'd quiz each other to see if anyone had developed any 'right' or 'left' tendencies overnight."

But the China craze was not an exercise in radical *chic.*

Peking, in the 1960s strongly supported communist undergrounds throughout Southeast Asia. Its propaganda broadcasts in the Tagalog dialect reached most of Luzon. Small but significant amounts of aid reached Philippine Maoists and many journalists, students and professors went to Peking (Sison made one visit as a journalist). Chinese aid was a factor in the revolution then gaining momentum in Indonesia not far away. Although the emulation of Mao reached laughable proportions in the Philippines, the belief that China would become the powerful godfather of their own rebellion was serious nourishment for Sison and his circle.

Far from encouraged by this rush of fresh ideas, the timid, aging leaders of the PKP were at first nervous and finally appalled. Jesus Lava had been arrested in 1964 but his heirs retained control, although Sison has said he managed the party's ideological work. The party elders counted for little in the arena of international communism, but they were Stalinists by inheritance and feared a schism with the young Maoists in their midst. The veterans also feared that Sison's clamorous KM partisans would arouse the government to new repression. The real division within the PKP was not over communist theory or choosing sides in the Sino-Soviet split. It was a generational gap: The young lions wanted action; the old guard did not. Sison wanted a revitalized party that would strike out again on the road to revolution. The Lavaites wanted no part of such adventurous nonsense. Nemenzo, who watched the rift grow into a chasm from a seat within the party, has written of Sison's group:

They were more daring and innovative, whereas (the party elders) tended to be overly concerned with how the government might construe their intentions. Moreover, the fresh recruits, mostly middle-class intellectuals, had a better grasp of the Marxist classics and the Maoist adaptations, while the old cadres derived their theoretical knowledge almost exclusively from Josef Stalin's *Foundation of Leninism*. [7]

Sison himself was to expend much energy excoriating the old guard's resistance to new initiatives, and two decades later still remembered the period with bitterness:

The only capital which the Lavaites had was the name of the party. I fought them because they were pro-Soviet but also because I thought of them as just weekend warriors. They really attended only one meeting a month. It took much patience dealing with the princes of the Lava dynasty. They were such mediocre men.[8]

In 1967, the animosities spun out of control and the inevitable breach occurred. Sison, who had by then adopted the party and pen name of Amado Guerrero, insisted that the PKP review its history, pursue a "rectification" to cleanse itself of past errors, and prepare for a new era. The party elders at first refused, but to avoid losing the youthful members who supported him they reluctantly empowered Sison to draft a critique. The result was far harsher than anything they had anticipated. Sison caustically and in considerable detail denounced a trail of errors leading back to the wartime Huks. Each of the three Lava brothers was assailed for specific mistakes, including the then-imprisoned Jesus Lava who had initiated the "single-file" policy that had dismembered the party. It was too much for the old guard. Sison was expelled by a special meeting of the Central Committee in April 1967. He quickly moved to establish an independent branch, forming his own politburo and issuing a May Day statement which praised Mao and denounced the "Lava clique" as pitiable revisionists. The expulsion of Sison was perhaps the PKP's last significant act. With him went its ties to both the avid young Marxists and the nationalist movement it had sought to control. The PKP became an inconsequential collection of men so timid and fearful that its most publicized act of the next decade was the endorsement of Ferdinand Marcos' proclamation of martial law.

On December 26, 1968, the seventy-fifth anniversary of Mao's birth, Sison and ten disciples gathered in a remote part of Pangasinan Province to found the new Communist Party of the Philippines—Marxist-Leninist (Mao Zedong Thought). By Sison's subsequent account, the eleven founders represented a total party membership of 75, most of them students but also including a smattering of workers and peasants. (A number of his associates in KM had defected, in part because of Sison's abrasiveness, to form a separate Maoist organization). The founding was officially entitled a "Congress of Reestablishment" to signify that it was not a renegade band but a reassembling of the one true Communist party of the Philippines. Under the guidance of Sison and his closest KM associate from the Lyceum, Arthur Garcia, the delegates adopted a constitution, added new members to the politburo, and approved a lengthy document, "Rectify Errors and Rebuild The Party." It largely rehashed the bill of indictment against the Lavas which Sison had drafted the year before. It also called for armed struggle against the government and a Maoist–style people's war in the countryside, culminating in seizure of the cities.

In retrospect, the Pangasinan conference seemed a preposterous affair: Eleven young radicals huddled in a remote nook one hundred miles from Manila, plotting revolution by the book written years earlier for Chinese peasants, proclaiming armed struggle without the semblance of an army. Only Sison's supreme self-confidence and sense of historical certainty lent an air of reality. Four of the participants later told a scholar that "Amado Guerrero alone was brimming with optimism; the rest silently nursed a sense of futility. They could hardly believe that their rag-tag army of student activists would grow into a serious guerilla force."[9] Sison himself admits to no self-doubts. "I felt confident always of our growth," he has since said. "I had watched it grow from nothing."[10] His wife, Julie, is perhaps more candid. Asked eighteen years later how such a pitiful force could concoct such an extravagantly ambitious plan, she laughed and answered, "Audacity." Most ludicrous was the absence of any armed force. The plotters had no weapons, no money to buy them, and no skills in using them, except possibly for Garcia who reportedly had undergone small-arms training on a visit to China. It was a revolution searching for a revolutionary army. Only Sison seems to have known where one could be found.

During the period when the old Communist party in Manila was splintering and disintegrating, its army in the provinces was experiencing a similar fate. In the popular shorthand of the day, there were "convenience Huks" and "ideological Huks." The former were those still led by Commander Sumulong in his

Mafia-style operations at Angeles City. The "ideological Huks" consisted of small bands in the countryside whose dwindling number of leaders clung to remnants of revolutionary idealism. Chief among the latter were Commander Dante and his closest ally, a Commander Freddie. When Freddie was slain in a Constabulary ambush, Dante was convinced that Sumulong was responsible. Their breach became inevitable when Sumulong instructed him to cease supporting poor farmers then being evicted from their lands to provide a site for a U.S. Voice of America transmitter. Dante's group, then controlling only a small bit of Huk turf in Tarlac Province, was also menaced by another enemy. A gang of government-paid thugs known for some reason as "The Monkees" was harrassing his force daily. (Manila sophisticates attuned to western music inevitably dubbed this mini-war a clash between the "Monkees" and Dante's "Beatles.") Discouraged and lonely, his little army hunted from one hiding spot to another, Dante broke finally with the Huk leadership and began his search for a new alliance.

Sison and Dante met in January 1969, soon after the founding party congress was finished. How they got together is not entirely clear. It appears that the initial contacts were made by Dante through the groups of young KM members who frequently encamped to central Luzon in those days. There has been a persistent rumor that the formal introduction was made by Benigno S. Aquino, Jr., then a congressman from Tarlac Province. It was not at all uncommon for quite respectable politicians to have links with Huk groups which were sources of votes and muscle on election days. The Aquino connection is denied on all fronts, although communist sources state that a congressman other than Aquino was involved, for reasons that are not clear. However their first encounter was arranged, the young Huk killer and the ideologue from Manila hit it off quickly and agreed to cooperate. Dante brought to the union only 37 guerillas and 35 guns. But the revolution had found its army and the apostate Huk his new ideological moorings.

The New People's Army, or NPA, was formally established two months later, in March 1969, with Dante as its first commander. It had by then doubled to about seventy armed fighters as small clutches of defecting Huks came over, each of them greeted by jubilant celebrations. With his customary zeal for grand organizational schemes, Sison had sketched out a paper army consisting of regular mobile forces, guerilla units, militia, and "armed city partisans," with the regulars structured into squads, platoons, companies, regiments, divisions and even corps. In fact, the first army consisted of nine squads each containing seven fighters. A lengthy document, "Basic Rules of the New People's Army," set forth its operating principles, which seemed to be a cross between Chairman Mao's puritanism and the *Boy Scout Handbook.* Soldiers were prohibited from drinking and gambling. They were not "to take a single needle or piece of thread from the masses" and were to observe Mao's "Eight Points of Attention":

1. Speak politely.
2. Pay fairly for what you buy.
3. Return everything you borrow.
4. Pay for anything you damage.
5. Do not hit or swear at people.
6. Do not damage crops.
7. Do not take liberties with women.
8. Do not ill-treat captives.

The new army's first exploits were not encouraging. Central Luzon units of the Armed Forces of the Philippines soon learned of its appearance in Tarlac Province and harrassed it mercilessly. Julie Sison remembers scuttling from one barrio to another in search of safe hiding. Then, as later, the principal military actions were raids and ambushes designed to obtain weapons. Some observers have referred to this time as the party's "Yenan Period," suggesting a plan to establish a central impregnable base as Mao had done in the caves of Shensi Province in China. Sison insists there never was any Yenan strategy and that his intent from the first was a dispersal of forces to avoid a wipe-out by the Constabulary. Whatever the strategy, it unfolded amateurishly. All of the vital party and NPA documents were concealed in an underground pit used at times by government troops for gasoline storage. The papers were discovered and their contents, revealing all of the plans for rural revolution, were published in a government book, *So*

The People Will Know. Sison himself had gone underground in February in Isabela Province, far to the north, where he established a training base and headquarters for his central committee. Things went better in Isabela. The cadres were welcome because they were among friendly former Huk families who had been resettled there as part of the old Magsaysay dispersal plan in the 1950s. With local recruits and new students arriving from Manila, the main NPA force grew quickly to include 300 fighters armed with rifles and another 500 with antique shotguns. Still, they barely survived a furious government assault involving nearly 7,000 troops.[11]

The skirmishes in the countryside were echoed by, and perhaps abetted, the radical protest movement in Manila. By early 1970, large and noisy demonstrations against the government and "U.S.Imperialism" were daily affairs, known as the "parliament of the streets." Several of the participants believed urban radicalism was greatly strengthened by the accounts of guerilla warfare in the provinces, accounts made more fearsome by extensive government publicity and warnings. For the first time, the notion of genuine revolution became a topic of serious discussion in university study groups. What had before been adolescent rhetoric and bravado now seemed real threats. Membership in the new Communist Party of the Philippines grew rather quickly from 1970 to 1972 and in the street demonstrations Marxist slogans began to drown out the old nationalist ones. The cadres struggling in Tarlac and Isabela became instant heroes and more than one street parade featured shouts of, "Dante for President." On January 26, 1970, thousands of students, banners waving, converged on Congress in the beginning of what would be memorialized as the "First Quarter Storm." Four days later, an even larger crowd used a stolen fire truck to batter through the main gates of Malacañang Palace. Jittery police opened fire at the nearby Mendiola Bridge and before the night was over four students were slain martyrs and scores of others were wounded.[12]

The same year saw the first appearance of Sison's *Philippine Society and Revolution,* published under his pen name of Amado Guerrero. "PSR," as it became known, is both his Marxist interpretation of Philippine history and his recipe for Maoist revolution. Still widely read today by young radicals, PSR was

Sison's attempt to provide an all-encompassing rationale for resorting to revolutionary force and to give form to his own self-confidence in its eventual success. The Philippines, he wrote, was a semi-colonial and semi-feudal state governed for the interests of American imperialists and rich landlords. His class analysis was drawn directly from Mao's description of China in the 1920s. At the top were the landlords and the "comprador big bourgeoisie," the rich businessmen ("local running dogs") who made foreign capitalism the scourge of their own country. Ranged against them were the proletariat and poor peasants who could expect some help in their revolution from "middle peasants" and even those elements of the business class—"the national bourgeoisie"—whose self-interests were naturally opposed to foreign domination of the economy. Only armed revolution led by the Communist party would rid the country of feudal and imperialist exploitation. It was essential to understand Mao's great thought: "Political power grows out of the barrel of a gun." First would come a national democratic revolution overthrowing the bourgeoise government, to be followed by socialist revolution in which feudal estates would be distributed to the peasantry and essential industry would be owned by the state. Mao's formula of a "protracted war in the countryside" must be copied faithfully. From bases in the mountains the peasant armies would advance "wave upon wave" until the countryside fell into their hands and the cities were encircled. Urban insurrection would automatically follow. The great value of PSR, like any good revolutionary tract, is not so much its specific prescriptions but its conveyance of an overriding sense of inevitability: Here is the Master Plan. If one sticks to it long enough, success is assured. A generation of Philippine radicals has been nourished by its certainty and promise of ultimate victory, and although parts of it are now dated—Mao himself has been downgraded to the role of one enlightened thinker among many—PSR remains the bible of the revolution.

Measured against the reality of the times, Sison's call to arms was an exercise in dream-work. There was no revolutionary mood in the Philippines of 1970. His party was a collection of noisy students long on sloganeering and short on public support. The New People's Army numbered a few hundred peasants, untrained and poorly armed. It would be ten years before it could begin to strike with enough force to be considered a serious threat in limited areas of the archipelago. But a foundation had been laid and it was testimony to what a determined few could accomplish in time of high emotion. Sison's hand was in all of it. His skill in organizing and manipulation, his clever adaptations of Mao, and most of all his exuberant self-confidence made a serious venture of what could have been mere radical *chic.*

These talents produced two overriding achievements. The first was formation of the link between student zealots and the peasants. This connection between an urban intelligentsia and agrarian rebels was an unusual phenomenon in the Philippines and one of immense importance. The peasants supplied the army and the students the ideological cement that held it all together, giving direction and purpose and a sense of ultimate victory. The students of the 1960s went on to become the leaders and disciplinarians of a mass-based organization which spread throughout the country. Now in their forties, they are the top- and middle-level cadres of the movement, trained Marxists and veterans of battle, their initial squeamishness at executing an enemy long since overcome. Without them, the new agrarian revolt probably would not have taken shape at all and most certainly would by now have withered into that peculiar form of banditry common to past Philippine rebellions.

The second achievement was in transforming the nationalism of the 1950s into Marxist ideology and support for armed revolt. How this transformation came about is still something of a mystery. Virtually every cadre I interviewed said that his activism began in the nationalist crusade that took its force from the preachings of Recto, Lorenzo Tañada, Constantino and Agoncillo. Still today, they discuss the "unequal treaties" that produced the parity clause and the American bases at Subic and Clark, and they continue to draw strength from the American failure in Vietnam. Most of those early nationalists, of course, did not take the leap into Marxism and revolution but the question remains of why so many of them did. Some recall their instant radicalization when police shot and beat their friends in 1970. Others recall a gradual intellectual change which came primarily from reading Marx in college. Still others made their personal leap only when President Marcos imposed martial law in 1972.

Perhaps the clearest answer came from one 1960s activist who did not make that leap at all. He had been a young nationalist leader at the University of the Philippines, a passionate opponent of the American role in Vietnam and one of those who organized the daily rallies outside the U.S. embassy in Manila. The demonstrations remained large and noisy, but there came a time, he remembered, when it all became a bit stale, when his friends began to talk of the uselessness of protest. Something more was needed and the friends began quoting a radical named "Amado Guerrero" who had said: "The only way to make a revolution is to engage in revolution." He remained a moderate, believing in protest and pressure politics to change the government. His friends drifted away:

I think that it was an inevitable climax of their intellectual growth. The only way to change things was to resort to violence. That was the big dividing line between us. Our position was that we could wait for reforms. They were like the Simon character in Rizal's *El Filibustero* who was for violence. People were affected by that. The way to freedom and dignity for them was down that road. We took the position that the people were not ready for violence and that they would be the ones to suffer most if it came. Sison's group would insist that the people in power would not surrender it voluntarily and would not "teeter easily into the abyss," is the way I think Sison always phrased it, but must be pushed. I think they became consumed by their own rhetoric. They felt they had to put up or shut up, and they followed that logic into armed struggle.[13]

5

★★★

By Asian standards of political life, the democratic system inherited from the United States by the 1960s had been adapted admirably to the Philippines. Just as in America, two major parties alternated in governing the country. Elections were regularly held. A majority of the people voted. Power was routinely passed to the victor after each election without turmoil and the Philippine army stayed respectfully in the background, something which could not be said for Indonesia, South Vietnam, Taiwan, Thailand and South Korea. Each election was a popular event. Each was also attended by much violence. The crime rate rose sharply as election day neared and even afterward, when old scores were settled. A high level of corruption was tolerated in the workings of government. Graft and favoritism were acknowledged to be widespread. An aide to the late President Roxas was reported to have said: "But what's the use of being the majority party if we can't have a little honest graft?"[1] If the Philippine government was not exactly the "showcase of Democracy" the U.S. had envisioned for Southeast Asia, it seemed closer to that ideal than that which prevailed in much of Asia.

The two dominant parties, *Nacionalista* and Liberal, were agglomerations of rich families and business leaders. Each was a non-ideological grouping of economic interests whose mission was to control the government for economic gain. Each believed strongly in the spoils system to reward supporters and each spent large sums of money to win elections. Philippine politics was an intensely personal affair. The loyalties of its participants were to relatives and close friends and it was rare to find an issue of principle coming between them. What Theodore Friend, the American historian, observed of pre-independence politics was still a truism in the new republic:

. . . the Filipino politician cherished in his friends not their principles but their proximity; he valued them less for their convictions than for their affections. The company he found himself among meant more than the side of an issue they took.[2]

At the national level, competition between parties was defined by the pursuit of specific economic advantages. Landlords from Luzon and the Visayas wanted safe men who would not take too seriously the demands for land reform or who would see that Congress watered down those reform measures which were enacted. They wanted presidents who would work diligently to maintain the generous American markets for sugar and other export crops. The new business class wanted domestic markets protected from foreign imports and they supported nationalists who promised just that.

This political framework offered little of value to the poor Filipino who lived in the countryside. His benefits were modest, consisting of patronage jobs for a few, bribes on election day, and occasional gifts from the government pork barrel. For these his vote was willingly swapped and he accepted docilely his exclusion from the greater play of politics. A series of farmers' parties and pressure groups were planned and launched but the land reform and distribution policies they advocated seemed always to dissolve into the mists once Congress and administrators had acted upon them. There was no concerted attempt to form a left-wing party of workers and farmers which might have claimed a share of the rewards. The Democratic

Alliance, formed by the communists when independence came, had been intended to do just that but the Roxas forces had shut it down. The great mass of Filipinos—perhaps three out of four—found no real place in this political landscape and did not, it seemed, make any great effort to find one. Sison's new Communist party scorned electoral politics as futile and dismissed traditional politicians as mere "running dogs" of imperialists, landlords, and "bureaucrat capitalists."

Although the rich often sat in the provincial governorships and Congress, they rarely competed personally for the presidency. The postwar system decreed that the country's presidents come from more humble ranks. Thus, Ramón Magsaysay had been elevated from lowly beginnings as a truck driver. Diosdado Macapagal had been a poor man's son treated to a college education by a wealthy benefactor. They and others needed large sums of money to run for office, for Philippine elections were scandalously expensive. To obtain campaign funds, the candidate had to pass three tests. First, he must have proved himself a skillful campaigner and officeholder, one who could manage the political process and control the Congress. Second, he must be judged safe on the issues dear to the men who financed him. Third he must have demonstrated his appeal to that great mass of Filipinos who were to be humored and made to feel important when their votes were needed. Thus, the field of eligible candidates usually consisted of ambitious, clever men of middle-class or poorer backgrounds who could be relied on to deliver on promises by exuding populism on the hustings and managing a fractious Congress.

Ferdinand Edralin Marcos fit the prescription precisely. He came from Ilocos Norte, a province known for its aggressive natives, and was the son of a shrewd but intemperate man who had been a school teacher, lawyer and Congressman. His mother came from a family of means. She was a stern-willed woman who held the family together with personal discipline and not a little of her own funds when Ferdinand's father, Mariano, ran out of money. Ferdinand's youthful career took extraordinary turns. He was found guilty of participating in the murder, in 1935, of the congressional candidate who had defeated his father. While the case was being appealed, he continued to study law. In 1939, he pulled off two remarkable coups simultaneously, graduating first in his law school class and winning a reversal of his murder conviction by arguing his own case before the Supreme Court. He became a celebrity overnight.

Marcos emerged from World War II claiming feats of heroism as a guerilla fighter against the Japanese armies in Luzon. American guerilla verification records which surfaced four decades later disclosed most of these claims to be fraudulent, but by then Marcos had long since covered himself with medals. Moreover, the guerilla experience provided his first postwar success in building a following. He got hundreds of fellow Ilocanos certified as resistance fighters, making them eligible for American financial payments, and parlayed their gratitude into a local political machine. He was elected to Congress in 1949, 1953 and 1957, by which time he and Macapagal were regarded as potential Liberal Party candidates for president. In 1959, Marcos was the country's top vote-getter in his first campaign for the Senate, an achievement not ignored by the rich man's club that picked presidential candidates. Marcos made a deal in which Macapagal would be the party's presidential nominee in 1961 and then bow out in Marcos's favor four years later. Macapagal won the election but welched on the agreement. Marcos switched to the *Nacionalista* party, won its nomination in 1965, and defeated Macapagal by a wide margin. Four years later, he became the first Filipino to be twice elected to the presidency of the republic.

Marcos extracted money from the rich and votes from the poor with equal skill and even today his many enemies remember him as the most accomplished of postwar politicians. More than any of them except perhaps Magsaysay, he had the populist's touch with crowds of poor farmers (his resemblance in platform style to Huey Long of Louisiana was striking). He was adept at convincing farmers that he was on their side, battling for roads and schools and medical services against an uncaring bureaucracy. In 1969, a journalist brilliantly captured his performance at a crossroads village in Camarines Sur Province. Marcos mentioned, with the local mayor present, that he had made 8,000 pesos available for a new road and the crowd murmured back the complaint that no new road had been built.

And it is then that Marcos stops and frowns across the plaza. "Hey!" he growls. "What's this? What are you saying? No money? You haven't got the money?" He roars: "What's going on here?" And the crowd, delightedly horrified, roars with him. The village officials on the platform are no longer beaming.

Marcos turns to the man standing next to him, the mayor. "I give you eight thousand pesos for the barrio road!"

"Yessir," squeaks the mayor.

"Is the road finished?"

"Well, er, not quite . . ."

"The road isn't finished?"

"No, sir."

Marcos glares at the hapless mayor. He extends one hand, palm outward, raises his bass voice one octave and says: "Where is the moneeeey?" The crowd in the plaza explodes into laughter, rocking in the sun. The mayor's mouth moves, but no words come. Marcos . . . holds the pose, his mouth a hard straight line.

"You're working on the road?"

The mayor, unhappy, nods.[3]

It was great theater, but the politics of Marcos and others in this period rarely addressed real problems in the countryside. The crushing of the Huk rebellion had seemed to settle the issue of peasant unrest and the political system preferred that it remain that way. The tenant farmer's life seemed on the surface to continue unchanged that pattern of high rents and usurious interest which had produced revolt three decades earlier, and the politician's promises of relief somehow never were realized. Two major land-reform programs purportedly guaranteeing farmers their dream of owning small plots failed because landlords used political power to weaken them. The first, drafted in 1954 when President Magsaysay sought to redeem his promises, was shredded after Magsaysay was killed in an airplane crash. A second, enacted in 1963, promised a gradual evolution in which the tenant would become first a leaseholder and eventually a landowner. It too failed. By 1971, only about 50,000 sharecroppers (five percent of the total) had become leaseholders and only 3400 had obtained actual titles of ownership.

In fact, the conditions of peasant life were not remaining static. They were deteriorating rapidly. For the Philippine countryside in the 1960s was afflicted with two changes of dramatic proportions, both of which had the effect of forcing the farmer deeper into poverty and further dimming his prospects of becoming a landowner. The first was a rapid postwar population growth which created an ever-growing number of people in search of arable land. Population was increasing at the rate of 3.4 percent a year, nearly equal to the growth in Philippine gross national product. The second was an equally rapid decrease of land available to small farmers on any terms. The trend toward large plantations growing crops for export, a trend first noted in the 1930s, became more pronounced after the war. Landlords bought or illegally seized vast tracts for sugar, coconuts and other profitable export crops, often using armed force and the historic vagueness of Philippine land titles to move tenants out. To work land at all, farmers increasingly had to sign on as day laborers at absurdly low wages. Even that kind of work was disappearing as landlords turned increasingly to mechanized farming for greater profit—and for a less troublesome work force. Benedict Kerkvliet, the scholar, returning to his researches in Nueva Ecija Province in 1970, discovered the landlord Manolo Tinio using tenants to farm only 35 of his 216 hectares and planning to replace the remaining tenants as soon as possible. The reason, Tinio explained, was simple: "If you tell a machine to do something, it will do it. It's not that way with tenants."[4]

The result of these changes was a Philippine peasantry deep in debt and often homeless, living marginal lives on the fringes of great estates or clustering in shacks in towns. The postwar period had brought the beginnings of rural prosperity in many other Asian countries like Japan, South Korea, Taiwan and even Thailand, where enforced land-reform programs offered security. But not in the Philippines. By 1971, at least half of all rural Filipino families earned incomes that kept them below the poverty line, below the level needed for adequate nutrition and other essentials. For many, the only alternative was to seek refuge in Manila and other cities and during the 1960s there began to appear the first urban squatter colonies, great collections of packing-crate hovels that were homes to thousands. The number of squatters increased from 60,000 to 800,000 during the decade. In the countryside, the rich got richer, the poor poorer. Between 1957 and 1971, the share of total rural income received by the bottom 40 percent of the people declined from 18 to 13 percent. Over half of that total income went to the richest 20 percent.

In 1968, Renato Constantino, the nationalist historian and social critic, arrived at an apocalyptic vision of the Philippine condition. The political system, he wrote in a popular essay, was "bankrupt" and cynicism and indifference lay all about. Filipinos in the years since independence had formed a society "without a central, common purpose, whose members are obsessed with the pursuit of idleness." They had failed to shake off their colonial past and still permitted the United States to control the country's destiny. The economy was deteriorating. Land reform was a myth and foreign corporations continued to siphon off the capital surpluses needed to build a sound economy. The rich flourished and the specter of class warfare loomed over all.

It is certain that the masses will continue getting poorer while a relatively diminishing minority of privileged individuals will enjoy the advantages of immense wealth. The plutocratic content of our social system will become more exposed and the anti-popular nature of our government will be unmasked for an increasing number of our citizens. We shall be a country with two distinct societies—the masses who will struggle more and more fiercely for change and the beneficiaries of the system who will fight back with violence and repression to preserve the status quo.[5]

Constantino's words were widely quoted as the decade neared its end, and many other commentators seized on the fashionable notion of utter decadence. A mood of collective flagellation took hold and a chase began to point out new instances of national failure. Crime was out of control. Radicals owned the streets and in the provinces Huks were regrouping. The universities were in turmoil, beset by student strikes demanding everything from national regeneration to better cafeteria food. Political life was hopelessly corrupt, the bureaucracy riddled with bribery and favoritism. In 1968, a group of intellectuals, politicians and nationalist businessmen formed the Movement for the Advancement of Nationalism (MAN) and at its second congress, in March 1969, adopted this statement: "Philippine society today is sick, plagued by the perennial and now explosive problems of poverty, unemployment, corruption in the public service, and the breakdown of law and order. . . . Ninety percent of the population live under conditions of virtual peonage and starvation while a very few wallow in sinful wealth."[6]

Politicians quickly adapted to the enfevered mood. A Liberal Party leader, John Osmeña (grandnephew of Sergio Osmeño), proposed a "national unity council" composed of distinguished elders "to restore order and sanity in this sick, scared and uncertain country." The new president, Ferdinand E. Marcos, was not to be outdone. "We have come to the point of despair," he said.

We have declared for peace in our time but we cannot even guarantee life and limb in our growing cities. . . . Our government is gripped in the iron hand of venality, its treasury is barren, its resources are wasted, its civil service is slothful and indifferent, its armed forces demoralized and its councils sterile.[7]

And a young congressman, Benigno S. Aquino, Jr., who was soon to become Marcos's enemy, pronounced the Philippines a country of haves and have-nots:

Here is a land in which a few are spectacularly rich while the masses remain abjectly poor. Gleaming suburbia clashes with the squalor of the slums. . . . Here is a land consecrated to democracy but run by an entrenched plutocracy. Here, too, are a people whose ambitions run high, but whose fulfillment is low and mainly restricted to the self-perpetuating elite. Here is a land of privilege and rank—a republic dedicated to equality but mired in an archaic system of caste.[8]

Stripped of hyperbole, there was still much in these descriptions that was accurate. There was a great chasm between rich and poor. The crime rate was high. Money did talk in politics. But the picture of a society suddenly floundering in decadence and poised for revolution was largely a concoction of the intelligentsia, the press, and a few politicians. A public poll early in 1970 found that less than three percent of the people identified themselves with such radical issues as imperialism and the lack of social justice.[9] The most searching examination of public attitudes was one conducted by social scientists from the Rand Corporation and they found little to support the view of an alienated mass careening toward revolution. They found, instead, that Filipinos held favorable perceptions of their government and were disposed to accept the idea that government action changed their lives for the better. Sixty percent of the adults voted. Nearly three out of four believed the court system was honest and efficient. Two-thirds of them did think that graft and corruption were major problems and Filipinos everywhere expressed a strong desire for honest and sincere politicians. The Rand team concluded that the Philippines compared favorably with other new countries in their transition to the admired western norms of a "civic culture." The political system, they reported, was stable and generally responsive to the desires of the people. "In short, the problems facing the Philippines do not appear to be greatly in excess of the government's capacity to solve them."[10]

But the predictions of doom, overdrawn as they were by those in position to mold opinion, had their effect, for they conditioned the public mind to accept what was to come. There was genuine fear within the Filipino elite that revolutionary forces had been loosed and that drastic measures were called for. Marcos played skillfully on these fears and did much to heighten them. We know now that many frightening events in the pre-martial law months were concocted by him and his coterie as part of a clever design to create a stampede psychology that would not only accept but welcome the dismantling of democratic institutions. It is tantalizing but futile to speculate on whether he could have succeeded without the backdrop of pessimism and despair created for him.

It is not clear at what precise point Marcos determined to suspend the constitution and declare martial law. His decision may have been made quite early in his second term, which began in 1969 after a reelection campaign that was outrageously fraudulent even by Philippine standards. (So great was the expenditure of campaign funds that the new money sud-

93

denly put into circulation set off a round of inflation.) Marcos was prohibited by the constitution from seeking a third term and he could not serve beyond December 30, 1973. He faced the prospect of being succeeded by his despised rival, Benigno Aquino, who had pilloried him in the Senate and in the press.

It was the communist New People's Army which provided Marcos with the immediate pretext for martial law. At the time, of course, the NPA consisted of a few hundred riflemen being chased and hunted by thousands of government troops and it required heavy propaganda to make this motley band appear a dangerous force. Malacañang and the Defense Ministry headed by Juan Ponce Enrile churned out reports of ferocious battles in the hills. In 1971, Marcos warned that the rebels had established "rural sanctuaries" and "production bases" in northern Luzon and were bent on seizing power, although he estimated their armed force at only "1,000 front line troops." The following year, the president declared that the insurrection had grown "by leaps and bounds" and that its timetable envisioned toppling the government when his term expired. *Apres moi le déluge.* In the late 1970s and early 1980s, when the NPA was twenty times larger and far more skilled in guerilla warfare, Marcos would dismiss it as a minor nuisance. But in 1972, his interests were served by the magnification of a small force into a threat to national stability.

In August 1971, there began a series of spectacular incidents which seemed to lend support to Marcos's warnings. Grenades were thrown at a Liberal party rally in Manila's Plaza Miranda, killing nine people and severely wounding several of the opposition party's leaders. Malacañang blamed it on the communists. In July 1972, the military announced a great shoot-out with a contingent of NPA guerillas at a remote fishing port in Isabela Province where the rebels were allegedly trying to land a shipment of high-powered weapons imported from some unidentified foreign power. During the next few weeks, Manila was rocked by blasts of more than a dozen bombs planted in municipal offices and private buildings. The Armed Forces of the Philippines announced that captured communist documents revealed a plot to kill many political leaders and assault the airport in Manila. On September 19, a bomb exploded inside Quezon City Hall where the Constitutional Convention was meeting. Reports that Marcos would invoke martial law were widespread. Senator Aquino revealed one version, entitled "Oplan Sagittarius," which had been leaked to him by a dissident general. On September 21, thousands of KM-led demonstrators gathered at Plaza Miranda to protest the atmosphere of "fear and repression" Marcos had created. The most alarming incident occurred the following day. The official limousine usually occupied by Defense Minister Enrile was shattered by bullets. Enrile himself was riding in a trailing security escort car because, he claimed, he had anticipated just such an attack. On September 23, Marcos appeared on television and radio to announce Proclamation 1081 authorizing martial law because, he said, the country was "in urgent danger of violent overthrow, insurrection and rebellion."

How much of the pre-martial law turmoil was real and how much was orchestrated is unclear. Enrile has admitted that the attack on his car was staged. A defecting Marcos aide, Primitivo Mijares, disclosed before his sudden disappearance that military crews planted many of the Manila bombs, including those at the Quezon City Hall and at the Manila water system plant.[11] It seems likely that the NPA attempt to land arms in Isabela Province was real. The ghastly attack on the Liberal party at Plaza Miranda is still unexplained. But there were enough frightening incidents, real and faked, to manufacture the red scare out of what was an almost insignificant force. Enrile has since acknowledged that the guerillas numbered between 400 and 900 at the time and Marcos's own martial law proclamation referred to a force of only 1,028 fighters. A year earlier, a committee of the Senate had found the subversives presented no real military threat. Marcos brought it off with remarkably thorough planning and a Machiavellian's sure knowledge of his people and how they could be fooled. In a shrewd judgment rendered before martial law, a former presidential aide, Rafael Salas, observed of Marcos: "He knows the average Filipino—to what degree (he) can be scared, what are the limits before he becomes violent. Within these limits, he will apply any sort of artifice."[12]

Marcos's spokesmen liked to call it "martial law with a smile" and, indeed, the outward appearances of the new regime seemed hardly oppressive. No tanks appeared in the streets and Manila bore no resemblance to an armed camp. But for thousands of men and women on the military's lists the face of martial law held no trace of a smile. Hundreds were seized the first night. Benigno Aquino, Jr., one of the first to be arrested, was picked up at midnight in a room of the Hilton Hotel where his Senate committee was examining the government's proposed budget. Taken to a military camp, Aquino was never to be a free man in his country again. Opposition political leaders like Ramon Mitra and José Diokno were hustled away. Chino Roces, the patrician president of the Manila *Times,* and his columnist, Maximo Soliven, were taken into custody. Hundreds of other targets—from the sons of prominent old families to the long-haired young radicals in KM—disappeared. Camp Crame and Fort Bonifacio were jammed with prisoners, many of them living on cots in gymnasiums. Astonishingly, the government ultimately admitted that perhaps as many as 50,000 people were seized in the early years of martial law. Most were released after days of questioning but nearly 5,000 of them were still being detained as subversives in 1976.

Only as the months unfolded did the full dimensions of the Marcos revolution become clear. Virtually every democratic institution erected since independence was attained in 1946 was dismantled: the Congress, political parties, the free and lively press, the independent judiciary. The American "showcase of democracy" in Asia was smashed. In its place was a new constitution with the markings of a British-style parliamentary system, wrung from the remnants of a Constitutional Convention which initially had intended to curb Marcos's powers. It was ratified on January 17, 1973, in a series of rigged "citizen conventions," Marcos having first decreed and then cancelled a national plebiscite. The constitutional provisions hardly mattered. Marcos, through various proclamations, one-sided elections and phony plebiscites, would govern by edict until he had stayed too long and ruled too harshly and the people of the Philippines decided they had had enough.

They are called today the "martial law babies," those hundreds of young students for whom Marcos's proclamation in 1972 was the signal to flee into the communist underground. For them, martial law ended the era of amateur radicalism. The period of street marches and earnest work in Marxist study cells was over and whether they were ready for it or not the days of real revolution had begun. Their motives varied. Some were mere romantics caught up in the emotional reaction to the military arrests. A few were serious Marxists whose readings told them that such a "fascist" crackdown was inevitable, an example of the "contradictions of capitalism." Whatever their reasons, their numbers expanded the ranks of the radical underground and the NPA. Some headed straight into the hills to seek out a place in the guerilla army. Others waited in Manila for the party to find them useful jobs.

Over the years, the myth has grown that this exodus of "martial-law babies" was the moment when the rebellion really began. It is the belief of many that the declaration of martial law by itself created the new communist insurgency and that without Marcos there would have been nothing to worry about. His proclamation sent the best from Philippine universities scurrying to the hills, it is said, where they became the leaders of the movement and the dedicated revolutionaries who a decade later would threaten the government. It is a comforting notion for those who believe communism has no real roots in the Philippines. But interviews with many of the middle-level cadres who do run the revolution today suggest a different pattern. For the most part, they are men and women who had become committed before martial law to the idea of Marxist revolution, who quite seriously believed in its inevitable success. They were not starry-eyed flower children suddenly impelled by the sight of guns and soldiers to seek refuge in an underground party. The ones who guide the CPP in the provinces today were for the most part already deeply involved in party work before martial law and it was to them that the "martial law babies" came running when the Marcos whip was cracked. They had the discipline and the organization to channel that exodus into a larger movement and they are the ones who exert the most influence today.

Jes is typical of the breed. He was born into a middle-class Manila family which had suffered financial reverses, a condition he now describes in Marxist language: "Our family fell from the national bourgeoisie to the petty bourgeoisie."[13] His older

97

brother had become a doctor and Jes expected to follow in his footsteps, despite the decline in family fortunes. As a pre-medical student at the University of the Philippines in the late 1960s, he became involved in anti-government demonstrations, initially as a young nationalist opposed to American intervention in Philippine politics. But he also drifted, at the prodding of friends, into several Marxist discussion groups then being conducted by the two radical youth organizations, KM and *Samahang Democratiko ng Kabataang* (SDK), or the Democratic Youth Association. Both were secretly controlled by the CPP, which prescribed a curriculum ranging from moderate nationalism to Marxism. They were rather formal courses with texts and discussion leaders and in one of them Jes encountered a collection of essays on political economy written by British leftists. "We all read this book and it had a great impact on us. It was the first time I had ever understood the theory of surplus value. I grasped the idea that workers produce everything and they are being robbed of everything they produce. So then I started researching Marxist thought. Things were so unjust. The toiler produces everything."

Jes had intended to complete his pre-med courses, but his life was suddenly changed on January 26. He had joined the large demonstration, the start of the "First Quarter Storm," and never returned to his classes. "I was beaten up [by police] and had bruises all over me. I was so infuriated, all I could think of was getting back at the police. It was then that I perceived the importance of organizations. I joined SDK on January 30. It was a legal organization, but I knew it was controlled by the party.

"I was recruited into the party in May 1971, and was put into a labor committee of the SDK, doing trade union work, working with the people. I loved it. I learned there that you must learn from the people. It is the only way. I learned to set up a union. My people were in Bulacan. They worked in small, almost cottage-sized industries of 30 to 40 workers."

From that beginning, Jes went on to become an influential party cadre adept at union organizing in Manila and its nearby industrial communities. When I met him in 1986, he was a boyish, handsome man in his thirties, married to a party propaganda worker who had been similarly converted to Marxism in the 1960s. He talked eagerly of his lifetime commitment to party work and was especially encouraged by the successful infiltration of trade unions in and around Manila. One reason for the success, he volunteered, was the operation of an NPA assassination squad which killed or intimidated employers and police officials bent on crushing unions. Only recently, he said with something approaching delight, the team had slain a high police official as he dined in a Quezon City restaurant.

The story of Jes reflects the extent to which the communist movement and Marxist teachings had succeeded in capturing the imaginations of the young before martial law. By the early 1970s, KM and SDK, were attracting the brightest and most militant among them and were transforming the early nationalism into serious Marxism. The effect on an older generation was limited. Many liberals of the old school considered Maoist proselytism ludicrous. F. Sionil José, the accomplished novelist, magazine publisher, and reformist of an earlier time, remembers the passionate ideologs drifting into his bookstore to argue politics in those days. "I would tell them, 'Look, you are pro-Chinese in a country where the anti-Chinese feeling is very strong and you are anti-American in a country where a lot of people would like to see the Philippines become the fifty-first state.'" Still, the drift toward radicalism was very strong in intellectual circles, especially in the colleges where KM and SDK recruited. "By the time of martial law," one professor recalled, "Marxism had become respectable in the better universities and that was no small achievement. A decade earlier, no sensible professor or instructor would have dared touch Marx."

Like Jes, others today holding positions in the CPP's middle ranks had been converted before Marcos acted. Victor, who was to lead the movement in Mindanao, had become a Marxist in KM as early as 1970. "There were both radicals and moderates then," he remembered, "but we radicals held the initiative and the moderates joined us." George, who pieced together the party's united front in Negros, had learned about Marxism in high school by reading Sison's early articles and, like him ironically, by taking a required course designed to disparage communism. "I remember reading the statement in our text where it said that communists believe 'The state is an instrument of the ruling class.' I thought: 'What's wrong with that? It's true.'"

The "martial-law babies" were different. Although some had wandered into the ubiquitous Marxist study groups, most had remained simply nationalists. They wanted the U.S. bases removed, an end to American intervention in domestic politics, and restrictions on foreign corporations. In the elite Catholic colleges they opposed the domination of foreign-born priests and texts which emphasized foreign interpretations of Philippine history. When they went underground after the September proclamation they carried with them little Marxist baggage. "Most of them were non-communists," recalled Jes, who was assigned to help many of them adjust to new lives. "They were what we called national democrats in those days. There was just a smattering of real Marxists. Lots of them had of course been in KM and SDK, which the party controlled, but most were just nationalists." In 1972, Julie Sison was in the country attempting to cope with the arrival of new converts fleeing Manila. "Most of those who joined us were simply nationalists," she remembered.

Some were intellectual converts who made instant personal choices to fight from underground what was by then an unambiguously dictatorial government. Marcos had clarified the choice for them. The midnight sweeps, seizure of the press, and dismantling of Congress confirmed for them the scary tales of fascism their more advanced friends had warned against. The communists were right, after all. Suddenly all of those earnest study groups, clandestine lectures, and even the relentless preachments in the *Little Red Book* seemed sources of real truth and not mere philosophical talking points. And the communists were prepared to act. They possessed an organization which had real guns; the nationalist groups had only slogans and banners.

But for many the decision to go underground was made for them. There was no place else to go. The rowdy nationalists' names were on government lists as subversives, along with those of real Marxists. They faced arrest and, as it turned out, torture. Many were barred from schools overnight and inquiries were being made at their homes. Hiding out was the only option and the CPP offered the only organized underground. The CPP had rehearsed for just such an event a year earlier when Marcos had suspended the writ of habeas corpus and had

100

designed a network to spirit its members away. The purely nationalist groups had never seriously considered waging a campaign from illegal cells or mountain hideaways. The CPP was their only refuge. "They had no place else to go," Jes remembered. "They were all threatened with arrests. Their names were on the military lists and their families had been visited by people from the military who instructed the parents to turn them in. The colleges had been ordered to blacklist them. That was their situation."

The party itself was delighted to discover this new flood of recruits running into its arms and tried to make room for them. Statements appearing in the pages of *Ang Bayan,* the party newspaper, a week after martial law was declared, exulted in the new developments and issued instructions to accommodate the newcomers both in the NPA and the united front. (The party had begun work on a united front strategy in 1971 but would not issue its first clear plan until the spring of 1973). The duty of revolutionaries, said *Ang Bayan* on October 1, 1972 was to "join up with all forces that are opposed to the fascist dictatorship of the U.S.-Marcos clique." A message directed at moderate democrats called for a restoration of civil rights, revived political parties, trade unions, and a free media. Even defecting military officers would be welcomed into the NPA.

The CPP found many practical blessings in martial law. It confirmed the old Marxist saw about capitalism containing the seeds of its own destruction. It would heighten the confrontations between classes and bring the party substantial middle-class support. "Despite what appears to be the tightening of the situation due to the U.S.-Marcos dictatorship," declared *Ang Bayan* on October 12, "the entire country has been made far more fertile than before for revolutionary seeding and growth." From the ranks of outlawed trade unions and middle-class youth groups would come future cadres for the NPA. The party's instructions were to "assign more cadres of workers as well as [those from] petty bourgeoisie backgrounds to the New People's Army." Those who were no longer able to conduct legal or underground work in the cities "should be dispatched to the people's army through the various regional party committees."

Easier said than done, the party quickly discovered. Its regional organizations which were supposed to manage this sudden exodus were too fragile to assimilate hundreds of the new rebels. A government military offensive, launched on October 10 to crush NPA squads in Luzon and KM cells in the cities, also disrupted the system of communications. Safe passage to the rural hideaways and new homes among sympathetic farmers could not be arranged quickly enough. As a result, many of the new recruits languished restlessly in Manila apartments or huddled in rural encampments where they were easily spotted. In Manila, a party leader of that time recalled:

Our mechanism for nationwide deployment was not very systematic. There were so many of the activists just sitting around waiting for regional assignments. Many of them waited in underground houses in Manila for two to three months. There would be 10 or 12 people in one apartment and they had no bread-earners who could go out to get money for food. They had to live on coffee and *pan de sal* which we bought them out of funds we solicited. Our courier systems were faulty and their trips were constantly being postponed.

In the mountains outside Davao, in Mindanao, the situation was chaotic. Before martial law, a small group of militants had left the city to form armed bands in the mountains of Davao del Norte and Davao del Sur provinces. The martial law proclamation suddenly brought hundreds more streaming into their camps. "They had no guns and no experience," a Mindanao CPP veteran recalled. "Groups of 50 and 100 of them were just camping there in the countryside, chanting slogans about the Cultural Revolution in China." Operating near them in the rugged forested mountains were members of a farmers youth group who had merely favored modest land reforms but who were suddenly cast in the role of radical revolutionaries by the martial law proclamation. It was all a bit disillusioning, another party veteran remembered. The CPP propaganda and the military's own warnings had created the impression of a massive well-oiled organization linked with a fearsome people's army. The reality was different. What the newcomers found was a skeletal organization, a ragged army on the run, and an overloaded recruitment system which could not place most of them in useful jobs. Julie Sison has said:

Yes, martial law created many new recruits for us. It was a real exodus. But there were too many for us to absorb. Many had to be sent back. There was no room for them and they would only have overloaded our forces in the countryside. We had to discourage so many of them from the idea of waging war. . . . There weren't even any guns for them.

6

☆☆☆

Scout Rangers are the elite fighting units of the Armed Forces of the Philippines. They are disciplined and aggressive, exceptional traits in an army of sloppy habits and a notable reluctance to enter combat against guerillas hiding in mountains. Most, too, have a reputation for restraint in dealing with the Philippine citizens they are assigned to defend. But the Ranger force based at the small town of Isabela, in the province of Negros Occidental, was not of the usual caliber. Its troops had a record of civilian abuse which had made them outsiders in the village, and they were believed to be responsible for the several cases of "salvagings," the sudden disappearances and deaths of townspeople. Obtaining a permit as required for all public demonstrations, the Isabelans marched one day in protest to the Scout Ranger outpost. The confrontation grew rowdy and in the confusion shots were fired. One townsman was killed instantly and two others were wounded.

On a Sunday afternoon in May 1985, soon after that incident, the streets of Isabela were unusually quiet and deserted, many of its citizens having been warned secretly that it would

104

not be safe to hang around the Rangers that day. At the head-quarters itself, no sentries were posted, which was not unusual, and many of the troops had wandered away in pursuit of what passed for recreation in that sleepy outpost. Some enjoyed the fights at the local cockpit. Others played basketball on an out-door court. At 4:30 P.M., a long truck belonging to a nearby sugarcane plantation rolled slowly down the narrow main high-way and turned into town center, stopping near the Ranger headquarters. Forty men dressed in the ragged garb of sugar workers sprang from the truck bed bearing M-16 automatic rifles and World War II-vintage American Garands. The first shots killed several Rangers who tried to defend the headquar-ters. One detachment of invaders shot its way into the townhall jail which stood across the street and freed several friends. In a matter of a few minutes, the sugarcane truck was speeding up the highway toward a mountain range. The score for the day: twelve Rangers killed, seven wounded; two guerillas from the New People's Army killed, three wounded. In the bed of the departing truck lay the prize—72 rifles and a machine gun formerly in the Ranger armory.[1] A few weeks later, the outpost was abandoned and the surviving Rangers were transferred to a central base in the larger city of Cadiz.

Francisco, commander of the central front, New People's Army of the Philippines, Negros Occidental Province, planned and led the attack on Isabela's Scout Rangers. He is a stocky, moon-faced man in his late thirties, a veteran guerilla leader whose adult life has been spent in the hills. In his student days in Manila, he had been a young nationalist swept up in the noisy demonstrations of 1969 and 1970. But he drifted gradually into the radical youth group KM and its Marxist study cells where he had learned about the three famous "isms": imperial-ism, feudalism and bureaucrat capitalism. Francisco (a party name) went underground in 1971, and in 1973 began forming the NPA's first successful front in Negros Occidental. In late 1985, his home was the central front's camp thousands of feet high on the side of Mount Canlaon, a volcanic mountain that towers over the lowland plains and the sugar estates that stretch out to blue-green Visayan straits and the Gulf of Panay. He is a calm, soft-spoken man who speaks with slow delibera-tion and personal modesty (he dislikes the title *Kumander*).

One morning, after a meal of rice and beans outside his *nipa*-palm-covered hut, he talked of the Isabela raid.

Francisco had planned it for two reasons. First, the Scout Ranger armory contained many modern automatic weapons, the one commodity his army lacked. His force consisted then of only one company of at most a hundred men and women, but it could grow quickly to hundreds, even thousands, if guns were available. "There are so many volunteers from down there," he said, sweeping his hand toward the cane fields below. "We have to turn them away." Recently, a trigger-happy government paramilitary unit in the town of Escalante had fired into a crowd of protesting citizens, killing 27 of them and wounding many others. The day after the killings, nearly 200 young volunteers from Escalante had tried to join Francisco's front. There were no guns to arm them and they had been sent back.

The second reason for the Isabela raid was political. The Scout Rangers were an arrogant, boastful bunch who bragged frequently to the townspeople that the NPA was no match for them in battle. "We planned our raid to show them they could not get away with that," Francisco said, "and to show the people there who are our friends that we could help them to get the Rangers away from their town." It was extremely important, he said, that the NPA demonstrate to its friends that they could be protected. People in Isabela secretly sympathized with the guerillas in the hills and aided them in many ways. They gave donations of food, medicine and money to the central front, provided safe houses where guerillas could rest between fights, attended propaganda meetings, and supplied daily intelligence reports on the Rangers' comings and goings. Without their support, Francisco's squads would be roaming aimlessly and eating roots for supper. Conversely, without armed support from the NPA, the villagers would cease to take such risks, and so the Isabela attack was, in the strictly political sense, a form of reassurance. Francisco meshed the fingers of his hands and explained, "We are all tied up in this together."

Later, Francisco led me to a break in the foliage for a better view of the lovely scene below, where the tropical forest broke off into gentle, sparsely wooded slopes, which in turn gave way to rows of sugar cane, much of it recently harvested. His front's

106

territory, he explained, encompassed fourteen towns in the foothills and lowland plains. Down there, propaganda teams fanned out daily on routine missions to win converts among the cane-cutters' families, teaching the "three isms" he had first learned in Manila. In some barrios of his fourteen towns, revolutionary committees already controlled the public life; in others, party organizing teams were just beginning. Theirs was the hard and dangerous work, Francisco said, for the military might seize them at any moment. He thought that sixty percent of the townspeople in those towns now supported the NPA and the number of sympathizers increased daily. But this was only one front in Negros Occidental and the northern part of the province lay almost untouched. The military balance was heavily in the government's favor, even though its troops fought fewer battles than at first. I asked him how much time would pass before the final victory of the Negros Occidental NPA. "Ten years," he said.

Sixteen years earlier, the CPP founders gathered at Pangasinan had approved Sison's document entitled "Rectify Errors and Rebuild the Party." Richly embellished with Maoist jargon, it was a brutal exhumation of three errors committed by the Lava brothers' leadership of the old Communist party, errors which had precipitated the failure and demise of the Huk army. One of the grave mistakes was the quick-victory, or "putschist," policy which had projected a series of sudden large-scale assaults to bring down the government in the 1940s. The Lavas had not recognized the necessarily protracted nature of peasant war, which moves slowly by stages to grind the enemy down. A second error was the failure to understand the political nature of guerilla warfare. The people must be taught through patient education to understand the cause for which they made sacrifices. Finally, the old Huks, guided by Lava doctrine, concentrated their forces almost entirely in central Luzon, becoming an easy target for the massed power of government troops. "Rectify Errors . . ." was not intended as a military master plan. Essentially it was ammunition with which to vilify the despised Lavas. But in time these three lessons became the basic strategic guide for the New People's Army. A generation of cadres have memorized and applied them and with some modification they stand today as the holy writ of revolution in the Philippines.

The protracted character of guerilla war was fundamental to all of the NPA undertakings. The army was prepared for the long haul. There would be no quick victories. Mao had started in the 1920s and knew success only in 1949. Vietnamese communists had fought the French and Americans for four decades. Acceptance of the long-war doctrine was central to the Philippine communist concept, too. Sison had borrowed the Maoist strategy of establishing stable base areas, or zones, where guerillas could hide in safety. From these they would advance "wave after wave," establishing new bases with each wave. The war would go forward in three lengthy phases: the "strategic defensive," when NPA forces are grossly over-matched and engage only in small-scale raids and ambushes; the "strategic stalemate," when it obtains more or less parity of strength and confronts the enemy in equal force; and the "strategic offensive," when the encircled cities fall and the government collapses. In 1986, seventeen years after the NPA was founded, it was still in the first phase of defensive warfare. This was accepted as natural. When Francisco stood on the Negros mountain and estimated that victory lay ten years in the future he was not being pessimistic, merely practical.

"The New People's Army is not only a fighting force, it is also a propaganda and organizing force."[2] This admonition is found in the charter of the NPA, written in 1969, and became the second operating principle for the army's leadership. It was Sison's thesis that the older Huks had ignored the duty of arming peasant followers with an educated commitment to the cause. The new Red Army must be educators as well as fighters, their first obligation being to teach people what they were fighting against. The initial infiltration of a barrio was usually by an Armed Propaganda Team (APT) which made friends and selected potential converts and then settled in to explain the nature of the enemy in clandestine seminars. They were not pistol-packing ideologues—even educated veterans like Francisco had little interest in theoretical Marxism. The first APTs preached the evils of feudalism and imperialism, but in practical terms a farmer could comprehend: his high interest rates were the inevitable product of an immoral system imposed on millions of farmers. The fighter as teacher was an innovation also borrowed from Mao and for a dozen years it was a formula rigidly followed in the NPA. In 1981, it was modified in a major CPP policy change which sought to step up the pace of the war by creating full-time fighting units freed of propaganda duties.

The third lesson learned from the Huk debacle has been perhaps the one of most lasting value. The Lava strategy for ultimate victory had assumed a single target: the government in Manila. Bring it down by a series of decisive strikes from forces concentrated in the nearby countryside and the war was won. In practice, this strategy exposed the Huk platoons to ferocious assaults and near annihilation. NPA strategy became the precise reverse. The war would be spread to many fronts throughout the archipelago, each front operating with great independence and little central direction. Government forces would thus be similarly extended and dispersed, incapable of delivering decisive blows. "In the long run, the fact that our country is archipelagic will turn out to be a great advantage for us and a great disadvantage for the enemy," Sison wrote in the CPP's most innovative document. "The enemy shall be forced to divide his attention and forces not only to the countryside but also to so many islands."[3] In each war front, Red soldiers must avoid set battles with larger enemy contingents. The NPA would choose each target so that victory was likely, if not absolutely assured. When outnumbered, they would fade into the protective concealment of the countryside. The enemy "is made to exhaust himself by punching the air . . ."[4]

In early 1986, the CPP leadership believed that fidelity to these three lessons had served it well. Hundreds of thousands of Filipinos had been politicized. Among the cadres, many of them in their late thirties and forties by then, the concept of a protracted conflict was well accepted. Most important, the NPA had spread to all corners of the archipelago, creating the first national insurgency in Philippine history. From the initial small base in central Luzon, the old "Huklandia," it had moved first to the far north, into the nearly impenetrable Cagayan Valley and the rugged Cordillera Mountains. An early foothold in the Bicol region of Southeastern Luzon had erupted into a major battlefront. The northern part of Samar, an impoverished island in the eastern Visayas, was rebel territory, the NPA control there so solid that government forces rarely challenged it. In the western Visayas, the islands of Negros and Panay swarmed with NPA soldiers who moved through many sectors unmolested. The big surprise, though, was the large southern island of Mindanao. Original NPA strategy conceived of Mindanao as a mere diversion. Its soldiers there were to cause only enough trouble to pin down government forces and thus ease pressure on more important rebel fronts in Luzon. But by 1986, Mindanao was the most active region. NPA fronts were spread across its eastern and northern provinces, and the sprawling city of Davao had become the movement's most successful experiment in urban guerilla warfare. Throughout the Philippines, only the capital of Manila seemed untouched, but its time was coming. Already, across the bay, communities in Bataan where labor troubles spread unrest came under NPA control. In late 1985, veteran cadres had established a new base only twenty kilometers southeast of the metropolis.

The advance in the 1970s had been uneven and marked by many setbacks. Repeatedly, the Marcos government had insisted that communism had been crushed, and these were not always idle boasts. As late as 1975, for example, the Mindanao NPA had been whittled down to a mere four squads. But the 1980s had witnessed a remarkable acceleration in the fighting. The size of both party membership and fighting units had expanded rapidly. From Dante's first force of 35 defecting Huks in 1969, the NPA had grown to about 20,000 full-time and part-time guerillas sharing about 12,000 modern weapons, the party said. CPP membership had reached the 30,000 mark, compared to the 75 novices on the rolls when the Pangasinan conference was held. Guerilla fronts had been extended into at least 60 of the 73 Philippine provinces and the mass base of active supporters, the party claimed, exceeded one million men and women. Nowhere in the archipelago could the NPA resist an all-out government assault. But nowhere did the Armed Forces of the Philippines seem capable of destroying the NPA. The slow, patient mobilization of sympathizers, accompanied by the murder or intimidation of local officials, had spread so widely that the CPP could realistically claim that about 25 percent of the nation's *barangays* were either controlled or influenced to some extent by the NPA and party organs. The Philippine government and American intelligence disputed estimates of the fighting force, but did not challenge the claims of political influence. The NPA and its political movement, all sides agreed, were expanding virtually unchecked. Confident party leaders asserted in 1985 that in three to five years the long crusade would reach the "strategic stalemate" stage, which meant a full-scale civil war. Alarmed American officials had reached a similar conclusion. Richard L. Armitage, assistant secretary of Defense for International Security Affairs, testified in 1984, "Although the combat forces of the NPA are currently inferior in numbers to the AFP, the insurgents are building their base and could tip the balance of military power within the next several years."[5]

On a rocky, uneven plateau two-thirds of the way up one side of Mount Canlaon was perched Francisco's camp of the NPA central front, Negros Occidental. It did not appear a formidable bastion. A disorderly assortment of small raised huts scattered under palms and other trees were the only structures and the visitor was struck by the insubstantiality of it all. A thin metal sheet braced by rocks was the camp stove and the water system was a rickety chain of halved bamboo poles leading to a pool and waterfall. Life there seemed to the outsider precarious. Meals were rice, beans and occasionally sweet potatos, all of it carried to the camp on the shoulders of boys from the friendly barrios several thousand feet below. There was no electricity and so the sun regulated the work day. Light faded each night around seven, when the NPA soldiers who were not on missions rolled into the rough huts six abreast, each clutching his loaded M-16 as he drifted into sleep. The next day began at 5:30, dawn announced by the bright, chirping sound of a young woman soldier calling out the cadence for calisthenics to her squad in Ilonggo, the native dialect. A slight figure with tiny forearms, she managed somehow to muscle her M-16 above her head, then to the ground, then straight out in front. After a half hour, she and the squad disappeared over a ledge and into the forest trail that led to the day's business in the plains below.

111

From the first, Negros had seemed to the communists a land of promise. "Feudalism" was no abstraction there, but an exact description of an enduring economic pattern which brought riches to a few and desperate poverty to the rest. Sugar barons lived lives of a regal quality in grand haciendas, their wealth assured by the world's demand for cheap sweets and their fiefs protected from threats of all sorts by large private armies. The sugar workers were all but indentured serfs, living in huts on the great estates, their large families dependent on daily wages as low as twenty-five cents. Their misery had become a national scandal in the 1960s when a Catholic priest wrote a painfully incisive account of field-work on the masters' plantations. The cane-cutters of Negros seemed of all Philippine farmers the most exploited. It was natural, then, for the new Communist Party of the Philippines to select them as objects of their strategy to spread the people's war throughout the archipelago. The southern rim of Negros Occidental Province, with its large estates and impoverished workers, was chosen by the CPP in 1969 as the first area outside Luzon for NPA infiltration. If the war on feudalism could succeed anywhere, certainly it would be among the cane fields of Negros.

Instead, the expedition was a disaster. The first emissaries (Julie Sison recalled) were two guerilla veterans from Dante's force who linked up with a KM student and a single local peasant to start the revolution. Dante's men from Tarlac, on Luzon, spoke no Ilonggo and stood out conspicuously. Moreover, they knew little about the art of political mobilization and set about doing what they did best, which was murdering police and members of the Constabulary. Within weeks they were spotted and slain and the government quickly shut down the embryonic support group that had formed in Bacolod, the provincial capital. But the lesson had been learned: No NPA fighters could survive outside the shelter of a political base. Farmers first must be convinced that the cause could help them. Then they would provide food, hiding places, and intelligence for the people's army; the killing could come later. In 1973, the southern front was reopened, this time by students, radical Catholics from the new Christians for National Liberation (CNL), and the island's first Armed Propaganda Team from the NPA. They began the long, patience-sapping work of organizing the peasant communities and barrios. Three teams of from three to five young men, all Negrenses, moved almost unnoticed among the sugar workers, preaching the "three isms," slowly winning trust and support. By the 1980s, the southern front of Negros Occidental was a model NPA territory, so efficiently mobilized that Francisco, who had organized it, was able to move on with a few veterans to Mount Canlaon and found the central front base.

A peasant army led by educated cadres is the NPA standard and in 1985 the central front generally was typical. All of its foot-soldiers were from Negros farm families and ninety percent of them came from homes lying within the front's territory in the lowlands, the sons and daughters of sugar workers. Francisco's company included between 60 and 100 members, the numbers varying by shifting assignments to other fronts. Almost all I met were in their late teens and early twenties. About ten percent of them were young women and they had formed their own squad to fight together. An exception was Guillermo, a cagey veteran in his late thirties whose tactical and killing skills had elevated him to second in command of the camp. He had deserted the Philippine army in 1978. A brother and sister sympathetic to the underground movement had swayed him into viewing his army as oppressive. The final breach, he said, had come when his unit, stationed in the Mindanao province of Lanao del Sur, committed a "massacre" against a group of civilians. He and 27 other soldiers made secret plans to defect and one night simply walked away; several, like him, went on to join the NPA.

The young soldiers he commanded had joined for a variety of reasons. Several talked of relatives and friends abused and even killed by the military—a 19-year-old boy's father had been dragged from home in the night and never seen again. The NPA was wary of those so emotionally motivated because they often lacked discipline and became trigger-happy. "We do not want anarchy and a bloody war," Carlos, a party leader in the Visayas had told me. "We have had troubles before with people who just want to avenge a death in the family. We tell them they need training to understand why it was their brothers were killed."

"If someone comes in with personal reasons only," Francisco explained, "he will not last long. We do not want some guy just because his brother has been salvaged, but of course it is easier to teach that kind what state fascism means." With a shortage of guns and a backlog of volunteers, the Negros NPA could be picky. Those selected had undergone political training and had been put to work first as unarmed organizers in the barrios. Those who demonstrated discipline entered a six-month probationary period and even then were not guaranteed selection because the front was chronically short of weapons. Some said they had served first in the front's militia, a sort of home guard whose mission was patrolling barrios below and the paths that led up to the base camp. One had literally shot his way into the NPA regulars. On his own initiative, he had killed a lone soldier and seized his rifle, which he then presented to the central front as a credential meriting his acceptance.

His experience was a revealing insight into a corner of the rebellion that was at first difficult to understand. The act of seizing a weapon is an extremely important feat, for in the Philippine revolution each new gun equals one new soldier. It seemed strange, in a world awash in weaponry, to come across a full-blown rebellion which had endured for seventeen years but which still had to struggle daily to find arms. So far as is known, the NPA received one shipment of rifles from abroad, a purchase from the Palestine Liberation Organization in 1981. All others had been taken in battle, stolen, or purchased on the black market from governmental soldiers. Some 10,000 high-powered rifles, pistols, and machine guns had been obtained in this fashion over the years. Each seizure was an event for celebration.

The raids and ambushes launched by Francisco's troops followed the cardinal rule of always massing in superior force. In a typical raid, a military outpost would be silently surrounded in the night by NPA squads that outnumbered soldiers three and four to one. Usually, the garrison surrendered without a fight and Francisco's men carted off its guns, ammunition, typewriters, and other equipment. Ambushes were more sophisticated and far deadlier operations. Guerillas would slip through the canefields at night and line both sides of a country road, digging foxholes at the edges of the fields and covering themselves with dirt and cane. At dawn, as the military patrol

114

moved along the road, the NPA opened fire and the shooting continued until the patrol was wiped out or its resistance proved too great to overcome. In virtually every ambush, Francisco said, the guerillas had advance intelligence on the patrol's planned movements.

The specific goal of each raid or ambush was the collection of weapons, but the cumulative effect was distinctly political. In many cases, the military stopped patrolling remote areas where they were extremely vulnerable and thus could provide no support for owners of outlying plantations. Unable to rely on armed force, the landlords in turn became more willing to agree to their workers' demands for higher wages, less inclined to resist. Many simply abandoned their farms and their former employees became de facto owners of small parcels. And so the political message became clear: NPA tactical offensives enhanced the workers' power, enabled them to stand up to recalcitrant *hacenderos*. Francisco explained:

The tactical offensives are mainly to get guns, but they also have an effect on the people. They back up the farmers in their confrontations with the landlords. The landlords are afraid now. People confront them on wages and benefits and then the landlords assume they are backed up by the NPA, even though sometimes they really aren't. And so then the farmers are in a strong position, they know they need the NPA. Without the NPA they would be nothing. As it was before, the landlords could just call in the military and be deaf to their demands.

The central front of Negros held the revolutionary record for what is called *agaw-armas,* or the massing of arms, in a single operation. One night in March 1985, Francisco led a party from the hills and an urban guerilla group from Bacolod to the Visayas Maritime Academy, a private coast guard training school near the provincial capital. Informers had described to them the cache of weapons in the academy's armory and there was inside help during the raid itself. Without firing a shot, the party carried off 421 rifles in a truck borrowed from a sugar plantation. Similarly favored with advice from informers, another party raided a copper mine headquarters partly owned by a Japanese corporation, Marubeni. The prize was two tons of explosives. Most *agaw-armas* operations produced less spectacular results. The armories of sugar estates had yielded a supply of AK-47 automatic rifles but little ammunition to go with them. Raiding them had proved easier than the alternative of ambushing military units. Carlos, the Visayan united front leader, described with keen satisfaction how a supply of Armalites and AK-47 rifles were taken from a sugar planter's home in Bacolod by four raiders from the city's urban guerilla team:

All of the local landlords are very macho. They like guns, and our intelligence had told us that this one kept a lot of them locked in his home. We knew everything about him and the house—even the time he and his wife would arrive home that night. Our people were waiting. They told him they would not kill him, that they only wanted his rifles. He showed them where to look. Then our people made him sit down and they had a discussion. They explained to him about conditions in Negros and why they were robbing him. When they left, they told him they were people who lived in the city, not far away from him, and that he should not report the incident.

Through these and other devices, the central front amassed a varied armory consisting of American-made M-16s, M-14s, World War II-vintage Garands, grease guns and machine guns. The only weapons on hand not manufactured in the United States were Russian AK-47s. Ammunition was in such short supply that each fighter was permitted to fire only five rounds a day, regardless of his mission.

At first, Francisco said, the central front guerillas had been too few in number and too lightly armed to attack government troops in anything but small units. The seizure of more than two or three army rifles in any single raid was unusual. But since 1984, with its armory growing and more recruits available, it had moved into full-sized company assaults involving seventy or eighty guerillas and the arms harvest had grown accordingly. A typical ambush took place near a market town where a military detachment was based. The NPA had a substantial intelligence network in the town and was informed that on a particular night an enemy platoon would be returning to barracks from a patrol. Its route took it along a narrow farm road bordered on both sides by sugar cane. Francisco's units moved in at dusk, dug foxholes in the cane field, and lay concealed for hours until the military trucks came along. The sudden ambush left several soldiers dead and netted the central front about twenty rifles. By the time a rescue team arrived, the shooting was over and the guerillas had faded away into the cane fields toward Mount Canlaon.

No one seems to know for certain where the NPA's "sparrow units" first began their deadly operations. Some say they sprang up informally in the city of Davao, in Mindanao. Whatever their origin, the sparrows had proved to be one of the NPA's bloodiest and most effective methods of getting guns. The sparrow unit was a three-member assassination squad assigned to liquidate informers or other enemies and kill isolated police and military men for their weapons. They were experts in the quick kill, the term sparrow denoting their ability to dart quickly toward a victim, kill him, and flee before authorities arrived. The preferred method was one shot in the back of the skull. In Negros, Francisco said, sparrows had killed off-duty soldiers while they were courting local girls, loitering in bars, or gambling in the small-town cockpits. Sparrow warfare had its unwritten rules, he explained: Any soldier was fair game for the assassin's bullet, but the ordinary policeman should first be warned and asked to surrender his pistol voluntarily.

Within the party, there was some nervousness about the sparrows' activities, especially in Davao where they murdered many traffic patrolmen to obtain pistols. Some of the more sophisticated propagandists have sought to soften this gunslinging image by suggesting that sparrows were carefully trained and disciplined veterans who selected as victims only those soldiers known for abusing civilians. Francisco was more candid. "Most of the sparrow killings are by young boys who have had no training," he said. "It's sort of an 'on-the-job training.' We select young unknowns for sparrow duty because they can move about easily without being noticed. Some of the people they kill are guilty of committing crimes against the people, but they also kill just to get guns." Some Negros sparrows were not even formally part of the NPA structure, according to a local party official, but mere free-lancers eager to help. "Of course, we encourage them to do it," he said. Carlos, the united front leader, stressed the importance of a decision in 1982 to move assassination squads into the city of Bacolod.

Killing urban police and soldiers was as much a political as a military advance. "They brought the fact of the war close to the city people," he said. "People in Bacolod came to know that the war really existed. Before, we had just operated in the country-side."

Killing for weapons was a casual, sometimes random action quite often planned at low levels of the NPA structure and requiring only a certain tactical expertise. The political murder was of a different order. The victim was selected with care by a special party committee, often after consultation with local cadres and peasant supporters. The impact of his demise was cautiously weighed, for the object was not the mere elimination of an enemy. A political "liquidation," as the party calls it, was performed for the primary purpose of enhancing the NPA's reputation as a protector of the people and a servant of their interests. It had to be a *popular* killing. The target might be a particularly abusive soldier, whose "crimes against the people" were widely known, or a ranking town official who habitually cooperated with the military, or an especially severe landlord.

Mayor Pablo Sola of Kabankalan, Negros Occidental, in the eyes of the NPA, was a natural choice. He was a "land-grabber" exploiting the vagueness of land titles to evict independent farmers and he had been at war with a small Christian move-ment which tried to defend them. According to the party's brief, Sola also had engaged the services of a mysterious hoodlum gang known as the "Long Range Patrol" to kill nine peasants who sympathized with the NPA. At 5:30 P.M. on March 10, 1982, Sola and a truckload of his armed guards rounded a bend on a country road leading to his hacienda. The NPA ambush killed Sola and four of his guards, incidentally netting a few guns for the movement. Several days later, the NPA took credit with a statement which said: "The revolutionary people have a cause for celebration on the execution of Sola and the NPA's confisca-tion of two carbines and three .38s carried by the butcher's gang. The people had one menace eliminated and added arms to boot." The execution of Sola set off a ripple effect. Six mayors of towns in southern Negros Occidental resigned and moved away.

On the scale of popular NPA killings in Negros, those of members of the Civilian Home Defense Force (CHDF) inevita-

118

bly ranked high. The CHDF is a national paramilitary force whose members are paid small wages to keep order and fight communists in their own barrios. Its ranks are mostly filled with community misfits and petty gangsters who have little training or discipline. Nominally a government force, it usually receives orders from a local mayor or police chief, although in Negros they had also functioned as an extra private army for prominent landlords. In 1985, witnesses testified, it had been CHDF thugs armed with machine guns who started the massacre in Escalante, which had left 27 people, many of them sugar workers, lying dead in the streets. Two days later, the training officer for that CHDF unit boarded a public bus in Bacolod for a brief journey to his home town in the north, not far from Escalante. Two young men also boarded and took seats at the rear of the bus. A few kilometers outside of Bacolod, one of the young men walked forward and asked the driver to stop. Simultaneously, his companion fired a bullet into the CHDF officer's head. The two NPA sparrows calmly descended from the bus and walked off into the canefields.[6] Within a few months, two other leaders of the Escalante CHDF had been similarly dispatched.

The murder of officials and soldiers had, by late 1985, become almost routine in Negros Occidental and, according to knowledgeable citizens, they were the main source of the NPA's appeal to poor farmers. "In the countryside," said one Bacolod businessman with many friends in the sugar lands, "the NPA is looked on as the protectors of people and the military is seen as the oppressor. I think that most of those who join are not communists at all. They are just the victims of the military and the landlords." It was not simply that the "liquidations" eliminated farmers' enemies, he said. They endowed the poorest peasant with a sense of power and control, with a conviction that he was not defenseless but could strike back through the NPA. That was of immense psychological importance, the businessman thought. Nothing else could explain the covert support given NPA operations. The raid on Scout Rangers in Isabela, the theft of rifles from the maritime academy, and many other NPA forays could not have succeeded without the help of citizens.

The formality of political liquidations was taken seriously. Each of the assassinations, according to Negros party leaders, was preceded by a judicial finding that the victim owed a "blood debt" to the people. The assessment of a blood debt was determined by a special district committee of local party members representing from three to five towns. In most cases, according to George, a united front leader in Negros, the ruling followed a hearing before a "people's" or "revolutionary" court, at which the views of several people—but not the accused—were taken into account. For the party, the hearing served a purpose other than mere guilt-finding. It provided assurance that the liquidation would be a popular one. In that sense, each had a political intent. The blood debts were not limited to enemy soldiers or landlords. They could be assessed on ordinary people who broke rules or committed crimes. George listed the most common of these:

1. Informing or betraying the movement to authorities.
2. Rape (a reflection, perhaps, of the importance of women cadres in the movement).
3. Repeated criminal offenses, such as cattle-rustling.

Wife-beating, George continued, was considered a serious crime in those villages controlled by party committees, although it was not usually judged a capital offense meriting liquidation. The incorrigible wife-beater was first criticized and ultimately expelled from the community. I asked George why the party concerned itself with that crime. "After all, we are restructuring society and wife-beating is an infringement of women's rights," he replied. "It is class exploitation of women and it is male chauvinism. We want the people to concern themselves with all sorts of problems."

Through these tactics, honed and refined for seventeen years, the NPA became a *political* success. In front after front throughout the archipelago, it had demonstrated by the mid-1980s that it could win friends by killing their enemies. Those who accepted the NPA as a worthy force which meant to do them well found that the guerillas could protect them from harassment, or at least avenge their losses. Cattle-rustlers, abusive soldiers, common thieves who preyed on the poor, land-grabbers—all of these came under the NPA guns. Hundreds of local officials were either killed or forced to abandon their barrios after receiving NPA warning letters. Hundreds of others saw the shape of things to come and tacitly cooperated with new local leaders who enjoyed NPA support. How many of these were actually, in the guerillas' vernacular, "enemies of the people," is a matter for conjecture, because such decisions were largely made by the NPA itself. Most significantly, the NPA had shown that it could usually defend the communist front organizers who moved from barrio to barrio spreading the party's propaganda and shaping underground cells which gradually became de facto village governments. As a *political* force, the NPA had proved itself resilient, innovative and very effective.

But what could be said of the NPA as a *military* force? Not nearly so much. After seventeen years, it was still essentially a raid-and-ambush army, desperate for arms and unable to defend territory anywhere the government forces cared to challenge it. It is true that by the mid-1980s the NPA could frequently mass its guerillas in company formations and could on occasion combine companies into battalion strength. It is also true that its ranks could be doubled, even tripled, overnight if guns could be obtained. But they could not. After seventeen years, it had at best 12,000 modern automatic rifles to turn against a combined government force of some 250,000 men, and in any prolonged battlefield test the strength of numbers would eventually prevail. Sison, Dante, and other NPA founders had, of course, reckoned on a prolonged period of defensive warfare, during which the guerilla army would be outnumbered and forced to retreat after each engagement. But they had also envisioned a time of offensive war when turf would be held and the tide turned, when in Mao's phrase the people's army would advance "wave after wave" from safe bases until at last the enemy's cities were encircled. It was apparent in the mid-1980s that nothing like that was happening or likely to happen for a long time to come.

This hard fact was recognized by many CPP cadres who had a grasp of what was occurring around the Philippines in 1985. The long war in the countryside, they saw, was not winnable in any classic military sense. It was not a fact acknowledged in party literature, and whether the highest-ranking party members on the central committee accepted it as true cannot be known. But there was a consensus among middle-level party

121

cadres whom I met in those months that some other formula was needed. They were not pessimistic, because to many of them a new formula already had been developed—or rather, had evolved—in their experience. Something new and unexpected was slowly taking shape down in the lowland barrios and in the cities and it was on developments there that they concentrated their hopes.

7

☆☆☆

I t was a revealing experience, the act of smuggling one foreign journalist into NPA territory and up the side of Mount Canlaon to Francisco's camp. My first Negros contact, prearranged in Manila, was in a hotel room near the airport at Bacolod where, precisely on schedule, a young Catholic priest knocked on my door one morning. We exchanged passwords and he instructed me to await a telephone call. Later I was taken to the comfortable home of a prominent Bacolod businessman where I waited for two hours while young members of the communist underground watched the streets to be sure no one had followed. Our next move was to a priest's parish house for a meal of rice, barbecued chicken, and Shakey's pizza, followed by interviews with leaders of the CPP national front. The next morning, three young party workers collected me in a bright red pickup truck, its bed loaded with sacks of rice for the NPA camp. Nearly two hours of driving on roads that led past small military stations brought us finally to a barrio at the foot of Mount Canlaon. There I waited two more hours in a farmer's home while the roads we had traveled were checked for follow-ers, and then began the seven-hour climb on foot to the central front headquarters. The trail passed through canefields and some sparsely wooded foothills, then disappeared into a dense tropical forest. There were way stations where friendly families offered jugs of water and checkpoints where armed men from the front's militia watched our passage.

At the base of the mountain, the 47-year-old farmer had fed me rice and sweet potatoes and we had talked of life in his barrio. He was clearly a man of some importance there and held a position of minor authority on a nearby sugar hacienda. He and all of his neighbors supported the NPA, he explained, and the two oldest of his own eight children had gone to join the armed guerillas, "Up there," he said with a wave of his hand at the mountain behind his house. The other six would follow when they finished school. His entire barrio had been meticulously organized to provide support for the NPA in one fashion or another and the people's commitment, he said, was very deep. Every family gave the army a few pesos each month, even though they were very poor and could hardly feed their children now that cane-cutting jobs were disappearing in the sugar depression. Yes, it was risky giving aid and shelter to the NPA soldiers who passed regularly through the barrio. There and in the nearby foothills they fought frequent small encounters with the Constabulary and members of a CHDF unit which came looking for suspected communists. The previous week, one guerilla and a Constabularyman had been killed in a firefight. Search parties frequently stopped at his home to ask questions. "I tell them that the NPA comes and goes, but that I do not know where they hide."

About three miles down the road from his home was a small military headquarters and I suggested that it would be a simple matter for troops based there to raid his home suddenly when suspicious visitors arrived. There was no need to worry, he said. The headquarters was closely watched at all hours by a network of young boys and old women who would notice any sudden movement. Reports of unusual activity would be brought swiftly by young couriers who rode horseback along the dirt road or raced on foot through the canefields to his home. "I would know within minutes if anything happened there at the headquarters," he said. As we lunched, the farmer occasionally leaned out of an open window to receive notes

124

from the hands of boys, all of them about ten years of age. He read each one carefully, then scribbled replies on a yellow pad and passed notes back out the window. After several such exchanges, he concluded that the area was free of soldiers and we slipped out the back door and into a canefield to begin the trek up the mountains.

In this little drama most of the cast—farmers, guides, student convoys, militiamen, hill families and a small army of spies, lookouts and messengers—were part of what the communists called their "mass base." It was a phrase of almost mystical importance in the CPP lexicon. Organizing the "mass base"— planning it, doing it, criticizing how it was done—occupied as much time and thought, if not more, than preparing NPA military offensives. It meant the transformation of whole villages from simple peasant groups into bastions of support for NPA guerillas and, ultimately, into self-sustaining communities virtually isolated from government influence. This was a complex process that often required years of spade work, political education, and no small amount of coercion. Nearly five years had been needed to transform the barrio at the bottom of Mount Canlaon into an NPA haven and support base. Others have required twice that time.

The mass base was the Philippine equivalent of Mao's famous adage about fish swimming concealed in water, guerillas being the fish and the water being the peasant masses. Its importance had become painfully clear very early in the NPA's existence. Several of the first squads had attempted to operate alone in the hills without protective cover or support in the villages, and they were quickly spotted and wiped out. So a grassroots organizing technique was designed and perfected over the years to assure support and concealment, and gradually this process of building indigenous mass bases came to be the party's greatest accomplishment, almost overshadowing in importance the NPA's military actions and becoming at last an end in itself.

In the successful formula that emerged over time, the virgin barrio was first approached by NPA Armed Propaganda Teams which made contact with friends, relatives or others known to be sympathetic. Casual chats extending over days or weeks ensued, during which the teams gained a general impression of issues troubling the residents. Then began the phase known as "social investigation," a thorough sort of local census often employing long questionnaires (early social investigating teams seemed to have drawn heavily from their college sociology textbooks). A profile of the village emerged describing the livelihood of all inhabitants, from the richest landlord down to the lowliest farm hand. This yielded a "class analysis" of every family which, through Marxist categorization, revealed who in the barrio was exploiting whom and which peasants were most likely to support the NPA. A sense of the survey's comprehensiveness was apparent in the following guide offered by *Ang Bayan,* the party newspaper:

The key point is to identify the existing classes and to point out exactly how they relate to one another. We seek to find out the situation not only among the toiling masses, but also among the classes with which they are in conflict, as well as the situation among the middle classes. . . . We seek to unearth the objective truth about society or a part of it so we can identify with precision those forces, institutions, trends, etc., which promote the interests of the people and the revolution.[1]

Once the class structure and the most pressing problems were identified, the propaganda teams embarked on programs of practical assistance. Some taught reading and math to the children and medical care, usually herbal remedies and acupuncture, to the parents. They helped with the farming, developed primitive irrigation systems, and experimented with homemade fertilizers and pesticides to replace the costly products sold commercially. The early teams were a kind of domestic peace corps. Some called it their "Robin Hood" phase. The goal was a modest one, merely to build a measure of trust and confidence. Propaganda was sown along with the crops, of course, but the message at first was muted and undemanding, its focus directed at the everyday practical problems of poor people trying to live off the land.

Almost inevitably, solving the real problems involved armed force, and at a fairly early stage the NPA's value as a fighting unit came into play. Squatters wanted protection of their lots from land-grabbers. Farmers wanted the bandit gangs and cattle-rustlers, or carabao thieves, driven off. The NPA took their side. A coconut farmer in Albay Province, in the Bicol region south of Manila, has described how the guerillas won his loyalty. He was visited one day in 1980 by thirty armed guerillas who asked how they could help him. He told them of the roving bands which each year stole one fourth of his coconut crop. The police and military would not help him. The NPA routed the bandits, saved his crops, and supplanted the local military as preservers of law and order. "The NPA has been very helpful to me," he said.[2]

There were more complex relationships in which the NPA provided the muscle to extract concessions from landowners: wage increases for hired hands, lower land rents, and interest costs for tenants. Such ad hoc land reform programs proved extremely successful in many areas of the Philippine country-side. On the island of Samar, in the 1970s, farmers usually were required to divide their harvest on a fifty-fifty basis with owners of the land. The NPA began a campaign to gain 75 percent for the tenant. It sent letters of warning to the landlords and often visited them in their city homes to explain that a new order of things was being established in the countryside. If the landlord still refused, and if the NPA was strong enough in his section of Samar, his lands and work animals were confiscated and distributed to the peasants.[3] *Ang Bayan* claimed in February 1984, that NPA coercion against *hacenderos* in central Luzon guerilla zones had reduced tenants' land rents by one-half.[4]

The most celebrated early breakthrough for the NPA was its defense of the Kalinga tribesmen who resisted the Marcos government's plan to harness the waters of the wild Chico River, which flows through the towering and remote Cordillera Mountains in northern Luzon. A rugged tribe of former head-hunters, the Kalingas were notoriously hostile to all outsiders. The government intruded in 1974 with a plan to construct four dams which would have diverted the Chico River and inundated thousands of tribal homes and farms and many sacred ritual grounds. The NPA moved in to help the Kalingas in 1976, ambushing government patrols, killing a mayor who had organized a 2,000-man defense force, and, some said, executing

127

engineers sent by the power company. Within a few years, after an abortive attempt to crush the resistance with a Constabulary battalion, the government abandoned the project. The NPA became local heroes to the Kalingas and its squads could roam the region unmolested except for occasional military encounters.

In Negros, the NPA role of enforcer and protector grew slowly. Sugar workers are perhaps the most docile of all Filipino farmers. Centuries of paternalism have left them reluctant to question the landlord's authority and their unions had been models of deference. The NPA's first appeal to them was as a defense against thieves and rustlers, not as a resistance to *hacenderos*. But the great world sugar glut of the 1980s forced a rapid change in all relationships in Negros Occidental. Half of the mills were shut down as the price of sugar collapsed and by 1985 more than 250,000 sugar workers were out of work. Those who had work were paid only 32 pesos ($1.50) a day at most. Unable to grow food crops on the planters' estates where they lived, thousands of families were in danger of starving and Bacolod hospitals began to fill up with children suffering from severe malnutrition. The unemployed workers turned to a new and more radical union, the National Federation of Sugar Workers (NFSW), which had ties to a leftist labor federation in Manila and, clandestinely, to the NPA.

The NFSW concocted a novel survival scheme, asking landlords to set aside plots of their idle lands on which workers could plant small food crops, mainly kamote (sweet potatoes), rice, corn, and cassava. The *hacenderos* at first refused. Suddenly they began to notice strange occurrences: the disappearance of a truck or the theft of parts from their tractors. Many received visits from NPA gunmen who issued blunt threats of worse to come unless the food-lot plans were established. Slowly the planters began to give in. At no time did the sugar workers union acknowledge its support from the NPA. "We have no relationship with the NPA, but there is a parallelism in what we do," was the rather ingenuous explanation of Serge Cherniguin, head of the NFSW in Negros. In fact, he said, many farm workers had failed to join the union, insisting they could get their food lots faster if they dealt directly through the NPA. In any case, other sources admitted, it was the NPA's muscle and implied threats of violence that caused most landlords to give in. "They want to avoid trouble with us and so they settle peacefully," said one CPP official in Negros.

Serving the poor by punishing and intimidating their enemies became the common NPA strategy in the countryside. It was perhaps the real key to building their bases there. In the city, however, it did not work as well. Under Marcos, the military was clustered in urban areas where it denied the NPA space to carry out such reprisals and coercion. The urban strategy called for armed guerillas to back up the more radical labor unions just as their arms supported peasants in the country. Because strikes were more or less outlawed by several Marcos decrees, employers were free to call in police and the military to bust strikes and it was against these uniformed strike-breakers that the urban NPA began to turn its guns. It was a development quietly applauded by the *Kilusang Mayo Uno* (KMU), the leftist labor federation which publicly disclaimed links with the communists but in fact cooperated with them secretly. In 1986 one KMU official spoke candidly to me:

There is now occasional tacit cooperation between us and the NPA, because many legal groups like ours are under harrassment from the military. Although this is not officially said, of course, there is natural cooperation between the legal groups and the underground. In certain areas where we have trouble organizing, the NPA puts pressure on company goons and the [police] officers.

One of the more prominent victims of such NPA-labor union cooperation was a tough, high-ranking police officer, Brig. Gen. Thomas Karingal. Karingal was the superintendent of the Northern Police District of Metro Manila, and included in his jurisdiction a number of small strike-bound factories and stores. His reputation for picket line busting, arrests, and armed confrontations had made him the principal enemy of organized labor in Manila. It was suggested to the NPA that his demise would be appreciated and the job was assigned to the Alex Boncayao Brigade, named, appropriately, after a deceased labor leader. One reason that Karingal was moved to the top of the NPA hit list was that his regular habit of visiting each night a restaurant which he owned in Quezon City made him an easy target. The

Boncayao Brigade tried once and muffed the assignment. But on the night of May 24, 1985, the brigade's sparrows walked into the restaurant and shot him dead. "We have meted out just punishment," said a special news release in *Ang Bayan* the following morning.[5]

And so the accumulated experience of years had produced, by 1986, the working formula for building the NPA's mass base: the base grows as the NPA wins the people's trust and demonstrates its benefits for them in practical ways. The larger that base becomes, the more shelter and support it provides for the soldiers. The expanded mass base in turn expands the NPA. This intricate, mutually supporting relationship flourished in the 1980s and was largely responsible for the mounting death toll which suggested a country on the verge of civil war. For increasingly it was observed that the "benefits" which the NPA could confer most often involved the coercion and liquidation of those deemed by the NPA to be enemies of the people. Murders of landlords, military men, local officials and ordinary citizens judged to be informers increased rapidly. So did the size of the mass base, which by 1986 was estimated to include more than one million Filipinos, most of them farmers. The NPA had learned many lessons in its seventeen years, but none was so important as the fact that selective violence wins friends and builds support.

These lessons had not been learned easily or quickly but through trial and error. In many areas, the NPA was all but crushed in the 1970s. Party documents examining those hard times concluded that the major reason for the losses was a repeated failure to achieve a proper balance of base-building and military action. In some cases, the cadres relied almost exclusively on the gun and ignored grassroots organization. In others, they spent too much time organizing and consolidating the barrios. This imbalance was sharply criticized in the 1976 essay "Our Urgent Tasks," which was published by Sison in the first issue of a party theoretical journal, *Revolution*. It denounced excessive gun-play as "adventurism," or "Left opportunism," and excoriated those who "fail to recognize that to support and ensure the success of any important action, military or otherwise, requires painstaking mass work." Others, declared the essay, were guilty of "Right opportunism." They sinned by avoiding guerilla warfare and relying solely on perfecting barrio committees.[6]

Finding the proper balance occupied the attention of cadres throughout the islands. In Negros in 1969 and in the Bicol region of southern Luzon in 1973, initial NPA contingents were eliminated by government troops. They had failed to establish solid bases and thus had nowhere to flee for protection when the military gave pursuit. The same problem shattered NPA units in several parts of Mindanao. The dilemma of too much or too little base building was described to me by a middle-level Mindanao cadre, "Victor," who had suffered through both phases:

At first, in our mass work there was a tendency to be haphazard. We were not being cautious. We had too many big assemblies of people and not enough small cells. We did not have enough patience and we felt it could be set up overnight. Some of us thought that military actions by themselves would be sufficient to rouse the people to our side.

The Mindanao NPA by 1975 had been reduced to a mere four squads, and the lessons outlined in "Our Urgent Tasks" were carefully studied as a guide to past mistakes. Overnight, the party organization began to concentrate on expanding base support. Then a new problem developed. Too *much* time was being spent in organizing and explaining the party program to people who had more pressing problems, such as the immediate one of military harrassment. The arrival of NPA propagandists in a new barrio inevitably attracted the military's attention and communist sympathizers were being picked off by troops guided by informers. The NPA had to protect them, and in doing so realized that military force was itself a valuable organizing tactic. As Francisco stated,

From 1977 onward, we had decided that the people should be organized fully before we started any armed attacks at all. But this turned out to be too conservative. We then realized that armed attacks did build up the confidence of people. They were popular. The people had more confidence in us when we showed them that we could kill *demonyos* [informers and military intelligence agents] and the military.

131

Beginning in the late seventies, the party central committee made a number of other tactical adjustments which enlarged both its military and base-building capacities. None was more important than a seemingly minor modification adopted in either 1980 or 1981 (accounts differ on the timing). To free more armed guerillas for tactical offensives against the Philippine military, the party decreed that most of them should cease propaganda and organizational work and become full-time soldiers. It was a rather heretical decision, because the party's founders had insisted that to preserve the political character of the NPA its fighters should also be propagandists. (Sison was by then in prison and the chairman was Rodolfo Salas, who seems to have favored more emphasis on "armed struggle"). Armed Propaganda Teams would still conduct the initial, dangerous spade work in new barrios. But when a certain level of development was reached, organizational work was to be turned over to local loyalists who had demonstrated proficiency in it. This had two important effects. It enhanced security, because military secrets were withheld from the citizen-organizers. ("We call it 'compartmentalization,'" Francisco explained in Negros. "The organizers do not even know where the fighters are at any given time.") The second and more important effect was a much larger force of full-time guerillas operating in the field. Freed from political work in the barrios, armed teams launched more ambushes and raids and began merging into large combined forces. Company-sized operations replaced squad and platoon-sized ones in the 1980s and the level of conflict was heightened dramatically. Several cadres with whom I talked described this change as the major reason for the marked escalation in fighting during that period.

Another major party decision hastened the pace of barrio organizing. The first cadres had worked on the assumption that an entire *barrio* population was to be mobilized simultaneously. Everyone—well-to-do peasants, poor peasants, young people and old—would be proselytized together and instructed to form the Barrio Organizing Committee. This proved to be awkward. Rich and poor peasants had little in common. There was also a tendency of the propaganda teams to concentrate first on the natural community leaders—"prestigious personalities," Sison called them disparagingly—and to ignore the lesser members. Friction was inevitable and it slowed the organizational work. In the late 1970s, the party adopted a policy of "sectoral" organizing, in which different groups within the barrio were approached separately: women, youth, poor peasants, richer peasants, fishermen, farm workers and the like. At a developed stage, all would be merged into a single Barrio Organizing Committee, or as it was later named, a National Democratic Front Council. The tactical change greatly accelerated organizational progress. Francisco explained:

We switched to sectoral organizing on the southern front [in Negros Occidental] in 1978 because we saw that it was easier to organize if the people see their common problems. In a hacienda we now have sectors for women, youth and farm workers and in a fishing village there will be a fisherman's sector. Women are treated as a separate sector because they have common problems—they are looked on as second class citizens. They have no equal rights. They are victims of rape and wife-beating. So they have these things in common.

Jes, whose student conversion to communism was recounted in Chapter Five was by his mid-thirties, an important figure in the Communist party's campaign to organize Metro Manila. Like any man who has achieved success in his career Jes could look back on the mistakes of his youth with amused detachment. He and the party had made many of them in the exuberance of the pre-martial-law days, a period of experimentation for young cadres assigned to organize and educate the poor. At the University of the Philippines, he had been excited by the works of Marx, especially *Das Kapital*, and of David Ricardo, the nineteenth-century British economist, and at the age of 19 he was eager to enlighten the Philippine working man about the nature of exploitation. The party gave him his chance teaching propaganda courses to workers in a noodle factory in Bulacan Province.

I was full of enthusiasm but all I really knew was what I had learned at the university and in the KM classes. So on my first day I began telling them about Marx and Ricardo and the theory of surplus labor

133

value. I looked up and most of them were asleep. I counted, and 27 out of the 30 were sound asleep, and the only three who were still awake were my contact persons, those who had set up the class meeting for me.

I explained the problem to my political officer. She said that that was no way to teach workers anything. So I visited her discussion group where she taught about 40 textile workers. She held their attention perfectly by getting them to participate. She would ask, 'How many pesos do you earn a day?' and 'How many yards of cloth do you produce?' Then she could explain where the profits of their work went to. So I learned not to be so bookish.

By the 1980s, there was no room in the party's education programs for such greenhorns as Jes and his amateurish, egghead ways. Propaganda work among "the masses" was for trained practitioners who followed carefully prepared teaching plans designed to explain the sources of poverty to farmers and workers. There was a "General Mass Course" for beginners and a "Special Mass Course" for each sectoral group—women, fishermen, youth and so on. For the quick and curious there was the CPP's "Basic Party Course," which offered a primitive introduction to Marx and Mao. Thousands of Filipinos have participated in the classes over the past two decades, gathering in groups of ten or fifteen in homes, churches, and other secret meeting places. In the countryside, the classes began as soon as the first NPA armed propaganda team obtained a foothold in the barrio and they continued long after the last guerilla had moved on to new territory. The party placed an enormous emphasis on political education and proclaimed great confidence in its success. "We like to say that any farmer can debate a college professor," Sison said.

The purpose of this elaborate and often quite sophisticated educational program was neither to pack heads with knowledge nor to create instant revolutionaries. It was to change attitudes, to foster new ways of looking at the problems of poverty and exploitation. The Filipino, many scholars have observed, is very personalistic in his politics; he views it as a clash between good and bad men or a choice between friends and enemies. The goal of Philippine communist education was to make him see that his problems were caused not by bad men

134

but by a bad system, a bad ism. Only then would he be willing to confront the system in alliance with other victims. He was guided to discover common ground with the farmer in the next barrio and even with the laborer in the city. I once asked Carlos, a national front leader, why so much time was spent burdening people with such concepts as feudalism, imperialism and bureaucrat capitalism. Why not merely show the peasant how the landlord gave him a raw deal?

As a tactic, making them understand the three isms will make them more apt to participate in a political action. They must not only understand farm issues. If they are only worried about that, they will not act with others. We want them to be nationalists. We do not want just activists. We want committed nationalists who understand what is happening in the world. It makes for a more broadly conscious revolutionary. It is very inspiring for them to know what is happening, even in Nicaragua.

Another veteran of national front education programs in central Luzon had a more practical explanation: The farmer who was not trained to see beyond his immediate problems was not likely to remain a faithful follower.

Of course we always approach them through their most pressing problems. Let's say it is cattle-rustling, we begin with that. And we drive off the cattle-rustlers. But if you just stop with that issue, the people will come to you and say, "Why are you still here? The cattle problem is solved." In Pampanga Province, we were trying to teach about feudalism. So we scared some landlords into distributing some of their lands. Then the people got some benefits and they came to us and said we could go away. So you cannot just stop with a single local issue. They must see the connection of local and national issues.[7]

Or as a Mindanao cadre put it:

It is not enough just to explain why fertilizer prices are high and interest rates are so high. We must explain that those are only manifestations of bigger problems and that the solution comes only through dismantling the semi-colonial and semi-feudal set-up. They come to realize that high fertilizer prices and interest rates are only part of a bigger problem. It is not so hard for them to see this.[8]

135

Most Filipinos living today came of age exposed to a peculiarly sanitized version of their country's history. Until recently, history texts used in public and church schools were written by foreigners whose view of the nation's principal events had an oddly detached quality, as if written from afar after viewing the archipelago through a telescope. The history of the Philippines was itself subordinated to that of the United States and the average student learned first of all about American heroes, only later about his country's own. One man who attended elite Catholic schools recalled that his introduction to history was memorization of Lincoln's Gettysburg Address, the list of American presidents, and the names of American states, state capitals, *and* state flowers. "I learned first about Washington and Lincoln and it was only in my final college course that I read anything about Claro Recto," he said.

Not surprisingly, the period of American rule was portrayed as one of benign enlightenment during which the natives were rescued from Spanish tyranny, introduced to modern medicine and education, endowed with a democratic system of government, and graciously granted independence. Little was recorded of the brutal American suppression of Philippine nationalism in 1900, or of the real purposes for which the United States seized the islands. A standard text used in better Catholic high schools quoted approvingly from the famous recollection of the Protestant President McKinley, who had sought divine guidance one night to determine a proper course in the Philippines. He had concluded, McKinley later said, that "There was nothing left for us to do but to take them all and to educate the Filipinos and uplift and civilize and Christianize them. . . . And then I went to bed. . . . and slept soundly."[9] The nationalist ferment of the 1960s sought to inculcate a more skeptical appreciation of the American experience, but the memories of most adult Filipinos are shaped by the earlier one. "I was already out of college before I ever knew that close to half a million Filipinos died during the fight for independence," said one man educated in Catholic schools.

Erasing this biased version of Philippine history was a primary objective of the Communist party's political education. In the General Mass Course taught in the barrios, a simplified Marxist version was used to illuminate the past and to prepare

136

the learner to understand the origins of his present misery. Much of the curricula was drawn from Sison's *Philippine Society and Revolution,* which portrayed American rule as one designed to continue and reenforce the exploitive reign of the Spaniards. American soldiers embarked on a policy of deliberate "genocide" in the Philippine-American War, during which fifty natives were killed for each American life lost. The supposed benevolences of the colonial period were in fact devices to tighten American control: Roads were constructed in rural areas to facilitate military suppression; education in the English language opened the way to political indoctrination and cultural dominance; mass media was developed to spread Washington's propaganda. Early Philippine leaders like Quezon and Osmena were not patriots but fawning sycophants whose own careers depended on appeasement of colonial administrators.

On a rainy afternoon in the Visayan province of Iloilo, I watched as this exercise in new history education was presented to the peasants of a barrio high up in the foothills. It was no slap-dash affair. First, a squad of rifle-bearing NPA soldiers warmed up the crowd with a melodramatic cultural show on the barrio's basketball court. There were musical skits depicting the NPA in action, stealing guns and raiding a Philippine army detachment, and "revolutionary dances" honoring peasants who gave food and shelter to the soldiers. One carefully crafted skit recreated a battle scene in which a local boy had died with the NPA. It brought moans and wailing from women in the crowd along the basketball court. The finale was a cheerful salute to victory in which local girls were coaxed to dance with the men from the NPA. When the show was over, the adults crowded into a tin-roofed shelter for the lecture on Philippine history, Marxist style. There was urgency in the timing because soon the afternoon rains would drum so loudly on the roof that voices would be drowned out.

The lecturer had been chosen with care. Javier was a local hero, a barrio boy who had made good as the party's control had spread through Iloilo's countryside. Eight years earlier he had been a high school radical leading protests of students who objected to school tuitions. (In this barrio, three out of four

137

elementary school graduates did not attend high school because parents could not afford an annual tuition of 200 pesos, about ten dollars). The CPP had spotted him as a likely prospect and soon Javier was fighting in the hills. He was bright and had a sharp sense of the political dimensions of the struggle in Iloilo. Soon he was rising in the party hierarchy, one of the native sons who replaced the college-educated cadres who first formed it. Now he was a member of the district CPP committee and a hit on the political lecture circuit in the barrios of the foothills.

Javier began with the basics. The Philippines were rich in natural resources, in gold, copper, nickel, bauxite, even uranium. The soil was fertile and easily produced food and export crops—corn, rice, sugar cane, tobacco, coconuts, pineapples. There were natural harbors, like the one at Subic Bay, and rivers enough to make hydroelectric power plentiful. Their country should be rich and strong; prosperity should be within the reach of everyone. Instead the people were poor. Too much of the wealth was drained away by imperialists, especially the Americans. "Filipinos are not the ones who benefit from this," said Javier. "Foreigners benefit."

The imperialists worked their will through native businessmen called the "comprador bourgeoisie," rich men who managed their businesses from Manila, ran their banks, gobbled up land for the foreigners' great agricultural estates. "And here we will see the leeches who suck the wealth of the country," said Javier. He named names: Atlas Mining, Pepsi-Cola, B.F. Goodrich, Philippine Packing, Dole. Finally, there were the rich Filipino landlords, exploiters in their own names. They controlled huge estates. If they leased their land to peasants, they charged high rents and practiced a vicious usury which kept the farmer in debt. But most hired day laborers to work their crops, paying wages so low that poverty and hunger were inevitable. Again, a litany of names: Benedicto, Gustilio, Floirendo, Montelibano, Cojuango, Alberto, Cinco.

On a blackboard facing the class, Javier and an assistant, Dennis, chalked a large pyramid, ruled by lines that divided it into segments to illustrate the Philippine class structure. At the very peak, occupying the tiniest segment, was the ruling class composed of landlords and the "comprador bourgeoisie." Beneath it were the lesser classes—the national bourgeoisie, petty bourgeoisie, semi-proletariat, workers and farmers. That tiny tip at the top of the triangle represented only one percent of the population. The remainder, ninety-nine percent, were to varying degrees exploited by the minority at the top.

The lecture had been dry and unemotional. Javier had been the patient schoolmaster, not the passionate demogogue. His class was passive but attentive. Teenaged boys and girls penciled notes on school tablets, asking occasional questions. Old women listened quietly, smoking homemade cheroots and nodding agreement. A group of older men filtered into the back of the shed, indifferent at first but soon caught up in the discussion. Everyone seemed to understand; it was impossible to guess how deeply they were moved, if at all. Javier seemed satisfied, and at the end offered a brief sermon on how the people would change all this, would turn the pyramid upside down. The exploiters would not, he said, give up their advantages without a struggle. Only a "national-democratic revolution" would force them to surrender. Then the clouds grew very dark, so dark that the blackboard could no longer be seen, and a downpour of rain on the tin roof blotted out all other sounds.

All of this might seem to demand rather heavy mental effort from a rice farmer who never got beyond the sixth grade. But the communists devised certain techniques for simplifying the themes and were careful to relate each lesson in the mass courses to the students' own experiences. Land-grabbing by *hacenderos* and local politicians was a phenomenon familiar to millions of peasants and it was explained as a product of feudalism, along with high land rents and usurious interest rates. The point was to make the farmer see these as systemic afflictions common throughout the country, not the machinations of a few "bad" landlords. The "good" landlord, one who still displayed some of the generous traits of the old paternalism, was to be distrusted as much as the "bad" one. The peasant was exploited by both, the difference being a matter of small degree. One communist organizer recalled a "chalk-talk" lesson he had routinely used with sugar workers in Negros. Each of them was asked to draw on the blackboard a sketch of his own landlord. One worker would depict his master as loathsomely fat (and hence greedy). Another would sketch a lean and handsome landlord smiling good-naturedly. The cadre would then explain that both drawings were of men who represented an oppressive system which kept sugar workers mired in poverty.

Imperialism, too, was explained with familiar examples. Almost all tenant-farmers bought expensive herbicides and fertilizers, usually with borrowed money. In barrio classes they learned from communist teachers that the high prices were dictated by foreign corporations which dominated the Philippine market. Much farm land had been acquired by large multinational corporations which grew pineapples, bananas, and coconuts for export and which paid the same low wages as domestic landlords. Workers were taught that the government deliberately maintained low wage rates, ostensibly to attract foreign investors. In Mindanao, communist lecturers pointed to the presence of Japanese and other foreign logging companies which exacted great profits from Philippine trees hewn and hauled by cheap local labor. One cadre dramatized imperialism by asking students how many of them had recently eaten the delicious large prawns which abounded off the coast. None had, of course; foreign fishing trawlers took so many prawns that their price on local markets was prohibitively high. In Nueva Ecija Province, on Luzon, one former national front organizer enlivened his class of tenant-farmers by blaming the high price of an especially desirable onion seed on the U.S. exporter, who, he asserted, had obtained a monopoly in the Philippines.

Preaching against the monster of imperialism, however, collided with one of the Filipino's cherished attitudes—his affection for Americans. Many Filipinos retain an almost child-like fondness for everything American—clothes, soft drinks, music—and still show a marked deference when dealing with Americans personally. "Down With The U.S.–Marcos Dictatorship" had been the party's most popular rallying cry since 1972, but it seemed to ring harshly on the ears of ordinary Filipinos (who in my presence used it only with an apologetic moue). The communists were aware of the average Filipino's disincli-

140

nation to hate Americans and they resolved the dilemma by explaining that it was the American government, not the American people, which was to blame for imperialist intrusions in the Philippines.

Within that limitation, however, the party zealously indicted "American imperialism." One issue of *Ang Bayan* was largely devoted to American atrocities during the Philippine–American War, including the oft-quoted admonition made to his troops by the American commander in Samar: "Kill and burn, kill and burn. The more you kill and the more you burn, the more you please me."[10] Philippine leaders from the first *ilustrados* through Quezon and Osmena to the post-independence presidents were routinely pictured as puppets of the American government. President Marcos was but the latest in a long line of collaborators who acted to protect United States interests in the Philippines. "U.S. imperialism continues to support and benefit from the fascist dictatorship of the Marcos clique," declared an *Ang Bayan* editorial on imperialism four months before Marcos was deposed.[11]

Marxist ideology as a system of thought and historical analysis was not a subject considered proper for the rudimentary classwork offered to peasants and workers. Marxist training schools were reserved for more educated cadres and a few of the unschooled who had shown intellectual curiosity. But the CPP injected simplified Marxism into beginners' lessons and developed a "Basic Party Course" to cover the fundamentals. It concentrated on instruction in the inevitability of class struggle. The text outlined eight classes in Philippine society, ranging from landlords down to a *lumpen-proletariat,* and depicted the role which each class was likely to play in the revolution. Since the state invariably upheld the interests of the ruling class, its military forces must be defeated through armed confrontation. Only then would the classless society of communism be reached. Dialectical materialism was the scientific thought process which guided people to understand the contradictions in capitalist society and prepared them for class struggle.

I once asked Carlos how he managed to teach the intricacies of dialectical materialism and capitalist contradictions to poor farmers. "I used ants," he said.

I put two ants—one of them black, one red—into a clear plastic vial. Naturally, they began to fight until one of them was dead. Then I asked the farmers why they thought the ants had fought. Why could they not live happily together? I would then list their answers on the blackboard. Some would say the ants fought because of different "interests" and some would say it was differences in their color—in other words, racism. I would tell them that the ants' fighting was the same as the relationship between them and their landlord. Struggle is inevitable, but in the present circumstances the landlord would always win. They would understand. I was trying by concrete example to get them to the level of revolutionary practice. Mao once said that unless you taste an apple you will not know what an apple is.

ne might look upon Dina as the underground mayor of Punta Dumalag, a village on the coast of Mindanao. She was one of the seven Communist party members who made up its National Democratic Front Barrio Council, the unit which the party called its "shadow government" in controlled areas. A stranger would quickly judge her a person of authority. She had about her an air of command and as she walked along the narrow village road people treated her with deference. She was dressed in a bright new T-shirt and designer jeans and her permed hair glistened, all signs of privilege and prominence in a poor community.

A true daughter of that squatters' settlement, Dina had been born and reared there by a family of early pioneers and had risen in the Communist party as one who fought government efforts to dismantle its seedy slums. She was the first important party member I met who had risen from a lowly background, and observing her self-confident domination of others one could sense what the party's victories could mean in personal terms. She had become a very important person in Punta Dumalag. She spoke both to me and her neighbors in a crisp, direct way, which suggested that she meant to be believed and obeyed. Dina was also the first party boss whom I encountered who conveyed the impression that she did not much care for me or the country I came from. She would do her duty in explaining Punta Dumalag because the party had asked her to do so. But I would learn only what she wanted me to learn.

It had all come together in Punta Dumalag. The pieces fit. The trial-and-error years of guerilla raids and barrio organization and mass education and arms gathering, all of that was in the past for this ramshackle fishing community on the Gulf of Davao. In early 1986, Punta Dumalag was a model communist village, a kind of Philippine commune where under the party's protection and guidance the dispossessed had taken possession. The killing days were over, for no longer did the government's army attempt to interfere and the NPA contingent had moved on to other battles. The revolution had come and conquered and then marched on, leaving behind this quiet self-contained enclave of outwardly satisfied converts. There were other communities like it scattered around the country, outposts where the Manila government's writ no longer ran, but none fit as neatly the CPP's definition of success. And so when journalists came to this far corner of Mindanao, it was there that the party delighted in displaying its handiwork.

The party had at first not known precisely what to do with a case of success. It was obvious, of course, that some areas of the country would be more vulnerable to NPA domination and indoctrination than others. Barring a miracle, the national struggle would occupy years, even decades. What would be done with these "advanced" areas which came rather quickly under party control? The dilemma was resolved, as usual, by experience. Very early in the 1970s, a few remote barrios in northern Luzon had become so completely politicized and so perfectly protected by NPA local forces that the Philippine military had tacitly ceded them to the communists. Unmolested from the outside, they became independent little havens governed by party committees with little pretense of secrecy. Punta Dumalag had been fitted to this model. Its affairs conducted by an underground committee of seven party members, the community governed and policed itself, organized a communal economic structure, furnished independent supplies of water and electricity, administered its own form of justice, and killed or expelled those who stood in the way. One cadre in Manila had explained that at that stage in the revolution the party hoped to see some barrios become "as isolated as possible." Punta Dumalag answered to that description. It had in important ways simply disengaged itself from the rest of the country.

Punta Dumulag was a village of squatters, landless Filipinos who had moved onto undeveloped lots, established residence, and by various strategems survived the authorities' efforts to evict them. There are now millions of squatters in the Philippines, the majority of them clustered in or near major cities in homes ranging from packing-crate hovels to rather substantial wooden and concrete dwellings having an aura of permanence. In theory they were vulnerable to others' claims of land ownership, but in practice they were largely left alone as de facto subdivisions awkwardly incorporated into the Philippine political structure yet usually denied public services. Thousands of squatters had come streaming to the Gulf of Davao area in the 1960s and '70s from other parts of Mindanao and the Visayan islands to escape the hopelessness of rural poverty. Many had already been evicted from farms when wealthy landlords who knew about lawyers and law courts came along. Punta Dumalag's "pioneers" (as they were still reverentially spoken of there) had chosen this sweep of the bay only ten kilometers from central Davao as their new community sometime in the late 1950s and had settled in to become fishermen. A collection of jerry-built structures was home for 160 families who lived beside a narrow, pitted and rock-strewn road winding along the gulf.

The land was legally claimed by a wealthy Davao entrepreneur whose use of it had been limited to a large sawmill located at one end of the beach. Having at first little need for the rest of the property, he had left the squatters alone for several years, and the residents' main concern was the large number of thieves and housebreakers, mostly outsiders, who roamed without fear of arrest since the closest police station was far away. In the late 1970s, however, a more ominous threat was presented. The owner conceived of a profitable new plan to develop the shoreline with a new tourist hotel, a drydock for small vessels, and a large motor pool. He also intended to transform the fishing waters off-shore into a huge log-pond, a kind of holding basin where logs hauled and floated down from mountain forests could be stored. The obstacle, of course, was the population of Punta Dumalag. By 1979 the bulldozers were at the gate and demolition had begun.

Enter the New People's Army. NPA Armed Propaganda Teams had been active for several years in Davao, its rural suburbs, and the mountainous province of Davao del Norte to the north. Among the squatter communities they had found eager allies. Squatters lived the most precarious existence of any of the Philippine poor because the threat of demolition and eviction hung constantly over them, and the NPA had perfected a special strategy to thwart intruders who came waving certificates of land titles. In Punta Dumalag, the NPA teams at first ignited citizen protests and instructed local leaders to carry petitions to local authorities. By the time the first demolitions began, the citizens were aroused, polarized and ready for a long fight. During the daytime, brigades of women formed lines across the entry road, facing the demolition teams and a military squad. At their sides were buckets of sand, stones, bricks and human waste which they were prepared to shower on the invaders should an attack begin. In the night, the village was patrolled by armed members of an NPA-organized militia. Their weapons consisted of six old rifles obtained in a raid on the landowners' sawmill. A negotiation team was organized, on NPA instructions, to engage the military in discussions and, as is often the case in confrontations between Filipinos, the talks dragged on for weeks and then months. A stalemate was established and the houses stood.

It was for such situations that the Philippine government had established the CHDF, the paramilitary units whose members lived within a *barangay* and attempted to extinguish local political uprisings, especially those connected with the NPA. In a great many instances, they were composed of local thugs and drifters, but they were prized by the regular military because they could spot local trouble-makers and radicals through a string of informers. Matina, the *barangay* in which Punta Duma-

146

lag is located, was the turf of a particularly aggressive CHDF and it was put to work ferreting out the NPA newcomers and local sympathizers. A bloody internal war ensued while the official military standoff continued, and several local men disappeared—some of them NPA guerillas, some not. The NPA and the new militia unit retaliated. As one CPP member succinctly put it: "If we found an informer, we killed him. If a CHDF man came in, we killed him. If we found an unarmed military informer, then the unit militia would handle him. If he was armed, we would coordinate with the NPA, which would kill him." I asked the member how many CHDF men had been done away with. He counted the fingers first on one hand, then on the other, and finally turned the palms of both upward. "About a dozen, I guess," he said.

Assisting the CHDF in Punta Dumalag was yet another armed group—possibly vigilantes, although they were suspected of ties with the military—called the Rural Reform Movement. An NPA sparrow team killed its commander, my acquaintance said, and his men deserted.

In September of 1984, five years after the initial confrontation, the regular military force prepared at last to act, not only against the squatters but against picket lines thrown up at the owner's sawmill in an NPA-engineered strike. Fifteen soldiers were based in an improvised garrison resembling a small fortress near the sawmill. Again the battle lines formed. Protesters came forth under banners screaming "Down With The Military Establishment." Defenders grouped in threes, buckets ready, the military commander called for reenforcements, and then, inexplicably, yet another extended dialogue began. For reasons that are not clear, the soldiers again backed off and thirteen months later the fortress was dismantled. Since then, December 1984, the military has not returned to Punta Dumalag.

"Shadow governments" in party-controlled areas effectively isolated those communities from the official government. They staffed and controlled the local armed militias, assumed all police duties, and determined how offenders from within and without would be punished. The economic life of the village was restructured insofar as possible under a plan for sharing

147

incomes and building small "alternative economies," which involved anything from growing food to making cheap soap. Health care and political education were administered by committees of the shadow government. Gradually, almost all aspects of life came within its purview. Its agents performed marriages, advised on childrearing, settled domestic disputes. One suspected that this assumption of authority must have entailed a large measure of coercion. The party, of course, insisted that there was maximum tolerance of dissent and that any important decree was preceded by discussion and democratic practice.

A shadow government inevitably came into conflict with the municipal boards and *barangay* councils. *Barangay* councils were the lowest political units and normally the ones most involved in neighborhood affairs. They were also linked in a cumbersome fashion with the central government in Manila, and their leaders, called *barangay* captains, thus wielded great power. Through them government welfare assistance was passed along to local residents and they were usually arbiters of law and order, controlling the quasi-military Civilian Home Defense Forces. The coming of communist control naturally undermined and displaced them and the captains were faced with the most perilous decisions of their political lives: Stay and fight, cut and run, or work out an arrangement with the new communist authorities. Since the captain was usually in control of the local CHDF, he was an extremely unpopular figure to the party leadership, and in most cases his area of choice was quite limited. Many captains were killed. Victor, a national front leader in Mindanao, told me that the party's first act, once control of an area was assured, was to expel or execute a *barangay* captain and dismantle the council. But in some cases, the captain proved amenable to party direction and was left in his position, if for no other reason than to retain the receipt of welfare and other assistance from the central government. A Mindanao party leader, Noli, who had extensive experience in Matina, the *barangay* which included Punta Dumalag, explained the party's attitude:

Our policy is that as long as the *barangay* captains are not a hindrance, we do not liquidate them. If they cooperate with us, we let them stay in their positions. But if they are strict in carrying out the policies of the government and if they go after us, we are forced to do some harsh treatment. We would let them carry out some social welfare policies that help the people, like drainage and health and the [government] dole-outs. But if they carry out policies like planting informers, we meet with them and tell them that they can stay only if they do not go after us. Actually, there is not much of a problem there [in Matina *barangay*] because they know we control. Most captains and *barangay* council members cooperate with us.

In Punta Dumalag, the *barangay* captain had proved to be no obstacle. At several points in our interview, Dina declined to answer questions and some she had simply ignored. But this was a subject she was pleased to discuss. "He supports the cause," she said. "He is from one of the pioneering families and was with us from the start." There were actually three captains for the sprawling Matina *barangay* and all three cooperated with the NPA, not surprisingly since at the time of my visit the communists were believed to control eighty percent of the turf. It was evident from Dina's description that the one whose jurisdiction included Punta Dumalag had been transformed into a sort of front-man or lackey, doing chores and running errands for the party committee. When there was a minor law-and-order problem, the captain brought it before the communist committee. If it became necessary to negotiate with military authorities, the captain was dispatched to meet them. If a local citizen unaccountably disappeared, the captain was sent to military barracks to make inquiries. I asked Dina what would have happened to the captain if he had been less cooperative. "There are 160 families in Punta Dumalag and all of them support the NPA," she said—a cryptic response but I got the message.

And so power had passed easily to the National Democratic Front Barrio Committee. There were ten Communist party members and seven of them composed the committee. Not all of the seven were local people, it developed, for with Dina as we talked was a man named Tony who was also a committee member, although he was from another village and had been in Punta Dumalag for only one year. I asked Dina how the committee members were selected. "Democratic procedures," she said. What procedures? She ignored the question and moved on to a description of the committee's duties, which were indeed numerous. It was responsible for political education, public safety, security, electricity, the water supply, and the development of a communal economic plan that was being designed to further reduce the villagers' dependence on the outside world. The committee settled family disputes, disposed of wife-beating cases, operated a new health center and allocated work shifts on the beaches where a fight against erosion was in progress. It collected taxes and it dispensed the revenue. In other words, the seven party members assumed control of almost every public and private affair that touched the lives of 160 families. And into their sphere of influence the official Philippine government intruded hardly at all.

Since the coming of the NPA and the party's assumption of power, no innovation had been more thorough and successful than the suppression of crime, Dina claimed. Punta Dumalag was technically an illegal squatters' community and the government's police had simply ignored its crime problems in the past. Crimes of all sorts—rape, street robbery, house-breaking and murders—had been the stuff of daily life. Most offenders came from outside, although at night the streets were roamed by local drunks. But no longer was crime a significant problem, I was told. The NPA had made the difference. The local unit militia performed all police functions and a separate squad of armed guards patrolled the village every night from 10 P.M. to 5 A.M. A strict curfew was imposed at 10 P.M. and no public drinking was permitted after that hour. No one thought anymore of calling the official police to Punta Dumalag, she said.

In the few occasional cases of robbery that still occurred, the party committee and unit militia meted out punishment, and from Dina's description I gathered that an informal criminal code had been established over the years. The robber who came from outside the village was executed immediately, for to delay punishment might permit an escape. There had been one such case recently. A man from a nearby village had broken into a home in Punta Dumalag and killed someone in the course of a robbery. The militia had apprehended him and promptly shot him. I asked if the militia had considered bringing him to trial. Dina thought the question odd. "He had been in here before and he had been warned," she said. In other cases, she continued, a suspected robber was brought to a hearing conducted by party members in front of many citizens. "When it is submitted to the NDF committee, we must have concrete data to determine his guilt. We inquire into when the robbery happened, what actually happened, how many times it had happened before. Sometimes the masses decide." Dina did not think it extreme to employ the death penalty against robbers, but she explained that in some cases a lighter penalty might be imposed. "If, for example, we decide that he has committed a robbery out of poverty, because he is poor, and if he lives within our *sitio* [neighborhood], he will merely be warned by the unit militia," she said. "But if we find out that he is a drinker and maybe chases women, and even if he lives in Punta Dumalag, he will be killed. He is exploiting people."

The one crime still prevalent, it seemed, was wife-beating. I had learned elsewhere in several conversations that wife-beating was widespread in the Philippines, a scourge so common that police regarded it as a facet of domestic disputes and hence outside their purview. The CPP, because of the influence of many women cadres from the middle-class, had classified it a crime punishable by death in certain circumstances. Dina acknowledged that wife-beating was still a problem in Punta Dumalag and explained the rules formulated to deal with it. A first-time wife-beater would be sent before the "open organization," or the official *barangay* council, where a warning was delivered. A repeat offender was brought before the underground party committee. "We would talk with him at first and suggest a separation from his wife. We'd encourage him to leave home. But if it is very grave, we give him the death penalty immediately." One reason for such summary execution apparently was the party committee's fear that a disgruntled husband denied the privilege of beating his wife might become an informer for the military. "We would do it immediately so that he does not go over to the reactionary side," Dina said.

Despite Punta Dumalag's virtual disengagement from outside influence, its rulers felt they had to be constantly on guard against "foreign bad elements"—a phrase Dina used frequently to encompass criminals, government spies, and informers. The unit militia and night watchguards were constantly on the alert

151

for suspicious intruders and the party committee repeatedly instructed residents to report the presence of unfamiliar persons. It had been observed that young children were often the best sources of information on unwanted visitors. Children played in the main road and would naturally notice someone who entered the village and began asking strange questions. All children between the ages of eight and ten had been organized into a special watch and given lessons on what sort of behavior to report. They would take the license plate numbers of strange cars and attempt to eavesdrop on anyone who seemed to display an undue curiosity. Dina thought the program very successful. Such children's spy brigades apparently were common in party-controlled areas. One of them in a community on Bataan had reported to the local NPA militia that an ice-cream vendor had asked about some local people as he pushed his cart through the neighborhood. The militia seized the vendor and executed him as a spy for military intelligence.[2]

By trial and error in some cases, by deliberate planning in others, Punta Dumalag had gradually moved toward the sort of political separation esteemed by the CPP. Similar processes were moving it toward a stage of economic disengagement. Although not spelled out explicitly anywhere, so far as I could discover, the party's goal for communities it controlled was a communal economic life disconnected as much as possible from the commercial economy. This was not a permanent goal. The ultimate victory would bring to the Philippines a national socialist economic system, with the major industries owned by the state, but for the interim years the party advocated a rather primitive communal formula to make poor farmers, fishermen and workers less dependent on the cash economy. Communal farming had been introduced successfully in Samar and parts of Luzon, I had been told, and farm cooperatives to market collective production were becoming popular. The party also encouraged development of crude small industries to make such necessities as soap and fertilizers. Propaganda organs urged the application of "alternative technology" to develop cheap substitutes for commercial medicines, pesticides, and an assortment of other commodities.

Punta Dumalag's contribution to this march of progress was a dingy wooden shed overlooking the gulf where two men used long paddles to stir a thick, milky fluid in a large vat suspended over a slow charcoal fire. Soap was being produced by boiling the oil of coconuts mixed with water and a cheap common chemical. The ingredients were inexpensive, since coconuts lay all about the coastline, and even the cooking fire was fueled by charcoal made of dried coconut shells. The soap could be produced for about two pesos a bar, half the cost of commercial soap, and the supply was sufficient for the entire village's needs with enough left over for sales elsewhere. A separate process used the juice of the coconut to make candy bars.

The real business of Punta Dumalag was fishing and, Dina explained, the party was forming a collective system in which income from the daily catch would be shared. All local fishermen were organized into a single association and the members divided into collectives, each consisting of five men. Upon returning home each night with the money earned from commercial boat-owners, each collective was expected to pool the funds and divide them into six equal parts, the sixth part going to the party committee. Another organization of collectives regulated the firewood industry, a source of considerable income. From the local sawmill, which could be subjected to various pressures by the community, the firewood collectives obtained long strips of thick bark sheared from the logs and cut them into kindling used in home cooking fires. One collective peeled the bark and a second sawed it into proper lengths. Each of these collectives contained thirty people and the income was divided into thirty-one shares, the thirty-first share being reserved for village expenses administered by the party committee. Most of the money, Dina said, was used to pay transportation costs for protesters who picketed government offices during political rallies.

Such enterprise might finance a few local operations, but running a national revolution required a far greater source of income. Guerillas must be fed and clothed, party newspapers printed, medicines purchased, and guns bought on the black market. So far as is known, the CPP has received no financial assistance from foreign communist governments, although it has obtained private aid through a European fund-raising organization headed by a former Filipino priest. The major source of funds was an elaborate but unevenly enforced system of "revolutionary taxes" paid voluntarily by supporters and involuntarily by large corporations and wealthy people. The taxes ranged in amount from a few centavos or pesos a month contributed by poor families to thousands of pesos paid annually by corporations and large landowners. In the latter cases, of course, the "revolutionary tax system" was simple extortion, although the party justified its soak-the-rich practice as a form of social welfare for exploited workers. A high-ranking NDF official, Satur Ocampo, has explained:

The basic idea is to impose some taxes on the big corporations, whether foreign or local, that are exploiting the natural resources and human resources of the country, so taxing them means expropriating part of the profits they got for the use of the people. . . . The general principle is that the corporations to be taxed are those whose operations greatly affected the livelihoods of people, like in the mining areas, logging areas that are denuding the forest, or huge plantations in Mindanao.[3]

George, the Visayan united front leader, had explained that the party used a graduated tax "on the ruling classes" to achieve the semblance of fairness. The usual levy in the Visayas was five percent on incomes ranging from 10,000 to 20,000 pesos and ten percent on those ranging from 20,000 to 30,000 pesos. For obvious reasons, the taxes were successfully imposed only in NPA-controlled areas where the rich victims' recourse to official protection was limited. I asked what happened to recalcitrant taxpayers. "If they are imperialists, *compradors* or landlords, and if they do not pay, we will either confiscate their equipment or burn it," George had answered. He insisted that lesser figures were dealt with leniently and that ordinary peasants were not coerced. I told him I had heard several accounts of poor families being badgered to hand over small monthly contributions. "Yes, there have been some excesses but not very many." George claimed the party had "rectified" such practices in lengthy meetings at which offending cadres had been subject to criticism.

The party's most lucrative tax sources were logging compa-

154

nies which operated in the mountains of Davao del Norte, the province north of the city of Davao. Access to their timber tracts lay along trails which wound through insurgent-controlled territory, and if a company wanted its logs brought down to the plywood and finishing plants outside the city it paid off the NPA. A Davao attorney familiar with the practice said the NPA was rather scrupulous in calculating its assessments and based them on the company's own production and income records. The lawyer mentioned one company which, he knew, paid fifty thousand pesos a year, about $2600, to move its logs. The company that refused to pay was warned. If it ignored two warnings, the lawyer said, one of its trucks was found burned. The CPP had encountered something of a moral dilemma in dealing with loggers whose operations ravaged and denuded large sections of Mindanao. Many of the party's members concerned with environmental issues wanted the NPA to put the companies out of business. But the party needed cash more than it valued environmental purity and so the loggers remained in business as a reliable tax base.

Sugar *hacenderos* in Negros provided much of the cash to run Francisco's war on the central front in that province, involuntarily of course. But the collapse of the world sugar market cut into the party's tax base there. Francisco said that plantation owners bargained hard to reduce their NPA tax bills, citing the loss of revenue caused by declining prices. Most paid regularly, however, to prevent their tractors from being stolen or demolished in the night. A few hold-outs maintained large private armies to resist extortion, forcing the NPA to resort to more drastic measures of raising funds. One of the fiercely recalcitrant Negros landlords was Eduardo M. Cojuangco, Jr., a man of vast wealth and a crony of former President Marcos. In December 1985, the NPA ambushed Cojuangco's payroll truck from fox-holes dug in a canefield, killed five guards, and made off with 500,000 pesos in cash and checks.

As so often happens with tax systems, the NPA's tended to become more elaborate and complex. Davao communists began imposing not one but two levies. The first was the ordinary tax based on a company's business income. The second was an "exploitation" tax assessed by calculating the difference between how much the company should pay each worker

155

under a reasonable minimum wage as compared to the actual wage paid. "Some pay regularly but some don't," said Luni, a party official in Davao. "If they refuse, we pressure them by destroying their heavy trucks and other equipment. There are some businessmen in the city who never pay because they know that we cannot mobilize enough force against them. But in rural areas, they usually pay."

Dina talked of the tax system in Punta Dumalag as though it were a model of equity. Individual taxes depended on the ability of each family to pay. The basic tax was two pesos a month (about a dime), with one peso going to the "open," or legal, community organizations. The other went to the underground party committee. She insisted that a family unable to pay in any given month would not be coerced. The industrial tax base consisted of a single company, the landlord's sawmill, and it was required to pay annually an amount based on earnings. Since several Punta Dumalag workers were employed at the sawmill and able to check on production, it was not difficult to measure the owner's income and profits. There were months when the sawmill earned no profits and was therefore not taxed. To expand this rather narrow base, the party committee placed assessments on enterprises not located within the village. These primarily were fishing boat operators who worked the waters immediately offshore and lumber companies which bought logs or finished lumber from the sawmill. Dina said the party committee took the position that these businesses owed local taxes simply because they profited from the environs. Even if the lumber buyer was situated miles away in Davao City, Dina's assessors visited him regularly to explain why he must pay taxes. "For example, we say to them that there are now two governments operating in this area and that there must be two taxes," she said. "There are now two armies here. We say that you are already paying taxes to support the (government's) military and that it is necessary for you now to support the NPA." These entrepreneurs, naturally, were not eager to accept responsibility for dual government and many balked. Ways had been found to assure their cooperation, Dina said.

If he is hard-headed, we paralyze his business. In other words if he has a fishing business and he comes to our waters, if he does not pay, we put a bomb in his fishing boat. Then they pay. Sometimes we must burn one of his boats. Then we always let him understand that we had burned it because that was our revolutionary judgment.

The history of Punta Dumalag has been one of almost constant conflict under the communists, and a readiness to use violence and threats of force seems part of the fabric of daily life. The military had to be repelled, spies killed, wife-beaters expelled, intruders watched, reluctant taxpayers harrassed. The sleepy little village on the placid gulf was in fact a kind of garrison city, ever on the alert to dangers without and within. I began to wonder how this state of perpetual emergency could be sustained. How could 160 Filipino families be constantly martialed to the defense of their strange new communal ethic? Dina had said that early polarization had occurred when soldiers and bulldozers came in 1979 to demolish the homes and that, later, the successful citizen-militia war on crime had hardened the feeling of cohesiveness. Maintaining that unity, after the early battles were over and won, required something more.

That something more, it turned out, was political education, constant large doses of it. Punta Dumalag was transformed into a sort of floating classroom where lessons shaped by the party committee went along with the splitting of firewood and the manufacture of cheap soap. Political classes were mandatory for everyone fourteen years and older. In the "legal," or above-ground, structure, the emphasis was on consciousness-raising issues, like Philippine nationalism and creation of the democratic coalition government advocated in National Democratic Front literature. Underground lessons went into Marxism, the revolutionary tradition, and the meaning of proletarian leadership, and such tracts as Mao's "Five Golden Rays" were earnestly studied in small groups which met clandestinely. Party instructors held a special class to pass on the skills of Marxist education to a new generation of teachers. Some had already graduated and been dispatched to classes in less advanced villages nearby.

The famous "three isms" were, of course, the meat of many lectures, and I had noticed that Tony, the other party committee member present during the interview, had spoken several times of lectures on "imperialism." I asked what imperialism

157

had to do with Punta Dumalag. It was the most evil presence, he said, and explained how this lesson was taught in underground classes:

We say that imperialism has a direct effect on our lives here. We can point out there [toward the gulf waters] and show that big ships come from Japan and Korea and other countries to take away logs that come from the mountains. Well, it was this big log business that made the landowner here want to take over this property. He was going to make a bigger log pond and build a drydock. That was why he wanted our homes torn down, to do that. So we can very easily say that imperialism is a big threat to us.

In other conversations with local communists, I had gained the impression that American military bases were not regarded as serious issues and played a minor part in the lectures about imperialism. A national front worker who had discussed Punta Dumalag before I went there had predicted I would find little interest in the bases among the rank and file. Only college-educated communists or those admitted to party ideology classes were much concerned with the bases, he had said. Tony, however, said the menace of American bases on Philippine soil was dealt with at length in the underground lectures. First of all, he said, the bases were an infringement of Philippine sovereignty forced on the country's "puppet presidents." They also spawned crime and prostitution in the base towns. The bases' presence drew the Philippines into the path of nuclear disaster, because in a war between superpowers the Soviet missiles in Asia would be targeted on the Subic and Clark bases. Finally, Tony said, the people of Punta Dumalag were taught that the American bases were training grounds for methods of repression used against Filipino dissidents. One lecture dealt with the Joint U.S. Military Advisory Group, or JUSMAG, which he claimed taught techniques in torture to Philippine military intelligence. "These are taught by the Americans in order to suppress the revolutionary movement," Tony said. I asked where the lecturers found proof of this and he said, "It is just something known by everyone."

It would have been nice to emerge from Punta Dumalag with a neat score-sheet summing up the good and bad in what was, in early 1986, the model community of the Philippine insurgency. It was not possible, because I had been permitted only the official view of its accomplishments and benefits. In themselves, these were of no small matter. One could not doubt that the coming of the NPA in 1979 had produced tangible achievements in the eyes of Dina and Tony. Homes had been rescued from bulldozers. Crime had been reduced, if not banished. Water and electricity had been introduced where none existed before. At what cost? One could only speculate on what would have been written on the other sheet of the ledger. Outsiders would not learn the amount of coercion and fear entered into the equation which produced collective fishing, income-sharing, monthly taxation, childrens' spy brigades, and the other trappings of communal life. How much of this was truly voluntary and how much decreed by party members remains unknown. When I asked Dina once about internal dissension, I was given a cheerful explanation of "democratic centralism," the Leninist principle by which collective decisions are supposedly reached through free discussion. There could be no dissent, she said, because all recognized the advantages of consensus rule and everyone was invited to state his views. We left it at that.

9

☆ ☆ ☆

Perhaps the most surprising fact about the death of Wilfredo "Baby" Aquino was that it took so long in coming. He was not a beloved man. In the huge Davao slum called Agdao, his family's interests were of the sleazy sort—cockpits, bars, massage parlors, and brothels—and in respectable circles his reputation was most unsavory. He was also the political overlord of Agdao, its *barangay* captain, and he ruled by favors, deals, and the force of a forty-man unit of the Civilian Home Defense Force. "Baby's" reign coincided with the growing influence of the New People's Army. Since the early 1980s, the NPA had been successful in organizing the poor squatters who lived there, and its propaganda teams roamed the *barangay* virtually untroubled by the regular police. NPA revolutionary graffiti covered the concrete-block walls, and by 1985 its control had become so nearly complete that the sprawling community was mockingly known as "Nicar-Agdao."

The contest of will between Aquino and the NPA was intense and, as time passed, it took on the character of a gangland war, the number of killings mounting on both sides. The NPA accused "Baby" of murdering strikers on picket lines and oppressing squatters' organizations. About thirty members of his CHDF unit were killed and others resigned, and although no one knew how many were actually slain by NPA squads and how many by underworld thugs it was widely assumed that the communists were mainly responsible. Aquino traveled with an armed guard and claimed to have survived five assassination attempts. His brother, "Pinky" Aquino, was shot in the head while attending mass in Agdao's Redemptorist Church and barely survived. (Local people, assuming the assailants were NPA hit men, renamed it the "Redempterrorist Church"). "Baby" Aquino himself remained stoic, once telling a reporter from the *Asian Wall Street Journal* that he was prepared to die with his boots on. "When you're a *barangay* captain you have three choices," he said. "You fight back, you abandon your post, or you get killed. I cannot run away." He was right. On April 22, 1986, as he left an Agdao brothel which he owned, his jeep was blocked by men armed with M-16 rifles. He and his girlfriend were killed instantly and the NPA gloated in a public statement that another enemy of the people was dead.[1]

It was but one bloody episode among thousands in Davao, which became the "murder capital" of the Philippines and acquired a reputation as a laboratory for urban guerilla warfare. In both 1984 and 1985, a rough accounting tabulated eight hundred violent deaths. Many of them were non-political slayings resulting from gang wars and routine street crime, but most were the product of the brutal conflict between the NPA and the authorities. In a single year, NPA sparrow units killed more than seventy city policemen, many in crowded central markets, and made off with their pistols, making law enforcement so dangerous that traffic police were removed from the streets. In one brief period, sparrows liquidated a police captain as he visited relatives in a relocation center, an investigator relaxing in a canteen, a patrolman waiting for a ride on a busy street, and a Constabulary officer standing in a hospital lobby. "The NPA can kill anyone in town with total impunity," former Mayor Luis Santos said.[2] In squalid slums like Matina, Agdao and Ma'a, the communists had sunk deep organizational roots and cadres boasted that 75 percent of all Davaoenos supported their cause.

The Philippine military fought back, usually in a ham-fisted fashion that served to create more enemies for itself and more friends for the NPA. Through informers, it sought to target the communist organizers and arrest them, but more often than not its dragnets bagged marginal sympathizers and the completely innocent. Salvagings by the Constabulary and CHDF units became increasingly common. People simply disappeared or their bodies turned up on a lonely road near the seashore. Throughout the city, military units performed dead-of-night "zonings," during which whole neighborhoods were emptied and homes ransacked for clues as to the movements of the NPA.

It was the Philippine military's intent to isolate the NPA through a combination of fear and persuasion, but it was the military instead which became isolated. Even respectable, moderate Davaoenos referred to it as "an army of occupation." In truth it occupied very little. Troops spent most of their time in barracks and patrolled only in large forces. Just how isolated the military had become was apparent one day in 1985 as I walked through the streets of a commercial district. It was a business-as-usual atmosphere, the open-air shops crowded with customers, the streets flowing with small dented taxis blowing tiny horns. Suddenly, around a corner swept two battered pick-up trucks. Standing in the bed of each were five or six men in civilian clothes, each wearing a handkerchief mask, clinging with one hand to the side of the truck and with the other to an automatic rifle. They rushed past me, ignoring a stop sign, and disappeared into the weaving traffic. An acquaintance explained they were a body-guard squad convoying a single military intelligence officer who had been marked for death by the NPA.

Davao, in 1985, appeared to be a city teetering toward anarchy, perhaps another Beirut in the making. The astonishing body count suggested mindless carnage. Lawlessness seemed somehow institutionalized, and although the old port city did not outwardly exhibit a mood of fear there was a sense felt even by an outsider of things coming unhinged, of some awful fundamental destabilization taking place. All seemed patternless. But that was not true. To the communist leaders hiding in the city and nearby rural areas, a kind of pattern was emerging. Perhaps the early killings by the NPA had been random tit-for-tat affairs or sparrow-unit arms-gathering missions, but over time the tactics of violence had come to seem rational, even productive. Selective killings triggered elephantine responses from the government and brought more and more sympathizers to the rebel side. There was a kind of flowering amid the gore. Political mobilization in the squatter communities progressed more swiftly in Davao than anywhere else. Underground shadow governments blossomed in community after community. With law enforcement dismantled and cadres free to come and go, the extortion of businessmen and other "class enemies" flourished and Davao became a veritable treasure chest of party funds. More and more petty officials offered cooperation. It was all novel and unanticipated and although the NPA could sense its new power it did not quite know how to measure it or what to do with it. But it dawned on them that they had stumbled into something very close to urban guerilla warfare, and so in formal councils they began to consider the question: Was urban insurrection possible in the Philippines?

In the early purist times, when the *Little Red Book* was the bible and Mao's injunctions the infallible guide to revolution in the Philippines, urban guerilla warfare was an eccentric, even heretical notion. The path to victory led through the forests, fields and mountain slopes. Cities were something to be encircled in the penultimate days before final victory. They would simply collapse from within, not because of internal uprisings but because of external pressure from armies in the field. Urban comrades had a role to play but not an important military one. They would build up the popular front through legal organizations and fund-raising but would leave the fighting to peasant soldiers in the countryside. In one of his earliest essays which became a key CPP document, Sison had written: "While the importance of urban revolutionary activity, both legal and illegal, should not be disregarded, it should be recognized as secondary but complimentary to the armed struggle in the countryside. Until the People's Army in the countryside is ready to seize the cities, the role of urban revolutionary activity is mainly defensive because the counterrevolutionary forces are here most concentrated and strong."[3]

As the last phrase suggests, it was Sison's fear of the government's massed forces in urban bases which largely dictated the countryside strategy and he clung to that formula for most of his career as CPP chairman. In *Philippine Society and Revolution,* published in 1970 as a guide for CPP recruits, he wrote that only "secondary stress" should be given to the cities. "Chairman Mao's strategic line of encircling the cities from the countryside should be assiduously implemented," he insisted, because rural areas provided the safety and maneuverability vital for an outnumbered guerilla army. Sison went so far as to suggest that the party and the NPA should create an "armed independent regime" in the countryside before the urban bastions were subjected to attack.[4] In the essay which cadres considered his most original, "Specific Characteristics of Our People's War," he wrote that ". . . it is our secondary task to develop the revolutionary underground and the broad anti-imperialist and democratic mass movement in the cities."[5] In a critique of the party's early failures and successes published in 1976 shortly before his capture, Sison at last spelled out in some detail what the urban cadres should be doing—organizing poor workers, students and teachers through infiltration of trade unions and community organizations to the point that government *barangay* organizations could be simply overwhelmed. Sison vaguely mentioned the possibility of a "general uprising" in cities as "preparation for the final day of reckoning," but he seems never to have thought systematically of such an event and even at that late date he referred to the urban underground's role as one of supporting the army afield by providing funds, couriers, propaganda and other services.[6]

Until the 1980s, this strategy of the city as a secondary front was accepted unquestioningly by cadres in the field. Urban centers, with their small and inactive undergrounds, were the "white areas" as opposed to the NPA spheres of influence, or "red areas," in the countryside. Victor recalled that "white areas" in the early 1980s were used essentially as support bases for the rural NPA:

They would organize small groups to give aid to the guerillas. They'd solicit clothes, money, ammunition, and prepare the propaganda materials that were needed in the country. This was a time when our resources were very limited and the red guerillas had many needs, like shoes, binoculars, even food. Because our formations were too big then to be cared for by the rural base people, or it was just that these things were not available there.

The city comrade's role as a behind-the-lines purveyor of supplies and propaganda material did not change quickly. Indeed, in some places it continued to be a largely non-military role, although almost everywhere the pace of both legal and underground mobilization was stepped up. The armed struggle in Manila and Cebu, the two largest cities, remained limited to sporadic assassinations and gun-grabbing operations by the sparrows. But this relatively passive condition for urban cadres was increasingly challenged, and the party as a whole gradually shifted in the direction of a strategy that placed the urban battleground on a par with that of the countryside. This came about, as usual, more by chance and circumstance, by trial and error, than by conscious planning. And it was due almost entirely to the bloody experiments in Davao.

The phrase has a pathetic ring to it today, but Mindanao, the large island at the southern end of the archipelago, was once known as the Philippines' "Land of Promise." When the great postwar land squeeze overwhelmed the rest of the country, thousands of emigres set out for the south where, the government said, land was plentiful and success assured for those who were willing to work. Tagalogs from southern Luzon, Ilonggos, Cebuanos, and other Visayans swept down by the thousands into Mindanao in one of the country's historic migrations. Some found the arable land they had sought, but most did not and the mass of migrants drifted on to the island's largest city, a sprawling metropolis on the Gulf of Davao. It seemed a likely spot in which to prosper. Davao City was the ocean gateway to the riches of Mindanao, the huge timber tracts and gold mines in Davao del Norte and adjacent provinces and the big plantations where pineapples, coconuts, and bananas were grown for export.

For most of the emigres, there turned out to be little more promise in Davao than in the rest of the island and by the 1980s the city was filled with thousands of poor families. Most were squatters who simply camped on the large vacant tracts that stretched out into the countryside (Davao is still largely rural today). Ignoring landowners' demands that they move on, the newcomers threw up ramshackle houses made of cast-off lumber, plywood, cinder blocks and bent sheets of metal plate and built tiny chapels for the patron saints of their native villages back in Cebu, Luzon, Panay, Negros. Life was very cheap. Fires swept the fragile communities, many of them, it was believed, deliberately set by landowners to clear out the intruders. "Hold-uppers" (street thieves) roamed the neighborhoods and armed gangs of hoodlums who affected a paramilitary style of operations dominated whole neighborhoods. Davao became a polyglot city of the very poor where refugees to the "Land of Promise" made out as best they could.

The mixture of rootless peasants and poorly paid workers was a volatile one, a likely combination on which to build the beginnings of a revolution, and to the youthful founders of the new CPP it seemed a genuine promised land. In the 1960s, Davao exhibited more signs of radicalization than any other city except Manila. Student demonstrations were many and large and attracted an element not found even in the capital in those days: workers. In Davao, protests did not stop at shutting down high schools and colleges. With help from taxi and bus drivers, they brought transportation to a halt and paralyzed the entire city. Almost all of the student leaders were nationalists and moderate leftists, although a few KM veterans moved in from Manila and Cebu to begin the conversion to more radical enthusiasms. Martial law brought a sudden crackdown and the movement leaders, aware that their names were on government lists, fled to the mountains of Davao del Norte and Davao del Sur. There they huddled in makeshift camps and were joined by an odd new bunch, members of a moderate farm youth organization who had been lumped with the urban radicals when the military launched its sweeps.

According to Davao underground veterans, it was from this motley assortment that the first sparrows were launched, the act which more than any other turned the city into a battlefield. The first sparrows were based not in the city but in the mountains of adjacent provinces where the several hundred radicals were stuck with the problem of launching a revolution without guns. Three-man teams would hike down from the mountains, stroll into the city center, and stake out their target, usually either a policeman or lone soldier. While two of them acted as lookouts, the hit-man shot his victim and seized his rifle or pistol. Then all three headed for cover. At night they walked around patrols back into the mountains, carrying one more weapon for the small armory in the hills.

In the city itself, the young cadres, following Sison's guidance and central committee instructions, concentrated on the usual tasks of supporting comrades in the nearby provinces. Supplying the NPA squads with money, food, clothing and propaganda materials was the first priority. The secondary role was organizing protests and legal front groups in Davao. This proved surprisingly easy to accomplish. It was apparent very early that Davaoenos had a taste for action, and unlike urban counterparts elsewhere they responded eagerly when invited by young activists to join the confrontation with the government. There was one problem. When sparrows from the hills entered the city killing for guns, they invariably provoked military reprisals and the victims most often were the unarmed organizers circulating in the *barangays*. Many were arrested, tortured, and killed. Finally, the party's central committee sent in a regional coordinator to arrange a division of turf: Sparrows were kept out of the neighborhoods where front-group canvassers were operating. The result was a rapid acceleration in the pace of recruitment and the growth of both front-group membership and street demonstrations.

The urban underground apparatus grew so large and tightly disciplined that the party decided to take another adventurous step. For the first time, in 1981, an armed NPA unit was established inside the city. Its purpose was not so much to gather weapons, a role still claimed by the sparrows, but to assassinate informers and military intelligence agents and to plan larger actions such as sabotage. But security failed, the group was infiltrated by government agents, and the plan collapsed. A new team was formed the following year and, with better security, became immensely successful. This was the first of the NPA "Armed City Partisan" units, a secretive clan whose members both liquidated chosen enemies and set to work organizing cells of supporters in the poorest communities. Thus there were two sets of organizing teams—the "legals" who worked the *barrios* unarmed, preaching non-military, united front tactics, and the partisans who carried guns and bluntly spoke of armed revolution. Between them there developed an informal competition to determine which method was better.

The results astonished even the hardcore NPA veterans. People responded more eagerly to the talk of armed revolt. The partisans who went quickly to the point of fighting Marcos with guns far outstripped the more discreet canvassers who spoke first of moderate tactics and only got around to the idea of force when they felt their study groups were thoroughly prepared for it. It dawned on the top CPP leaders in Davao that they had been underestimating their audience all along. What the people wanted was not elaborate "social investigations" and propaganda about the three isms. They wanted to grab a gun, or at least to support those who had guns, and get on with toppling the government in Manila. Victor, a front leader in Davao at the time, recalled:

It turned out that the organizational methods of the ACPs were superior to those of the legals. The legals would start on specific issues and political education and doing social investigations. But the ACP would come in with guns and introduce themselves right away as from the NPA. In one night they could explain the revolution. It was much faster. We were very surprised at the acceptability of this blunt approach. So a new style was born, in which there was little discussion of politics without talking about armed struggle. We'd go right to the armed struggle routine. Then this became standard practice, even for the legals.

This newly discovered penchant for force was strongest among Davao's teeming squatter communities which had the least to lose and which had been radicalized by experience even before the NPA teams were on the scene. Military demolition teams repeatedly came with bulldozers to root them out. Teaching the people of Agdao and other squatter camps how to resist such intrusions became the NPA's strongest organizing technique. The strategy was described to me by a slender young cadre who had been an organizer then and, by 1985, had risen to become a member of the executive committee of the Davao City Provisional Party Committee. He called himself Luni:

Our main thing [in Agdao] was teaching people how to defend themselves against the demolitions. At first we taught them to try legal actions in courts and then they'd send massive delegations down to the city government and lots of them would write letters. To save their homes. But their demands were never acted upon and the military kept demolishing their houses.

So then we taught the people how to defend themselves. They'd form human barricades around their neighborhood and some would lie down in front of the bulldozers. Others would throw stones and human waste at the soldiers. Some even carried bolos.

It all taught the people that the government would always take sides against them and that they needed to be organized. So then we could teach them the lessons. We'd talk about poverty and point out that the demolitions were just a part of the bigger problem of poverty. And then we'd move on to talk about feudalism, imperialism and bureaucrat capitalism.

The process led inevitably to military reprisals and these, Luni thought, did more to solidify the squatters' support for the NPA than anything else. The NPA's willingness to defend the communities against military incursions was not merely of practical value, he said. It was psychologically important for people to sense and feel the power of the movement, to know that there was a way to strike back. Partisan teams killed military officers who planned the demolitions, gunned down planted informers, and staged retaliatory raids in one neighborhood while the soldiers launched a dragnet in another. The death toll mounted and the familiar cycle began: The more the military raided, the more people turned to the NPA for support and protection. The "mass base" expanded and in turn became capable of supporting and concealing more Armed City Partisans. Violence and armed resistance became the best organizing tools. In Davao, perhaps more than in any other place in the Philippines, the power of selective violence as a mobilizing tactic was proved.

The Philippine military's contribution to this cycle of violence came in several forms—abductions, torture, sudden arrests. The Armed Forces of the Philippines was a large presence in Davao, but its combat groups had no enemy formations to confront and it concentrated on rooting out the shadowy citizen-soldiers who were concealed in the slums. Its favored tactic was the sudden sweep of neighborhoods where it hoped to identify, through informers, the NPA organizers and supporters. The AFP called such operations "dragnets" but most Davaoenos called them "zonings." The terminology was important because a "zoning" had been the despised method used by Japanese occupation forces to capture resistance leaders during World War II and the practice merely reenforced the Filipinos' view of the AFP as another army of occupation. In its usual application, Constabulary or CHDF units surrounded a neighborhood, rousted residents from their homes, and made house-to-house searches, hauling suspects before a hooded informer for identification. In some periods, there were two or three "zonings" in the city each day.

By coincidence one morning I was discussing this practice in a Davao attorney's office when two middle-aged women from one of the poor neighborhoods burst through the door and angrily plopped down beside me. They had come to report a zoning the previous evening, which occurred as they walked home together through the community of Santo Niño. Seven jeep-loads of Constabulary soldiers swooped in and cordoned off a section of fifty homes. Residents were ordered out and herded into a street while the soldiers searched each house for NPA suspects, arms, and subversive literature. When they had finished they brought all of the young men before an informer who wore a paper hood over his face to conceal his identity. "They said they were looking for a *demonyo*," one of the women recalled. It had been a slow night, however, and the man in the hood could spot no *demonyos*. The troops went away empty-handed.

Wandering through the sprawling squatters' slum of Agdao in the mid-1980s one rarely encountered anyone who had not suffered some embittering experience with the government soldiers, and many of them spoke willingly of incidents which turned them toward the NPA. One woman I met by chance began talking of the day the Constabulary came and searched

170

three houses, including her own, ostensibly seeking information about a policeman who had disappeared. She and three men were taken to headquarters for questioning—she was included because, they said, she had been seen talking with the missing policeman. She was released, but the three friends were held and tortured, one of them so severely that he later died. The effect had been to enhance her appreciation for the NPA and its brand of rough justice in Agdao. The NPA had brought a sense of order and discipline to the community, she thought, unlike the police and military. "Maybe some in the military are good men, but everytime I see a man in uniform I feel fear. I am not ever afraid of the NPA man."

Such accounts of NPA justice called for a measure of skepticism—even some communists I met acknowledged that mistakes were made—but it was not difficult to understand that its version might be preferable to the sort dispensed by the military and local courts. There seemed to be no ordinary remedies for the frequent disappearances and salvagings that plagued Davao's poor. In December 1984, four young men were picked up on the roadside early one morning as they returned home from an all-night wedding party. Cynthia Adao Prat, an attorney representing the men's wives, said witnesses identified one of the arresting party as a member of the local CHDF, easily recognizable as a hunch-back, and another whose long hair had earned him the nickname "Tarzan." On the morning of the disappearance, relatives had traced the four arrested men to police headquarters in Davao but were prevented from entering by soldiers who pointed guns at them. A Constabulary lieutenant arrived and was asked to produce the missing four. His response, according to papers filed in the families' law-suit, had been to order the relatives herded to Constabulary headquarters for questioning. Months later, the missing men had not been found and a local court was still considering an appeal for a writ of habeas corpus.

As the mayhem piled up and the NPA obtained a firmer grip on Davao neighborhoods, an even bloodier element was introduced. Armed paramilitary gangs whose sponsorship was unclear began appearing in Agdao and other squatter slums. Some made fantastic claims of religious origins and boasted of mystical powers to eliminate evil-doers. Such bizarre groups were rather common in the remote countryside of Mindanao where, claiming that immunity from death was assured by magic amulets or sacred oils on their bodies, they looted and pillaged under the guise of eliminating the unholy. It was widely believed in Davao that these intruders were secretly hired by the government to destroy the NPA and its sympathizers in radicalized slums which uniformed soldiers of the AFP feared to enter. I never found any evidence to support this, but the communist organizers eagerly spread the message that the "fascist state" had unloosed a new instrument of terror against the people.

The most ferocious of these pseudo-mystics was a certain "Kapitan Inggo," who allegedly had been a Muslim rebel leader in the secessionist movement that sought to create a separate Islamic state in Mindanao. Many like him had been co-opted or simply bought off by the Marcos government as the separatist insurgency petered out. "Kapitan Inggo" had surfaced in Davao under the new banner of anti-communism and with the aid of some 200 armed followers set about exorcising Marxist devils from slums such as Agdao and Mandug. He was on an NPA wanted list for allegedly having fired into a picket line of striking workers. The centerpiece of his campaign was a series of anti-communist polemics which he delivered to groups of bewildered slum-dwellers who were herded periodically onto an outdoor basketball court by his armed gangs.

Inggo was believed to be responsible for the killing of one of the more popular slum leaders. Alexander Orcullo, an anti-Marcos activist and crusading newspaper editor, was a local hero in the Mandug area where he may or may not have been in league with the powerful NPA forces there. Inggo had publicly labeled him a communist and threatened to kill him. Such threats were not taken lightly—Inggo had a reputation for delivering on them—and Orcullo for a time moved his family out of Mandug to a safer haven. Later he moved back in. On the night of October 19, 1984, Orcullo was driving along a lonely road with his wife and small son when a band of ten armed men stopped his car. Orcullo was ordered to get out of the car and turn his back. He did so and was shot once by each of the ten men. A statement issued in Inggo's name claimed credit for the murder of a dangerous communist. No proof emerged to link him to it and he was never prosecuted by Davao authorities.

The conviction that such vigilantes operated with official sanction and encouragement was strong in Agdao, the scene of many gangland slayings. The victims were usually not NPA members at all but local activists who had achieved prominence in community campaigns. One of them was the husband of a heavy-set, belligerent woman, Luz Tac-An, whose anger had driven her beyond the fear of speaking out. Her husband had been the leader of a squatters' anti-arson squad which patrolled Agdao's streets at night to halt a wave of mysterious house burnings. Their headquarters in evening hours was a crudely constructed Catholic chapel tucked in among the huts that bordered R. Castillo Street, a main thoroughfare. At 11:30 P.M. on December 2, 1984, the squad was having coffee at the chapel when a band of men armed with automatic rifles arrived, ordered several women to lie down inside the chapel, and told four men, including Luz's husband, to remain standing outside. The ringleader killed all four with a quick burst from his Armalite and then sprayed bullets around the chapel entrance, wounding seven women. The identity of the killers remained a mystery, although the people of Agdao were certain that both the military and a local political boss were responsible.

Noli, lean and tall, brusque but articulate, was a member of the regional CPP executive committee whose territory embraced Davao and surrounding areas; Monching was on the preparatory committee of Davao's national front; Luni was a member of the executive committee of the Davao City Provisional Party Committee; and Sammy, whose boyish face seemed not to fit with his job, was chief of Davao's Armed City Partisans, the unit responsible for most NPA killings in Davao. These four people had played a large role in putting together the pieces for the CPP in Davao and, early in 1986, they agreed to meet and do a bit of stock-taking for a visiting journalist. The manner of the meeting, as much as anything they said, told of the confidence

173

they had in their handiwork. It was not a furtive gathering. We had simply driven in a truck a few minutes from downtown Davao to a sort of amusement park, which was closed for the day, and convened in a room set aside by the management. A sudden pounce by the military would have netted the party's top leadership in Davao, but the four seemed unconcerned. I was unaware of any sentinels posted to provide a warning. We were interrupted once by several loud explosions nearby. Sammy wandered outside for a few minutes and returned to report casually that the military was conducting target practice in a nearby field.

Noli, the ranking party officer, described the evolution of the NPA in Davao, from the first few cadres huddled in the nearby mountains to the deployment of sparrows and the slow barrio-by-barrio mobilization of the people. He might have been a businessman describing the founding and growth of his company. There had been mistakes and failures, but the party had profited from them, changing tactics as the years unfolded, until the proper mix was found. The bad years were over, he managed to suggest, and Davao—the Philippines third largest urban area—was settling into a kind of routine. The large rural area was almost completely controlled by National Democratic Front barrio councils which the military rarely bothered. The same was true of most of the poor neighborhoods in the urbanized sections. The difference was that the NPA could militarily defend the rural areas but not the urban ones. Overall, Noli said, about 75 percent of the population of 800,000 supported the NPA. Only the very heart of the business district and the few walled and guarded residential areas of the rich seemed off limits. The great slum *barangays* like Agdao and Matina were almost totally controlled.

The years 1984–85 had been the time of great violence when on the average two Davaoenos a day were killed in some encounter or another. In mid-1985, however, a lull had developed and it was apparent that the NPA had curtailed its assaults on police, military agents, and other enemies. The AFP had taken this as a sign of retreat and Brig. Gen. Jamie Echeverria, the army commander in Davao, had talked of rolling back the NPA in sixteen neighborhoods.[7] Noli dismissed that as government

174

propaganda. The NPA had reduced its attacks, he said, because fewer were necessary. In the country and the urban poor districts most of the one-time opponents had been "neutralized" and had come around to cooperate with the new party committees. The national front had proved its power, paralyzing the city at will with huge protests and transport strikes; the *welgang bayan,* or people's strike, had been most successful in Davao and could, if the party wanted, immobilize the city. Recognizing the NPA's power, some of Davao's leaders secretly dealt with its representatives, often conceding peacefully on demands that once would have meant bloody encounters. For with its control of the slums, the party had become a clandestine political power. In Noli's view, a tacit accommodation was taking place.

This turn of events in Davao had a profound effect on many in the CPP, especially the national front organizers, and set off a debate not merely about tactics but about the entire grand strategy for final victory. The traditional assumption that only rural-based warfare could succeed was brought into question. Davao obviously was not the passive urban enclave whose revolutionary role was limited to that of a logistical base for the real heroes in the countryside. It possessed the ingredients for its own revolution. There was a large, politicized mass of people angrily polarized against the military and the Marcos government, a "mass base" which frequently showed itself to be more inclined than the party leaders to get on with the struggle. Large areas of the city were under the communists' de facto political control and the shadow governments were sufficiently entrenched to negotiate with and extract concessions from the official government. Most important, the national-front mass mobilizations—the *welgang bayans*—on several occasions had paralyzed the city, flooding the streets with protesters in such numbers that the military was helpless in dealing with them.

These were the conditions that provoked some in the CPP to begin thinking of a new kind of finale for the rebellion, an urban insurrection. They were vague in describing it, at least to outsiders, but they talked of simultaneous uprisings in major cities which would paralyze the governments. The formula called for mass outpourings to halt traffic and normal com-

175

merce while NPA partisan squads sabotaged military installations, cut power lines, occupied public buildings and liquidated government leaders. The established order would simply collapse, in this vision, and somehow in its place would surface a new authority composed of underground cadres and leaders of the legal national front. No real confrontation with the military would occur because, the insurrectionists assumed rather casually, thousands of soldiers would disobey orders and defect. The uprisings could not occur singly. They would be timed to erupt in all major Philippine cities on the same day. In 1985, the cadres who favored this formula admitted that only Davao, Bacolod in Negros Occidental, and a few cities in Mindanao and the Visayas were ripe. Most believed then that the great convulsion would take place within three to five years.

How widely this view was held within the party hierarchy is not known. The central committee never accepted it as worthy of formal adoption and it seems that as late as 1985 a majority on the committee opposed it, clinging still to the original theory of victory in the countryside. One middle-level cadre said that the urban insurrection scenario was first discussed at lower levels in 1981–83 but was endorsed by only about twenty percent of the leadership. By 1985, its acceptance had reached forty percent, he said. One reason for its slowly spreading popularity, it seemed, was a certain impatience with the pace of rural NPA development, a growing doubt that a peasant army could ever defeat government forces. Francisco Nemenzo, a scholar with excellent access to CPP leaders, wrote as early as 1982 that the old formula of rural conflict was obsolete:

The truly decisive task is to build the party's capacity for mass mobilizing outside the guerilla zones, especially in the cities; in other words, to gradually improve [the party's] capability for launching simultaneous insurrections at some future date. The NPA obviously has no illusion of beating the AFP in the battlefield. It can only hope to seize power by simultaneous insurrections and the armed struggle is probably viewed as a means to achieve this strategic objective.[8]

Victor observed that the insurrection theory had at one time been taboo within the party, but by 1985 was freely discussed in party literature, not so much as an alternative to the traditional rural guerilla concept but as complementary to it. "You never read about this in the '70s, but it has developed as an important component in our thinking in the past few months. It is Davao that has provided us with the vision of how this could come about."

10

☆ ☆ ☆

The revolution first touched him one day in 1975, the shopkeeper recalled, when two young strangers came to his store and asked for a donation to the New People's Army. He pledged two pesos a month, which he still paid a decade later, and agreed to attend their political indoctrination classes, which he quickly reckoned to be boring. As the years passed, he grew to respect the strangers, whose numbers increased and whose adventures grew bolder. They killed robbers and extortionists who for years had preyed on his friends in Agdao, the poor community in Davao. They also "liquidated" policemen and soldiers who had reputations for brutality. For the most part, they were polite and respectful young men who never robbed. Although their political lectures were tedious, they were accepted as friends and sheltered from the authorities.

Perhaps most appealing, the shopkeeper went on, was the disciplined nature of their "revolutionary justice." It had an orderliness and sense of purpose, unlike the random killings committed by crooks and soldiers. There was, for example, the case of his neighbor, a known troublemaker who cheated on his wife and identified communists for the military. One day in 1984, the neighbor received a written warning which admonished him to cease both philandering and informing. He ignored it and became so incautious as to meet military agents in his home. A second warning arrived and it, too, was ignored. At 11:45 P.M. on December 24, 1984, fifteen minutes before Christmas, the neighbor stepped into the street from his home and was shot to death by three bullets fired from a pistol. As the shopkeeper concluded this vignette, a woman friend listened, nodding approval. "Yes, yes," she said, "the NPA—they know who to kill."

The casual acceptance of murder by people on the periphery of the Philippine revolution was for a time puzzling. The shopkeeper's account was not an uncommon one, nor was his friend's enthusiasm unusual. In my efforts to trace the NPA's appeal to non-communists, I heard many such stories and a pattern emerged: In village after village, the NPA's initial appeal was its role as dispenser of punishment against the ordinary man's enemies. The NPA killed cattle rustler, "hold-uppers," coconut thieves, molesters of women, arrogant soldiers, even wife-beaters. Usually, but not always, the penalties followed investigations, warnings, and hearings before a "people's court." In the eyes of people who described such executions, the NPA had introduced into their communities a crude form of legal discipline—a vigilante's justice, true, but still a form of justice.

It flourished and became popular only because it replaced something worse, utter lawlessness. The typical poor community of urban squatters or subsistence farmers was often beyond the reach of civilized law enforcement. The government's writ simply did not run. Neither local police nor the Philippine Constabulary bothered much with crime in these places, had never bothered with it, in fact, and the protection of life and property usually fell to ordinary citizens. The NPA filled this gap.

In a communist-controlled barrio on the island of Panay, a 36-year-old public official and president of the Parent-Teachers Association described his first attachment to the NPA. The village had been molested for years by carabao thieves, he said. One afternoon he had tied his own carabao to a tree while he

179

visited a friend's home. The animal, which was the source of his family's livelihood in the fields, was gone when he returned an hour later. In 1979, he said, the first armed NPA squads arrived in the barrio and promptly killed three known rustlers. The deed impressed him and he joined the movement, rising in time to local party office and, with the NPA's help, to an elective position in the *barangay.* He cared little for the NPA's lectures; he was not even sure that they were communists, he said. But since 1979, no carabao thief had come near the barrio.

Nothing enhanced the NPA's Robin Hood image more than the contrasting behavior of the Armed Forces of the Philippines. Incompetent, corrupt, and abusive, the AFP had by the mid-1980s established itself as an oppressive force in much of the Philippine countryside, especially in areas where communist guerillas were active. Its troops, underpaid and poorly disciplined, were more at war with the citizenry than with the NPA in countless villages and were looked upon not as a protective force but as an army of occupation. Its torture of suspects was widespread. In 1983, Amnesty International concluded after many interviews that torture was "so prevalent as to amount to standard operating procedure for security and intelligence units."[1] AFP units detained citizens without charges, murdered many of them, conducted unwarranted searches of entire *barrios* and even engaged in a form of "strategic hamletting" similar to American practices in Vietnam. Measured against these standards, the NPA came off a model of chivalry.

This military monster was the creation of President Marcos, his chief of staff, Gen. Fabian Ver, and a clutch of favored generals who ruled the Regional Unified Commands like Caesar's pro-consuls. Before Marcos, the Philippines had maintained a small army with an erratic military tradition—the old Philippine Constabulary was little more than a police force. To defend his martial law regime, Marcos created a combined army and national police force which, including reserves, totaled 350,000 men. Nominally ruled from Manila by Ver and Defense Minister Juan Ponce Enrile, it became a loose aggregation of regional commands whose chiefs conceived their military role largely as one of pacifying villages where the NPA had obtained footholds. Even this role was a modest one. AFP commanders preferred to ignore the guerilla forces whenever possible. By the 1980s, the NPA was originating far more encounters than the AFP.

This disinclination to engage the guerillas appalled American military leaders who by 1983 had become alarmed by the growth of the NPA. Accustomed in the past to arming and advising the Philippine military, often looking upon it as a surrogate force serving American interests, U.S. officials closely examined the AFP in 1983 and sensed a catastrophe in the making. In June of that year, Admiral Robert L. J. Long, commander in chief of U.S. forces in the Pacific, told Congress: "I can categorize the Armed Forces of the Philippines today as incapable of performing what I would call organized functions that any armed force should be able to provide for its own self-defense."[2] AFP forces did not pursue the enemy, or when they did they had to borrow a logging truck; Manila kept many personnel carriers and helicopters handy to guard the presidential palace. Defections were common and, it was discovered, some local garrisons had reached tacit agreement with the guerillas not to attack. American officials grew increasingly fearful and critical. "It took ten years for the AFP to decline to its current dismal condition," observed Assistant Secretary of Defense Richard L. Armitage.[3]

Uninspired and undisciplined, ignorant of the political aspect of guerilla warfare, the local AFP forces came to be viewed as common thieves and arrogant bullies. They stole chickens from poor farmers, molested local girls, killed hapless villagers in drunken barfights, indeed committed all of those crimes common to foreign armies occupying a conquered land. "They are viewed not as soldiers of the Philippines but as the soldiers of Mr. Marcos," observed a Davao politician, Zafiro Respicio, in an interview. Staff members of the U.S. Senate Foreign Relations Committee, after extensive interviews in the Philippines, came to this conclusion:

The AFP tends to act toward the people as if they, the people, were the enemy, not the object of protection from a hostile force. . . . The

181

AFP and the government seem to act from fear and distrust of the people; the NPA appear to act from concern and confidence in the people.[4]

The pattern was worse where the NPA had made gains. Frustrated and fearful, the Philippine army countered not with battlefield confrontations but with civilian arrests, zonings, salvagings, and evacuations of entire villages. Distrust and hatred of the military grew and so did the number of recruits for the NPA. Perhaps the first to note this "vicious cycle," as he called it, was Bishop Francisco Claver, the liberal but anti-communist churchman who had opposed both the military and the guerillas in Mindanao's Bukidnon Province:

The chain of events is most predictable: Since the military are everywhere, their abuses are everywhere too—there is a direct ratio between the size of military groups in any given area and the number of crimes committed. These abuses help to make the NPA option all the more attractive to the people. . . . So the NPA make capital of them. But where the NPA are in strength, there the military presence increases and their abuses proliferate even more. In all this, it is the people who bear the brunt of the conflict.[5]

Gongonia Canabuan's experience fit the cycle which Bishop Claver described. She was 64 years old when I met her, a weathered and lined face peering attentively at the communist cadre delivering a propaganda lecture in a small bamboo chapel. In 1986, her barrio in Panay had for two years been safe NPA territory and she regularly participated in its front activities. But in May 1984, the barrio had been a battle zone, infiltrated by the guerillas but still contested by a military detachment which periodically arrested NPA sympathizers. Gongonia's conversion had begun one night at a dance and box supper suddenly interrupted by the arrival of a Constabulary squad. The soldiers had lists of names and picked out one of her husband's friends, a man who, she said, had once been with the NPA but who had become disgusted and returned to his small farm. Gunshots were heard and the friend was found severely wounded in a clump of trees. Gongonia's husband, Demetrio, 68, and another farmer managed to get him to a distant hospital. A few nights later, the PC came to the Canabuan home, searched it, and found an old rifle. Demetrio explained the gun was for defense against carabao thieves. The PC marched him away to a point outside the barrio where a huge rock of local legend stood at the edge of a ravine. He was found dead there next morning. Gongonia recalled making two decisions on the spot: To send her son far away for safety and to devote her life to revenge through the NPA.

The Canabuan case was not exceptional. Many like Gongonia turned to the NPA because of some fierce personal grievance. But many, too, did not see the NPA as a source of salvation. They ended up in its mass base out of fear or intimidation or simply a willingness to go along with the tide. There were many who had a stake in the old system—small landlords, middle-class peasants, petty politicians, local bureaucrats, the conservative churchmen. Some simply disliked being bossed around or taxed by the new authorities represented on NDF underground committees. For them, communist control offered not deliverance but a loss of status and independence and they did not embrace the new era with enthusiasm. Some did not embrace it at all and were killed or forced to leave home or taught to keep silent. For obvious reasons, the reluctant followers were not easy interviews and it was never possible to sort out and quantify, in any given place, the extent of passive acceptance. The mixture of conviction and coercion that went into the making of a communist-controlled barrio was not something the outsider could measure.

Bishop Antonio Fortich of Negros Occidental had lived with the NPA presence for many years and seemed more knowledgeable than most about the mixed motives of those who supported it. Outspoken and colorfully articulate, he devoted many sermons to explications of the guerilla's appeal: the grinding poverty of Negros sugar workers, abuses of government soldiers, indifference of Manila's government. (Conservative planters, who thought his sermons rationalizations for revolution, called him "Kumander Tony.") His diocesan residence had been destroyed in a fire which many believed was set by arsonists in the military to destroy records of human rights abuses, including one infamous massacre of nine young men. Through his priests, several of whom sympathized with or condoned the Marxist as defenders of the poor, the bishop had learned much about what converted simple peasants to supporters of revolution.

"They join first of all because of this massive poverty," he said one day in his office near a seminary that had become his temporary residence.

You have here a whole island of malnourished children. Next, it would be the torture by the soldiers. A farmer is taken away and never seen again and what happens? The next day his son is in the hills with the NPA. What would you expect? But it is not always like that. In this province, you have more than 200,000 in their mass base and it is through their gifts that the guerillas survive. But not all of them are hardcore Marxists, of course. Many are in this mass base because they are afraid. If you do not give, you become a marked man. The NPA marks them as "anti" and sometimes they just disappear. In the southern part (where the NPA is strongest), seven mayors have been forced to pull up and leave. They have moved away out of fear.

The issue of supposedly "voluntary" taxes levied by the NPA produced convincing accounts of intimidation. The party insisted formally that "taxes" were levied only on the rich while peasants made "contributions." But the mere presence of armed men made the term "contribution" dubious and blurred the line between voluntary and compulsory. The amount seemed small—two pesos a month was a common levy—but it was not insignificant to a farmer on the brink of absolute poverty. It was apparent in interviews through the Visayas and Mindanao that the problem of taxes was a serious one for the party. On the island of Panay, a school teacher in one communist village told me, when no one else was around to hear him, that for a brief period the NPA had insisted on mandatory "gifts." A tax revolt erupted and the party had backed down. The issue was no longer disruptive, he said. Several cadres admitted that such revolts were not uncommon. The party's practice, it seemed, was to reduce the pressure and rely on voluntary gifts when the resistance became heated. "Yes, there have been excesses," said George, the NDF leader on Negros.

184

"We have had to rectify these and they are frequently discussed in our self-criticism meetings."

The forced taxation of poor farmers, of course, tarnished the communists' Robin Hood image. So, at times, did their practice of eliminating political enemies. It was their claim that "liquidations" were measured punishments deserved by enemies of the people and carried out only after searching consideration. As political warriors, they attempted to avoid the appearance of indiscriminate killings and they sought the moral high ground that would contrast their behavior with the casual, random abuses of the military, especially the CHDF forces. CPP policy prescribed an elaborate system of warnings and trials by "people's courts" in cases involving death sentences.

There was little evidence that the party and the NPA encouraged or condoned indiscriminate killing of civilian officials. But there was evidence that in actual practice the liquidation of enemies was not as discriminating as the party claimed. The truth seemed to lie somewhere between the party's assurance that only the guilty were punished and the government's assertion that the NPA killed, as one military officer maintained, "anyone who got in their way." In general, there was nothing in the NPA's methods to suggest systematic terrorism, certainly nothing to compare with the Vietcong's tactics of murdering the uninvolved merely to create destabilization and chaos. One American official who had extensive experience in both Vietnam and the Philippines concluded that the methods of the two revolutionary armies differed greatly:

The NPA are not terrorists. Their killing is selective and usually designed to make a political point. They don't roll grenades into movie theaters [as the Vietcong had done]. The killings are not indiscriminate. They are usually very carefully considered. These are pretty sophisticated people. There is a high level of education, not like the Vietcong.[6]

In the NPA code of justice, certain defined "blood debts" merited liquidation. The list included informers, government intelligence agents, rapists, habitual cattle rustlers and other types defined as "incorrigible criminals." "Warlords," rich farmers who maintained private armies to protect their property, were automatic targets unless they secretly agreed to cooperate with the NPA (and several did, I was told). All, in theory, had to be formally judged guilty and all had to be warned.

Anyone in military uniform was assumed an enemy, and this blanket verdict was extended to local police who under Marcos had been integrated into the military command. CPP policy toward police was at best ambivalent. Officially, the cadre named George told me, only police who actively opposed the movement were considered targets. In fact, many were killed on the streets by sparrow units coveting their service revolvers. It was difficult to square the supposed policy of painstaking discrimination with what happened in Davao in the early 1980s when dozens of policemen, including traffic cops, were slain for their guns. Indeed, the pattern that unfolded there suggested that the degree of NPA control and influence determined the death toll—the greater the control, the less discriminate the killings. There seemed to be more indulgence in liquidations to make political points, and at times the behavior bordered on terrorism. In one especially chilling incident, a military instructor in a Davao high school was shot to death one afternoon amid a crowd of students and teachers on the school grounds. Instead of fleeing, the assailant and his partner launched into a lecture on the evils of militarization of the school system.

Nor was it true, as several cadres insisted, that the sparrows were skilled professionals subject to NPA discipline and limited in their targets. Some were, some were not. One NPA commander readily acknowledged that a number of the assassination squads operating in his territory were composed of teenaged boys eager to prove their credentials by killing police. "It is not official, but actually we sometimes encourage them to do this," he said.

There was also evidence that even disciplined sparrows were careless and prone to mistakes. One NDF member in Davao talked of such errors. He was a middle-class professional man and seemed more than a bit squeamish about his alliance with hardened killers, although intellectually he had come to terms with the consequences of armed revolution. In one case he cited, a squad had planned the liquidation of a police officer judged guilty of torture. Two rather popular policemen who usually accompanied the intended victim were to be warned to stay away from the scene. The warnings were not delivered and all three men were killed. In another case, the NDF member said, the wrong police target was shot to death because of a mixup over license plates on an automobile.

Many civilian officials—mayors, *barangay* captains and members of *barangay* councils—have been killed by the NPA and many more have been forced to flee their villages to avoid punishment. In the party's hierarchy of enemies, these officials were not automatically assumed to be class enemies and were usually given warnings. In villages controlled by NDF committees, they were given the options of working with the communists, remaining neutral, or leaving. The large number of *barangay* captains killed or driven away was justified by the claim that they often were in tactical command of the paramilitary CHDF units, with which the NPA had frequent encounters. The captains were looked upon as military, not political, chieftains. "The captain is the boss of the CHDF in his area," said Luni, a high-ranking Davao communist. "What action we take depends on what damage the captains and the CHDFs have done to the masses there. We hold the captain responsible for what the CHDF does and so this is why the captain is often liquidated."

The process of uncovering and liquidating informers was a major concern for the NPA. The military from the first had had little difficulty penetrating both the guerilla armies and the barrio party structures. (One ranking general boasted that both the real names and aliases of 17,000 NPA soldiers were known to AFP intelligence.) A few pesos per month had proved enough to buy agents among people who lived in NPA-influenced territory and the names they supplied were turned over to CHDF and Constabulary units for punishment. It was easy to identify the party's propaganda teams and organizers assigned to infiltrate a barrio and the local families which sheltered them. The casualty rate among these exposed organizers was said to be extremely high.

The NPA's elimination of military informers was complicated by the fact that many victims were prominent and popular members of their communities. Executing the wrong person could be a serious political setback for the organizing teams, and for that reason the party units responsible for village de-

187

fense were said to make intense efforts to identify the truly guilty. "Before liquidating an informer, we must have data to confirm that he really is an agent," Luni said. "Either they must admit their guilt in a confrontation with us or we must have the testimony of someone—his neighbors maybe—who has seen him talking with the military. Sometimes we have a public trial, but sometimes we do not. It is up to the top NPA unit in the community to decide." Once convicted, the informer was often put to death in front of assembled villagers to emphasize the penalty of collaboration.

The NPA had not always been so vigilant and quick to act against spies. In the early days, when many top commanders were middle-class young men fresh from the universities, there was a reluctance to kill farmers caught working with the military. The young pioneers cherished the belief that with enough proper education anyone could be reformed and converted to the cause. The result, said Jes, a veteran of those times, was the loss of several highly motivated leaders. As times passed, however, the university-bred commanders learned their lessons. Too, more of the peasant-born were elevated to top military ranks and they proved far less squeamish. "We had to learn not to be lenient and that it was a matter of life and death," Jes recalled. "Eliminating informers is a matter of survival—you must kill them." The young guerillas most likely to survive, he said, were those who had the good fortune to be trained by veteran Huk fighters brought over by Dante who taught that one's life depended on liquidating informers.

But some did not learn the lesson until it was too late, and in Mindanao the price paid for laxity was large and gruesome. In early 1986, the graves of more than 200 persons were discovered, most of them in the province of Misamis Oriental. At first the word was spread, mainly by the Philippine military, that the NPA had murdered hundreds of innocent civilians who resisted its approaches. Exactly what did happen was not clear, but the CPP's embarrassed explanation was a tangled story of military spies and botched attempts to ferret them out.

Several cadres provided a similar account. The Mindanao NPA and NDF had grown swiftly and haphazardly in the late 1970s and their leadership was less cautious than their Luzon counterparts in enlisting recruits. Many volunteers were military agents from the beginning while others were bought off soon after they joined fighting or propaganda units. They remained undetected for several years, some of them rising to positions of considerable importance. Beginning in October 1985, several of these "deep penetration agents," as they were called, were uncovered and a thorough purge was ordered. In one version explained to me by a cadre who had participated in the purge, the crisis was compounded by the discovery that some initially assigned to investigate suspected informers had themselves been on the military's payroll. The result, he admitted, was the false identification of many innocent party members as government agents. Infiltrators under AFP control pointed the finger at loyal veterans who were then executed as spies. The dimensions of the Mindanao calamity remained unclear, but it was acknowledged that many falsely accused workers were liquidated and a number of party leaders with years of experience were removed from their posts, criticized at length for their oversights, and dispersed to minor jobs in other regions.

Guerilla wars in Third World countries are almost by definition wars of the poor against the equally poor and the Philippine rebellion was no exception. It perhaps could not have been anything else in a country where three-fourths of the families which produced soldiers for both sides lived at the poverty level or below. Both the government and the CPP fielded armies from the lowest social rungs and the conditions of their service extended their lot to the battlefield. A common joke which contained a vein of truth had it that the lowly AFP private was more poorly fed and clothed than his adversary in the NPA.

The military build-up of the Marcos years expanded the size of the AFP but did little for its foot-soldiers. Much of the budget was drained away by high-ranking officers who relished comfort or went to purchase exotic command helicopters instead of trucks for the movement of troops. The ordinary fighter went into battle poorly equipped and aware that if wounded there would probably be no medicine or hospital attention to save his life. A soldier earned about 1,000 pesos a month, or fifty dollars, and even that was usually delayed in payment. It was not uncommon for troops in remote provinces to replace worn-out army boots with tennis shoes bought from their own pockets. Except for his rifle and ammunition belt, his battlefield equipment was usually in short supply. Military observers have noted that AFP units rarely pursued a routed enemy force. The reason was that the means of pursuit—trucks, jeeps, armored personnel carriers—did not exist, at least not in the field. The account of one typical encounter in northern Luzon described how a band of guerilla raiders escaped pursuit while a PC detachment waited for the arrival of trucks borrowed from a plantation.[7]

It was, then, little wonder that the AFP private fought only as much as he had to and seldom risked his life in pursuit. Nor was his penchant for looting difficult to understand. Stealing food from poor families whom he was supposed to protect was a common practice, not because the foot-soldier was greedy but because he needed the extra nourishment. Petty extortion became routine in far-flung garrisons where supervision was lax. One of the more notorious examples was a PC checkpoint on the outskirts of Davao. It was on the farmers' only route to the city's markets and they routinely turned over a chicken each day as the price of passage. The stop became known as "Chicken Point."

Many, too, supplemented a meager salary by selling rifles, machine guns, mortars, and ammunition to the NPA. Black-market sales were the second largest source of military hardware for the guerillas (the first being weapons captured in battle). These were not isolated deals consummated by a few corrupt soldiers. In several provinces, they were well-organized operations involving entire units which provided a permanent undercover market. In Panay, party officers told me that the NPA could purchase almost any type of AFP armaments if it could raise the money and that Armalite rifles were in steady supply, the cost of each being 18,000 pesos (about $1000). One party member expressed irritation that recently this price had been raised from 15,000 pesos. The reason, it seemed, was that AFP black-marketeers had discovered other clandestine customers in the ranks of rich landlords who began forming private armies when the Marcos regime was displaced in Manila.

If the livelihood of the AFP soldier was meager, so was that of his adversary in the mountains. From the start, it was an NPA maxim that "Red fighters" must sustain themselves on the contributions of food and cash from the "mass base" of peasants and farm workers. In time, as the party apparatus became more sophisticated in raising money, most guerilla fronts were partially subsidized from Manila. In either case, the support provided a bare subsistence living. In the mountain camps I visited, meals invariably consisted of rice, an occasional vegetable, and root crops. A piece of dried fish was a luxury. Rice was severely rationed because it usually had to be carried up mountain trails on the backs of young couriers. A recurring problem was the feeding of babies and young children of NPA soldiers who had married and formed families in the hills. There were ingenious solutions. In some cases, sympathetic nuns fed and educated the young in church boarding schools. In Negros, a large number of NPA infants subsisted on handouts from a UNICEF feeding program of a nourishing gruel called "Super Snack."

Because the guerilla regimen was spartan, CPP propaganda organs devoted much space to the encouragement of "self-reliance" and austerity throughout the movement. *Ang Bayan,* the party newspaper, regularly published admonitions against loose spending and frivolity and urged local branches to be creative in developing new sources of financial support. It also advised those guerilla fronts subsidized from the national headquarters to take care that their standard of living did not exceed that of local peasants, lest class envy be aroused. As an example of the necessary frugality, one issue of *Ang Bayan* published the daily budget prescribed for each guerilla fighter in Negros Occidental. It included:

Rice	2.55 pesos
Viand	2.25
Bath soap	.21
Laundry soap	.12
Toothpaste	.20
Tobacco	.30
Kerosene	.06
Batteries	.20
Lighter fluid	.02

| Flint | .02 |
| Gun oil | .05 |

The total came to 5.98 pesos a day, about 30 cents.

Being exclusively a war of the poor, the rebellion impinged only infrequently on the Philippine middle-class. There were cases, of course, in which well-to-do Filipinos were affected: landlords who no longer deemed it safe to occupy their estates, businessmen who were subject to communist extortion. There were, too, the prominent families of those college-educated radicals who had slipped into the underground in the 1960s and '70s. And not a few well-heeled Manilans were secretly contributing funds to the NDF, most of them out of hatred of Marcos and a conviction that only an armed force could rid the country of him.

But throughout the Marcos years, the Philippine middle-class was relatively untouched by the fighting and ignorant of the extensive politicization carried on by the communist front groups. In Manila, especially, the reports of raids and encounters in the mountains had a distant quality, as if these were occurring in some other country. There were many reasons for this sense of detachment. One was the widespread feeling that what was happening in the countryside was not a *communist* insurgency at all but merely an outpouring of resentment against the Marcos government; it would disappear once he was dethroned. I thought, too, that the notion of Filipino farmers being radicalized into communists was simply too far-fetched for non-ideological Manilans accustomed to looking upon politics as a game played only by the elite. Communism had disappeared with the Huks, had it not?

The Marcos regime encouraged this passive response to the rebellion that gathered force in the 1980s. Marcos himself, after all, had on several occasions declared the communists defeated and the war successfully completed. He could not very well pronounce the NPA a threat to the nation. Under the tight censorship imposed until 1983, when Aquino's assassination provoked a revolt of the media, the Manila press reported battle bulletins issued by the military but almost never explored the NPA's appeal and strength. Readers in Manila became vaguely aware of a spreading insurgency—battle datelines changed from northern to southern Luzon, then to the Visayas and Mindanao. And they would be momentarily jarred by friends' accounts of country estates abandoned because of NPA death threats. But the size and complexity of the communist-organized military and political movements never were recognized in the cities.

It was only where the NPA was powerful that the urban middle class sensed cause for concern. In the cities of Davao and Bacolod, the NPA's influence was too strong and its mass bases too large to be ignored. Even there the reaction of business and professional people was not one of fear that an actual communist revolution was overtaking them. This NPA outfit, they would say, was pretty strong and caused a lot of trouble and it was all President Marcos's fault, but it would go away in time. I met one Negros sugar planter whose estate was used routinely for NPA political gatherings and whose own foreman had developed a friendship with the fighters in the hills. The *hacendero* thought such developments a nuisance. But asked if he thought a social revolution was taking shape, he merely laughed.

It added up, I think, to a willing suspension of disbelief, an unformed conviction that nothing so serious as a Marxist revolution would be considered by poor Filipinos in the provinces. It was the ultimate in patronizing attitudes. That the poor had just grievances, the middle-class did not doubt. That the poor might be converted to a philosophy as complex as communism was a thought hardly to be entertained. At the height of the assassinations in Davao, when communist local committees were assuming control of barrio after barrio, I interviewed one of that city's prominent merchants, a man whose business was disintegrating around him in part because the communists had made his city unsafe for foreign tourists. We met in a bunkerlike office built into his company's basement where guards searched visitors for concealed weapons. A sensitive man deeply disturbed over his city's growing paralysis, he spoke in despairing tones as he ticked off the more recent incidents: Merchants threatened with extortion. Death threats from the NPA. Traffic police withdrawn from the streets because so many had died of assassins' bullets. But it was the work of ruffians and bullies, not of revolutionaries, he thought. It was random terrorism, not disciplined insurgency. "All I know," he said, "is that Filipinos are out there killing Filipinos."

11

☆☆☆

In his novel *Noli Me Tangere,* written in 1886, José Rizal drew the character of Father Damaso to represent all that the native Filipino hated in the Spanish clergy who dominated his country. Rich, mannered, haughty, and disdainful of the *indios,* Father Damaso ruled his parish like a feudal lord, punishing his flock for the most minor offenses. A memorable scene found him rebuking a humble schoolmaster who had dared address him in Spanish rather than in native dialect. Describing the dreadful tongue-lashing later to a friend, the schoolmaster assessed his own helplessness:

What could I do against him, the chief moral, political and civil authority in the town, supported by his Order, feared by the government, rich, powerful, consulted, listened to, believed and obeyed always and by all. If I am insulted, I must swallow it; should I dare reply, I would be thrown out of my job, ruining my career forever and, for all that, the cause of education would not be advanced. On the contrary, everyone would take the side of the parish priest, and heap abuse on me, calling me presumptuous, proud, and haughty, a boor, a bad Christian, and, more likely than not, anti-Spanish and subversive.

. . . God forgive me if I have betrayed my conscience and my reason, but I was born in this country, and I must make a living in it, I have a mother to support, and I must go along with my fate like a drowned man borne by the tide.[1]

The schoolmaster's lament was not the exaggeration it might seem today, for the friars from Spain did in fact control parish life to its last detail. The tenacious soldiers of God had arrived in the footsteps of the *conquistadors,* determined to play their role in the quest for "God, Gold, and Glory." Dominicans, Franciscans, Augustinians and Jesuits, they quickly became more than missionaries of the Church. In a vast and sparsely settled country to which few Spanish civil servants ventured, the holy fathers assumed sweeping temporal powers as the agents of the Spanish governor-general who sat in Manila. They were supervisors of schools, tax commissioners, overseers of public health, creators of public works, arbiters of all that was correct in both spiritual and worldly affairs. They also were rich, having assigned to the church the finest farming land in the provinces. Denied positions in the Catholic hierarchy, *indios* bitterly resented both the ecclesiastical and economic power of the friars and the latter days of the Spanish reign were marked by frequent although modest rebellions. During a brief uprising in February 1872, three native priests named Burgos, Gomez, and Zamora became martyrs when they were publicly garrotted for having pressed for Filipinization of the clergy.

The reign of the friars ended when American rule replaced Spain's. Indecisive in many other matters, the Americans were determined to diminish the authority of the clergy, the hatred of which, William Howard Taft reported, "was well-nigh universal and permeates all classes."[2] The United States insisted on separation of church and state and confiscated agricultural estates in which the church's economic power was anchored. To dilute Spanish domination of purely religious matters, American Jesuits and other foreign orders were encouraged to establish roots in the archipelago, and for the first time Protestant missionaries were dispatched to challenge the control of Rome. The purpose of this disenfranchisement was as much political as religious, for it was widely perceived abroad that the

Spanish church, even more than the Spanish civil governors, was responsible for the reactionary, anti-democratic spirit permeating the Philippines.

But although nominally stripped of its political power, the Catholic church remains today the most influential force in the Philippines. For most Filipinos, it is the rock of constancy. Through revolution, colonialism, war, occupation and martial law, the church survived, an edifice intact, always at the center of their lives. Despite eight decades of Protestant missionary work among them, at least four out of every five Filipinos still look to Rome as their spiritual home and to its representatives, the bishops and parish priests, for comfort, guidance and absolution. The Spanish friars are not today remembered with affection, but the legacy of their mission has withstood time and every imaginable test of the devil. With the disgrace and fall of the Marcos regime, the church stands as the only national institution commanding broad respect. It is a common joke in the Philippines that the Catholic church is one of only three national institutions that actually work with any semblance of efficiency and order. The others are the San Miguel brewery and the NPA.

The church arrived in the late twentieth century a remarkably conservative institution. Rather isolated in Asia, it was at first untouched by the winds of doctrinal change blowing in European and Latin countries. It was unyielding on such social and ecclesiastical issues as divorce, abortion, birth control, the celibacy of priests and the role of women. It was, too, in some ways still a "foreign" church. American and conservative European orders played an intrusive role, particularly in the high schools and colleges which ranked among the elite educational institutions. One student of church history has pointed out that although the Dominicans came to the Philippines in 1611, the first Filipino ordained a priest in that order was still alive in 1985. It was not until 1971 that a Filipino was chosen rector of the University of Santo Tomas, a Catholic college older than Harvard. The church was rich, the owner of valuable real estate in Manila, and it was politically opposed to any threat to change its status.

But in the 1970s the Philippine church went through a divisive upheaval, one which was perhaps all the more wrenching

197

because it had been delayed so long. A new breed of social activists emerged from its seminaries to spread a radical gospel in its parishes, especially in the rural areas. They espoused a fundamental revision of the church's social role, proclaiming its mission was to serve man and not God—or, more precisely, that only through serving man could they serve God—and they adopted the unsettling notion that their flocks were to be agitated and radicalized, not pacified. Within the church itself, they rejected centuries-old dogma, challenged the conservative bishops, insisted even that the traditional liturgies and sacraments give way to commonsense practices relevant to people facing hard times. The most extreme among them, frustrated at the slow pace of change, began talking of a "church within the church" and some sought to force the issue of a new church completely severed from Rome. As the Marcos years marched on, the radical left in the clergy became closely identified with the Communist Party of the Philippines and its underground ally, the National Democratic Front, accepting the call to revolution as equably as they once, while obedient young seminarians, received God's word from the bishops.

Father Noel is a product of these schismatic times. A slight almost tiny man in his early thirties, he is at a glance the picture of the loyal priest—gentle, polite, calm-spoken and endowed with a warming good humor. He had graduated from his seminary in Manila a docile servant of the church, prepared, he told me, to carry the traditional message to his first parish, a remote farming village in Mindanao. There he had been caught up in a confrontation between peasants and a landlord seeking more land. One night a young friend who had been trained to teach farming techniques was taken away by military agents who said he was a subversive preaching communism. He was not seen again and his disappearance started Father Noel off on a radical path which, by 1985, had brought him to membership in Christians for National Liberation, a pillar of the communist national front. The mission of this mild-mannered, diminutive priest when I met him was to convince fellow priests to accept revolution and armed violence in the name of the Lord. Of these truths he himself no longer had doubts. He said he was surprised when associates had trouble with the notion and objected to his argument that some evil could be cleansed only by taking human life. His response was to recall the days of the Spanish friars who, he reminded his friends, had endorsed torture and merciless punishment to rule their flocks. "The history of the institutional church in the Philippines," said Father Noel, "is one of great violence."

The first rebellion to shock the church was a manifestation of the nationalist ferment sweeping Philippine society in general. Young priests, seminarians and some laymen began in the 1960s to agitate for less foreign influence in church affairs, especially in the preparatory schools and colleges where the reign of American and European educators was far from ended. American Jesuits, for instance, still ran Ateneo de Manila, one of the elite church colleges, and to a surprising extent the scholastic view of the Philippines was one filtered through a foreign lens. American history preceded Philippine history in the curriculum and even Philippine history was of the version prepared abroad. (A Spanish Dominican still taught Philippine history at one Catholic college.) The nationalist movement sought replacement of foreign-written textbooks, a Filipinized curriculum, and the gradual elimination through attrition of foreign teachers. They wanted foreign bishops removed in time—about one-fourth of those holding office were foreign born—and the replacement of American, Irish, German, and Italian priests with Filipinos. There was in all this clamor no whiff of xenophobia and one is struck today by the relatively modest nature of the young nationalists' platform.

Just how modest is illustrated by an anecdote from the seminary life of Father Conrado Balweg, who would later become the most celebrated of the "rebel priests" who bolted the church to become rifle-toting soldiers in the New People's Army. In many interviews (the NPA finally disciplined him for his habit of self-glamorization in the news media) Balweg has spoken of his disaffection with the church, maintaining that it is historically indifferent to the poor. In one interview he touched on the personal encounter that first provoked his alienation:

The surge of nationalism had a strong influence on us. At that time the seminary did not have a flag pole. We Filipino seminarians wanted to fly the Filipino flag. The German superiors objected, claiming the congregation transcended national loyalties. We were accused of secularism. Our reply was that we were Filipinos, therefore we must learn how to serve the Filipino masses. We must be conscious of that to serve concretely. They wouldn't budge. So what we did, we gave up our *merienda* (the Philippine afternoon refreshment period) and soft drinks for a month. This saved enough cash to buy the materials to construct the flagpole.[3]

The second and far more divisive rebellion within the church was a consequence of Vatican II, the Church of Rome's new approach to worldly affairs, specifically the problems of poverty in the Third World. From it was spun a bewildering variety of liberalizing theories which the church is still attempting to sort out. The common theme was approval of a new theology that was to have a powerful effect on many priests, especially young ones in Latin America and the Philippines. It held that the priest had an obligation to serve the poor not merely as children of God but as victims of poverty and oppression and to minister to their desires for salvation from both. He had a duty to "opt for the poor"—a phrase taken by thousands of young priests to license social protest and agitation on behalf of the poor, even if it meant confrontation with civil authorities. The new "liberal theology," as it was broadly designated, conferred on the priest the right—even the duty, some contended—to engage in social revolution.

The Philippine church had traditionally been one of Catholicism's strictest in insisting that the priest attend to a man's soul, not his worldly predicament, and the new liberation theology struck with almost incendiary impact. Young priests had, in small voices, criticized the hierarchy as a pillar of the establishment which served the rich. Here in the words of church scholars was ammunition for their cause. The more adventurous were attracted to radical Latin American interpretations which were colored a bright Marxian red, and one of them assumed the stature of holy writ in country parishes. This was the work of Gustavo Gutierrez, the Peruvian priest who saw in liberation theology an endorsement of the class struggle. "To opt for the poor," he wrote in a statement widely circulated in the Philippines,

is to opt for one social class over against another; to take cognizance of the fact of class confrontation and side with the oppressed; to enter into the milieu of the exploited social class and its associated cultural categories and values; to unite in fellowship with its interests, concerns and struggles.[4]

The new theology cracked the Philippine church monolith, but did not sweep all before it. Even today, official church policy prescribes only the more conservative forms and most bishops have been keen to see that priests abide by them. Of the 110 bishops in 1985, only a half-dozen were regarded as "progressives" who encouraged social activism. ("No progressive is ever elected a bishop," one church official observed. "Those who are progressive today became so only after they were elected.") Liberation theology in many parishes is practiced only in the liturgical sense, such as admonitions to uplift the poor. There is great geographical variety. Mindanao parishes use the most radical forms; those in Luzon are tamer. But throughout the 1970s, a growing number of young priests in rural areas adopted liberation theology in its most advanced, agitational interpretations and set about rousing parishioners to near revolutionary acts. They also explicitly embraced Marxian analysis, usually called "structural analysis," to teach the poor about the nature of class exploitation. The overall result of these years of uneven change and adaptation was a confusing flow of messages to the Catholic faithful. "In the course of a few weeks, I will normally attend five different parish churches," said one conservative Catholic in the Visayas, "and I will hear priests deliver five different sermons, all with different messages."

Liberation theology came to a small riverside village in Negros Occidental in 1978 in an unlikely, almost comic encounter. A rich *hacendero* laid claim to the untidy village that was occupied by families who had lived for years among their mango trees. One Sunday the villagers turned the parish mass into a prolonged discussion of their rights and, encouraged by a young priest, agreed to protest at the municipal hall. Before they could do so, a contingent of police and Philippine Constabulary troops arrived in a small river launch, arrested five ringleaders, and marched them to the boat for the trip to jail. Whereupon nearly 120 villagers leapt into the launch, sinking it in the river flats. Five days later the PC came again, arrested the same five men and proceeded to march them by land and a bridge to a military jeep across the river. Villagers quickly piled into their canoes, sped across the river, seized the jeep, drove into town, and packed the jail with their bodies. In the end, the *hacendero* abandoned his attempt to seize the land.[5]

The riverside rebellion had been ignited by the local Basic Christian Community, one of hundreds of such church-sponsored groups which, during the 1970s, gave organizational form to the new theology of liberation. Led by local priests and laymen, the BCCs, as they are usually called, became the cutting edge of the church reform movement. Their mission was to awaken parishioners to the causes of poverty and to encourage them in the belief that their lives could be changed through social action. Some were conservative and ventured little more than discussions of the relation between Christian faith and social crises. But others became bastions of radicalism whose leaders preached a primitive Marxism, encouraged demonstrations and sought confrontation with the authorities. They spread the doctrine of the "social sin" which defined such practices as low wages, land-grabbing, and usury as evils to be fought with the same righteous conviction as drunkenness and adultery. Jesus Christ became an apostle of land reform.

Putting this doctrine into practice inevitably brought the BCCs into conflict with local authorities which saw in them merely another aspect of the social revolution being waged by the communists. Just as inevitably, attempts by police to curb them made parishioners more determined. Following the trail of BCC expansion, one is struck by how many communities were sparked into genuine agitation by the military's retaliation against rather minor gestures. In Bukidnon Province, the first BCC was launched after the death in the local jail of a farmer involved in cooperatives and credit unions sponsored by the church. In 1981, when Bukidnon authorities jailed the leader of an illegal election boycott, four hundred villagers marched six miles to protest at the town hall, forcing the mayor to release the man.[6] The military became convinced the mini-rebellions were part of a broader communist conspiracy and their suspicions in several cases were confirmed by evidence that BCCs indeed had connections with the New People's Army. By the late 1970s, the Ministry of Defense's expert on religious agitation had concluded:

What is now emerging as the most dangerous form of threat from the religious radicals is their creation of the so-called Basic Christian Communities in both rural and urban areas. They are practically building an infrastructure of political power in the entire country.[7]

His alarm exaggerated the strength but not the intent of the BCC movement, for it traveled an ever more radical path. After a long church debate, during which conservative bishops tried to rein in the adventurous, a "progressive faction" bolted, proclaiming itself impatient with the "seminar armchair theology" of the church hierarchy. It established in 1978 the Basic Christian Communities—Community Organization, or BCC-CO, the addition of "CO" serving notice that its supporters believed in more action and less talk. Well-funded with money from European church groups, including the German Bishops Conference, the BCC-CO won financial independence from the Philippine church, giving it the power to ignore Manila's instructions. It developed radical Christian organizations in more than 2,000 parishes and developed an education program calling for no less than the total transformation of Philippine society. "Our message," said former BCC-CO Executive Secretary José P. Dizon, "is that you have nothing to lose but your chains."

Its literature is contemptuous of the established church. One of the guidebooks for BCC-CO lay leaders contains this passage:

The present function of the church and the parishes in particular don't differ much from the operation of a gasoline service station. You drive the jeep or the car in to purchase gasoline or crude oil, have the water and oil checked, have flat tires vulcanized and occasionally have minor repairs done. The station, then, provides services for its customers. The attendants are active, the customers are passive.

The parish is similar to a service station. . . . The eucharist is offered daily. Those who want can attend. For people who want their children baptized, the priest is prepared to do so. As for young couples who want to marry, just set the date, and the priest is present. . . . This sort of service establishes a "service station mentality" of activity on the one side and passivity on the other.[8]

The BCC-CO evangelical mission is to train workers in the practice of community activism and to that end it operates several training schools for the select. Lay leaders are told to choose only the poor as their followers and to use middle-class adherents merely for support work. Total devotion to the group is insisted upon because the work will be dangerous and the authorities hostile. "Today," declares one advisory, "the main forces are those who are willing to love until death and to risk all."[9] Analytical material used is explicitly Marxist. Trainees are taught that the church historically has played a part in their exploitation, that "structural analysis" is the way to the "Reign of God," and that traditional prayer is no more than "begging" and should be discarded. Beware of instruments of deception used by the exploiting class. "The capitalist press is an ideological weapon . . . employed by the ruling class in oppressing workers, the peasants, and all the struggling sectors of society," warns a BCC-CO paper. Its purpose is to "keep its readers in a state of ignorance" about their real interests.[10]

It was no great leap from such preachings to the advocacy of social revolution and there were many priests whose mission it was to make the connection explicit. They were a minority in the priesthood, but their influence in several areas was great for their numbers. The ones whom I met were zealous men full of self-certainty and commitment. Some seemed more fervently devoted to the theme of armed revolution than party cadres in the national front. The absence of doubt was striking. Of all the radical temperaments I encountered in the Philippines, the one formed by the mixture of religious commitment, Marxist ideology, and enthusiasm for deadly combat was the most hardened, the least yielding.

Father George was representative except for his nationality. He was a European who had spent twenty years in the poor parishes of the Visayan islands. Immensely self-assured, as dogmatic in his beliefs as the most rigid Jesuit, he had divided the world into good and evil. Even the church hierarchy did devil's work, for it was as exploitative as the moneylenders and land-grabbers who preyed on the poor. He also seemed fearless. His friend, another radical priest, had been grabbed by military intelligence agents on a public street and never seen again. Father George accepted his loss stoically. I spent many hours talking with him in his busy office, which was a contact station for the party underground, and he led me patiently through the steps of radicalization which his BCC-CO workers used to educate the poor.

They began with the Bible. It was a sort of back-to-Christian-basics course in which farmers were taught that their church had "sanitized" the Bible's original meaning. The foulest perversion was that which separated the church's ministrations to man's soul from its concern for worldly life. It had left man to fend alone in his hostile temporal world, a victim to his oppressors. "We start by interpreting the Bible to show that salvation, in the original sense, meant economic and social salvation and that the idea of saving the soul only is a departure from early Christian teachings," Father George said. "We teach that the separation of the body and soul was a feudal capitalistic development of the Middle Ages. We want to destroy that concept and teach that economic salvation is part of the original meaning before it was corrupted. That has a lot of consequences."

The question then placed before the parish became: What kind of economic salvation? The proper answer began with a damning critique of capitalism. "We in the BCC-COs believe quite simply that capitalists are the devils and that there can be no compromise with them," he said. "And so we must help design the new socialist system. There is no alternative to a socialist society." Father George produced training documents which described in very simple language the attractions of a socialist economy. One of them approved state operation of *all* industry—a position more extreme even than the Communist party's. I asked what the peasants were told would bring about this socialist heaven. At first his response was vague. "We have no big theory on that," he said. "So far, we have acted only in a manner to let the people decide, to let the answer grow out of collaboration with them." He paused, weighing his decision to divulge what he apparently supposed was a big secret. Finally, he said, "But the New People's Army and the Communist party have a definite program and there is no alternative but to go with it and try to help them."

The ice broken, Father George talked at length about the appropriateness and morality of armed revolution. His was a straight-line logic: The government and capitalists were evil oppressors who would not surrender without struggle. The formal church was no stranger to violence. Remember the Spanish friars? Men of God could and should support armed combat to free their followers. There was moral violence and there was immoral violence; even the formal church accepted the notion of violence as a last resort against Godless tyranny. I asked whether he personally was troubled by the act of taking human life:

I accept it and I support it. And so does almost everyone else in our movement. I have been to more than a thousand BCC-CO meetings and I have heard the issue of violence often discussed. But I have not heard a single voice against it. When it comes up, the people usually say that their experience with violence committed by the military prepares them to accept violence in return. In my experience, there is no one at the grassroots level of BCC-CO who is opposed to violence.

All this was said in the faintly weary monotone of one who had answered such questions many times and wondered vaguely why anyone still asked them. A final question provoked a moment's contemplation: How could salvation through killing be accommodated within the Catholic church? "We are not thinking of the traditional church at all," Father George said finally. "In three or four years there will be a group starting a separate church, one which will openly support the Communist party. I see this coming. It will be the church of the people of God. It will probably not be aligned with the church of Rome. We will have to accept the dark night of not being united with Rome. It is inevitable."

Control and direction of the radical priesthood was centered in Christians for National Liberation, or CNL, a clandestine organization of clergy and laymen which was one of the strongest pillars of the National Democratic Front. It was formed by Father Edicio de la Torre and other priests on February 7, 1972 (the anniversary of the execution of nationalist priests Burgos, Gomez and Zamora) and went underground when martial law was declared. Its program was frankly revolutionary in content and messianic in tone. Revolution, CNL asserted, was a "Christian imperative" and in advancing it members were striving to "help build God's kingdom." True Christianity required struggle and death. "Our belief in Jesus Christ calls us to incarnate our Christianity, to give it flesh and blood. This we seek in the passion, death and resurrection of the Filipino people—the people's democratic revolution."[11]

Using official positions in the church, CNL became over the years a major logistical support base for the NPA. Its charter enjoined members to "mobilize as much of the church's resources as we can for the people's struggle."[12] CNL priests' quarters provided cover and shelter for armed cadres moving about the country and church automobiles for transportation. In the countryside, parish offices were often the contact points for journalists and other visitors smuggled into NPA fronts. Bags of rice destined for mountain base camps were routed through parish homes, some of whose back rooms resembled improvised granaries. Priests were logistical organizers of urban protests whose primary purpose was to tie down military units that might otherwise have been chasing the NPA. Overseas, CNL representatives acted as fundraisers for the CPP, tapping radical and human-rights-oriented groups for contributions. Priests are naturally talented in indoctrination and administrative work and skills honed at the seminaries were valuable to the party. One former national front leader said: "CNL is very powerful within the party. They have resources and that is very important. They are skilled and professional and political work comes easy to them. They have lots of influence for their numbers."

The Communist party made extraordinary efforts to infiltrate and use the church, especially its human-rights organizations. A nineteen-page party document explained that, "The ideal situation is to have at least one national democratic collective within each progressive mass organization, justice-oriented church office or project, religious congregation, seminary, etc. The collective would form the underground network within the sector."[13] The purpose of this penetration was not simply to make use of church facilities and priests' time. The grander plan, in which CNL was the cutting edge, was to appropriate the church's power and moral authority for the revolution. While the CPP regarded the Catholic church as merely an arm of the exploitative establishment, the people they sought to educate revered it as the source of ultimate wisdom. The priest's word carried enormous weight. Where his preachings could be translated as endorsement of social revolution, the party's advance could be swift. Aware of this, the CNL excelled in transforming rituals and liturgy of the established church into social messages to radicalize peasant congregations. One CNL priest described how even the *novena,* or service for the dead, could be used to raise the social consciousness of mourners:

We use the period of novenas for the dead to dramatize the cause of his death. We ask, was it hunger or the lack of medicine that caused his death? What had the church done to help him? In this way, we make the novena relevant, to show that the man was the victim of an evil system. It is far better than using the novenas simply to pray the dead out of purgatory.

The specter of a radicalized church naturally frightened the Marcos government which saw formidable threats in the rebel priests, the BCC-CO infrastructure, and CNL propaganda. "The potential of the clergy as a base for subversion cannot be over-emphasized," warned Defense Minister Enrile in 1978.[14] Throughout the 1970s and '80s, military units raided parish houses and BCC meeting halls, arresting priests, nuns, and lay activists. They found conclusive evidence of communist infiltration—a plum was the arrest of a Samar priest, Father Edgardo Kangleon, with documents showing he had used a social action center and church funds to aid the underground. But military sweeps also resulted in the arrests, torture and disappearance of many on the fringes, especially lay leaders active in the BCCs. The inevitable cycle began: The presence of military forces brought new abuses which in turn sparked sympathy for the NPA which in turn became not an intruder but a defender. By the early 1980s, a virtual war between the church and the military was underway.

It was in the remote provinces that the real confrontation between church and communism was played out in hundreds of little dramas. The pressures on the rural priest to cooperate with the NPA was intense. He daily encountered experiences of military abuse and the indifference of military commanders. The church had no guns to defend the farmer. The NPA did. The temptation to accept armed insurgents as a de facto defense force, to give them food, shelter and logistical support, was often too great to reject. More and more priests began sheltering guerillas and inviting propaganda teams into parish social programs. The conflict which these presented to church policy usually landed in the bishops' laps.

One bishop who lived through those pressures for years was a stocky, pipe-smoking man who in normal times possessed a wry good humor, great patience, and much common sense. Bishop Francisco Claver was, in 1980, the bishop of Bukidnon, a province in Mindanao where some of the first BCCs were organized among poor farmers. He was a leading "progressive" on social issues and a frequent critic of President Marcos. Other bishops thought him radical and frowned on his encouragement of social protest. In 1980 he was in constant confrontation with the military, which had closed down his church's radio station on grounds that it spread information to the NPA, and he had developed a keen understanding of how the government soldiers' intrusions and brutality had angered people:

A lot of it is just casual violence, when the soldiers shoot at random. They shoot just to frighten people, but several have been killed in that way. We have documented cases of people being shot like pigs and then the soldiers go scot free. The military whitewashes everything. Just recently, three people in our community were seized because the

209

military thought they were cooperating with the communists. They just disappeared. We have found their graves now, but the people who know what happened are afraid to testify. Often the soldiers are drunk, and because they have the guns, they have the power. If a farmer complains when his chickens are taken, he may be beaten or shot. Only the military has the guns.

Many priests and nuns approached Bishop Claver to ask whether violence should not be met with violence. Some had already befriended NPA soldiers and argued spiritedly for collaboration with them as the best defense against the military. He told them the church sanctioned violence only as a last resort. Besides, poor unarmed farmers would be the real victims of violent retaliation. Two priests became Marxists and told him so. "They said we should go with the people who have the power and that was the people with guns, the NPA. They asked me, what was the alternative to communism or martial law." Claver's response was to sanction all forms of civil disobedience except violence, and for a while he turned his head when maverick priests brought communists into church action programs. But finally, he drew the line for one priest: "I told him, you are not just sympathetic to the NPA, you are in league with them. I will not stop you, but you will not do this and be in charge of a parish."

Nearly six years later, in December 1985, I interviewed Bishop Claver again. He had left the diocese in 1983 for a quiet position in the church's East Asian Pastoral Institute in Manila. He was still a passionate critic of President Marcos, but the Bukidnon experience had left him embittered about communist influence in the church. Masquerading as social activists, he said, they had taken over several church programs which they used for Marxist indoctrination.

The thing that turned us off, what finally convinced me that I was right, was that the church was being used for their own ends. We would hold meetings and they would be present and all the time we would think they were there to help us raise people's consciousness about injustice. We would organize a community health program and they would offer to help. Then we would find that our health program had become ten percent health and ninety percent indoctrination. We were just

210

being used. They used the cloak of the church to appeal for support for their own cause.

Throughout the Marcos years, the church's crisis was Bishop Claver's experience on a larger scale. It was caught in one of those monumental cleavages that destroys lesser institutions. Indications of this surfaced rather soon in the martial law period. Marcos' declaration did not greatly alarm the church hierarchy, which was prepared to accept the new regime in a spirit described as "critical collaboration." Reports of dissatisfaction began streaming into Manila, particularly from the lower clergy and laity in the Visayas and Mindanao where the policy was regarded as more collaborative than critical. A survey conducted one year after martial law by the Association of Major Religious Superiors found that many loyal Catholics resented their formal church's acquiescence. The Association wrote:

Some feel the church cooperates because of fear or weakness or indifference; others think she wants to protect her own interests; still others feel that the church approves of martial law and The New Society because she feels that discipline and order are needed for economic development. Whatever the reason, the church is seen as going along with the present situation in spite of oppression and injustice. She has no plan of action, no clear stand.[15]

That warning was mild compared to the events that followed. Publicity centered on the "rebel priests" who denounced the church's cowardice and took up guns with the NPA. They were in fact few in number. Far more threatening was the steady leftward drift within the church infrastructure, those parishes and quasi-independent church institutions which made the faith a living force throughout the Philippines. Bishops reported more parishes welcoming and assisting NPA guerillas and noted the inherently radicalizing nature of the Basic Christian Communities. A semi-autonomous group, Task Force Detainees, became renowned for collecting and publishing statistical accounts of military abuses, a service which probably did more to radicalize young priests and nuns than their clandestine Marxist training sessions. Finally, the church had to take seriously the initially faint but later clear threat that unless it ceased collaboration with Marcos it faced schism and a separate church. A hint of things to come was revealed in 1981 when Mindanao bishops repudiated their own island-wide social action organization, the Mindanao-Sulu Pastoral Conference, on grounds that it had become politically subversive. The Priests and laymen who ran the conference simply ignored the bishops, created a new conference, and pursued their radical ways outside church jurisdiction.

The task of healing this breach fell on the rounded shoulders of a portly man with cherubic features and genial mien, Jaime Cardinal Sin, archbishop of Manila, dean of the church in the Philippines. Cardinal Sin (the unlikely name is a Filipinization of his Chinese father's, "Hsien") seemed to be born for the job. Politically shrewd and fundamentally conservative, he was not disposed at first to challenge Marcos. But he also sensed the leftward lurching of his church and he feared more than anything the incipient signs of schism. pacifying the left without angering the majority of bishops who were still quite conservative became his mission. In 1979, he told one interviewer: "The progressives in the church are the ones giving life. The conservatives are the brakes. If they are all brakes the church will not run. If they are all accelerators, the church will crash. So I, the driver, will decide when to use the brakes and the accelerator."[16]

The archbishop was more and more compelled to apply the accelerator and appease the left. He complained publicly of military abuses, urged mass participation in anti-government street marches, called on the president to release political detainees and abolish authoritarian decrees. He refused to sanction violence but also, despite the government's demands that he rein in church radicals, refused to censure those priests and nuns openly hospitable to the communist national front. He even bucked Rome. In 1982, one year after Pope John Paul II admonished priests to refrain from politics, Cardinal Sin advised Filipino clergy that political action was a moral obligation: "Politics is a human activity. Ergo, it has a morality. And who would be better equipped to explain this morality than a priest?"[17]

The assassination of Benigno Aquino, Jr. left Cardinal Sin in tears and he seemed, in the eyes of those close to him, to have become mordantly convinced of greater disasters to come. He was still the conciliator, still saw himself as the bridge between government and the left, and he obligingly celebrated Marcos's birthday only a month after Aquino's death. But his private comments grew bitter and his public ones more stinging; he once said the government record of repression recalled "memories of Mr. Goebbels of Nazi Germany."[18] He seemed for a time almost resigned to the coming of social revolution: "I feel that the people are already tired. I feel there are conversations going around in every corner of our country, in the barber shops, in the coffee shops, about civil war."[19]

12

☆ ☆ ☆

I f the Philippine revolution were merely a shooting war, it would likely fail. For all of its tactical skill, the New People's Army remains, after 18 years of skirmishes and ambushes, a badly outnumbered guerilla force which lacks modern weapons, sanctuaries to hide in, reliable logistics and foreign support. It is a raid-and-hide army which, without a sudden infusion of foreign weaponry, might continue fighting for years and still own no territory. But like all modern guerilla warfare, the one in the Philippines is a political-military show, a struggle more for popular support than turf, and it is on the political side that, it seemed to me, the real victories were being won. The agent of these political successes was the National Democratic Front.

Founded in April 1973 by a handful of party members and radical clergy, the NDF was somewhat of an afterthought. CPP founders, including Sison, seem to have shown little initial interest in classic political front work and their charter document, "Programme for a People's Democratic Revolution," mentioned only in passing that "in the course of the protracted people's war, a national liberation front *may* be created. . . ."[1]

But it grew rapidly in the late 1970s and early '80s to a point at which numerically it dwarfed the NPA. Its leaders in 1986 estimated its strength at approximately one million men and women, of whom about 50,000 were more or less full-time active members. (The Philippine military put the total at 500,000 to 700,000). In its ranks were thousands of farmers, workers, teachers, priests, nuns, fishermen, office-workers, students, and civil servants.

Unlike the classic communist front, which seeks to operate openly as an assorted collection of left-leaning sympathizers and non-communists, the NDF is an illegal, underground organization. Officially, it is a broad umbrella embracing many different underground groups of which the Communist Party of the Philippines is merely one. The party is, in fact, the dominating force in the NDF and its leadership is composed of experienced cadres. But it is incorrect to judge it as a mere arm of the party. There is considerable evidence that the modern NDF occasionally follows an independent path and that its leaders often differ with the party's Central Committee in both tactical and strategic matters. The NDF, because of its rapid growth and political skills, has become something of a force of its own in Philippine communism, has achieved its own peculiar dynamic and even its own agenda for victory.

Although led nationally by middle-class educated men and women the great number of NDF members are poor, most of them farmers and workers. The largest groupings under the umbrella are the Association of Revolutionary Workers and the Revolutionary Movement of Peasants. Allied with them are KM, the militant youth group founded in 1964 by Sison and revived in 1977 as a clandestine organization, and Christian for National Liberation, the underground movement of radicalized priests, nuns and laity who helped found the NDF in 1973. Radical teachers, health workers, women's groups, lawyers and businessmen fill out the ranks. NDF claims to have moles working in government bureaus and even in military compounds, but their existence is impossible to confirm.

At the grassroots level, the NDF plays two distinct roles. The first is barrio organization and management of those local units where control is generally assured. Most of the propaganda, education and organizing work there is now performed by NDF teams, from the first "social investigations" in new areas to the advanced stages where Communist party lectures are given. (This organizing role grew swiftly after the CPP Central Committee's decision in 1980 to increase NPA fighting strength by relieving armed fighters of much of the political organizing work). Eventually, as the local barrio becomes thoroughly influenced by party members, their actual government is turned over to an NDF Barrio Committee which administers justice, launches communal economic enterprises, and directs political protests against both local and the national government. An internal NDF memorandum from Mindanao, issued in 1985, boasted that, "In over 1100 organized barrios, NDF committees have emerged as the new organs of the people's power. NDF Committees . . . are also rising up at the municipal, district, regional and national levels."[2]

These clandestine committees, usually guided by local leaders elevated to party membership, have come to be considered the basic political cells of the communist movement, the building blocks of that distant goal, the Democratic Coalition Government. The 1985 NDF Program refers to these "local organs of democratic power" as the fundamental political units which "are already creating the basis for a nationwide democratic coalition government and a democratic republic."[3] It is the party's intent that these units will spread and become linked together in a national network, forming the political base of a new government. A 1984 tract attributed to the then-imprisoned Sison declared that these local organs "will rise from the barrio to the municipality, from the municipality to the district, from the district to the province, and from the province to the region, until the Democratic Coaltion Government can be established."[4]

The second grassroots role of the NDF is the penetration of existing organizations whose members are not communists but who have grievances against the government. They range from associations of poor squatters to church and human rights organizations. This is the more classic communist front technique, requiring secretiveness and tactical skill. The most enduring successes, according to NDF leaders, have come in the infiltration of labor unions of large cities. The work is concentrated in newer, more militant unions which are not affiliated

216

with the government-dominated Trade Union Center of the Philippines. The script calls for boring from within, attempting by slow, patient manipulation to win control of locals. Sometimes the NDF organizers attempt to elect their own members to local offices. Sometimes they seek the elections of non-communists who will at least not hinder the party's work. Jes, the Manila party leader who specialized in penetrating unions and organizations of the urban poor, described the process candidly:

We are basically trying to transform existing unions into party-led unions. We weed out the oldline union leaders who are mainly in office to make money by selling out the workers. We want to replace them with honest unionists who are at least sympathetic to the National Democratic Front lines. It is a long haul in the bigger unions. We start organizing even two or three years before the union elections to get our candidates elected. Sometimes we put up party members but other times they are only sympathetic to us—good unionists who we know will not interfere with our organizing. We try to get national democrats and party members onto every local union board, even the shop stewards.

A successful communist front requires most of all a common enemy, some despised man, institution or political system against which disparate groups can rally. French colonialism and American intervention performed the role in Vietnam, giving rise to a National Liberation Front, as did Somoza's authoritarianism and corruption in Nicaragua. The front's purpose is to broaden support among non-communists for the purpose of overthrowing dictators and getting rid of foreign interference. In its classic form, communist organizing concentrates on the visible evils, keeping their program of revolutionary government obscure. The essence of communist appeal is that political differences among front groups should be submerged for the greater good of combatting the common enemy.

In the Philippines, Ferdinand E. Marcos and his martial-law rule provided the ideal target. The NDF was formed six months after the martial law was declared to take advantage of the hostility aroused by the dismantling of democracy and through-

217

out Marcos's tenure the demand "Down with the Marcos–U.S. Dictatorship" was its battle cry. Hundreds of students and middle-class dissidents went underground to struggle against the regime, and many became the NDF's most gifted organizers. The poor farmers and workers whom they organized were easy marks for they were the most injured. Factory workers and field hands felt the oppression in the government's union-busting policies and anti-strike labor code and in the perilous decline in living standards. Farmers saw the failure yet again of a true land-reform program and the enormous land-grabbing enterprises Marcos tolerated among his cronies. Both groups, finally, saw the military and nationalized police turned against them to break strikes and evict tenants. It did not require a book-bound Marxist to tell them who the enemy was. It did require mobilization by an efficient, sophisticated force to teach them how to strike back. The NDF performed this role.

But from the start, the NDF was less successful in another respect. It had difficulty enlisting large numbers of those in the middle class who despised Marcos but who also feared a communist revolution. It was no real secret that the NDF was a party-dominated organization committed to socialism, and relatively few wanted to make that leap. There were, it is true, many converts—radical students, leftists in the church and the universities. But the great majority chose not to join, preferring to struggle ineffectually in street protests and in the rigged elections which Marcos periodically arranged. The traditional democratic leaders of the past, although aware of their own ineffectuality, chose to oppose Marcos in word but not in deed, and to them NDF was anathema. As late as 1986, I was told, more than ninety percent of the NDF membership in Manila, where the Philippine middle class is concentrated, was made up of workers and the urban poor. The result was a front that was not a front in the sense of embracing non-communist liberals but one formed by and composed of the already committed. Its failure to spread its umbrella over the uncommitted middle class was noted by the perceptive analyst, Francisco Nemenzo, as late as 1984:

Despite its impressive achievements, the NDF has yet to become a real united front because it consists almost entirely of party-led mass organizations. Other revolutionary groups have stayed apart and the few attempts to act jointly with them did not develop into a lasting relationship. . . . Its leading organ—the Preparatory Commission—is packed with representatives of party-led mass organizations, thus provoking fears in other groups that within its framework they will have no meaningful participation. . . . It is futile for the party to forge a "united front" with its own mass organizations.[5]

One reason for this failure may lie in the deep distrust with which Sison and his early comrades regarded most of the middle class, especially what he termed the "national bourgeoisie." "Programme for a People's Democratic Revolution," the early blueprint, had warned that although this element might be of some assistance it possessed a "dual character, revolutionary and reactionary," which rendered it a dubious ally:

To some extent it can accept anti-imperialism and anti-feudalism. But it still has a bourgeois class character to which the working class and its party must always be alert. The party can cooperate with it within certain periods and to some limited extent but it must be on the alert for its betrayals and basically opportunist class character. . . . The party must be cautious towards it although concessions may be given to it without sacrificing the basic interests and principles of workers and peasants.[6]

Sison had struggled with the shifting allegiances of the bourgeoisie in 1967 when he helped to form the Movement for the Advancement of Nationalism (MAN), which included many nationalistic but non-leftist businessmen and intellectuals. From that encounter, he developed both a disdain for liberals and, more important, a concern that the party would fritter away valuable energies trying to placate them for the purpose of maintaining a common front. It would be "senseless," he wrote, to consider MAN a united front "and worry most of the time about the tolerance and attitudes of bourgeois allies for the sake of preserving some weak and artificial unity."[7]

Therein lies the key to the party's subsequent debates and divisions over front-building: How far should the party bend to accommodate the uncommitted? Is it worthwhile participating in a front that includes liberal non-communists and to soften the party's revolutionary message to keep them in that front?

These questions have never been fully resolved within the CPP and they remain today a major point of division, both within the party and between the party's hard-liners and pragmatists in the NDF. The argument over front work created a fissure in the movement and led eventually to a major schism.

On August 21, 1983, Benigno Aquino, Jr., the former senator whom Marcos had imprisoned in the first hours of martial law, returned from a self-imposed exile in the United States, landing at Manila International Airport in a China Air Lines passenger jet. As he was led down a flight of steps by military agents, Aquino was shot in the back of the head. He died quickly, his body sprawling on the airport tarmac. The government announced to an appalled and disbelieving public that Aquino's assassin was a sometime-communist gunman named Rolando Galman, who had been quickly dispatched by airport guards at the scene of the murder. Most Filipinos knew instantly that either Marcos or his military henchmen had ordered the killing and took to the streets in protest in massive numbers. Within days, millions were in open, although unarmed, revolt, defiantly ignoring martial-law edicts which barred political demonstrations.

Other than their size, the distinctive characteristic of those demonstrations was the presence in them of large numbers of middle-class Manilans. There had been protests before, but they had mainly involved committed leftists leading peasants and workers. The post-Aquino protests brought out teachers, office workers, businessmen, even blue-blood socialites. On Ayala Avenue, the cavernous main thoroughfare which dissects the corporate and financial center of Makati, thousands of office workers and executives paraded in defiance of police orders. From the offices of banks and corporate headquarters, their supporters showered down clouds of yellow confetti snipped from telephone books. Jeepney drivers, civic employes, clerks and clerics poured out to join what had become a rebellion so large it was dubbed (like the ones in 1970) the "Parliament of the Streets."

Here at last was an opportunity long awaited by the Communist Party of the Philippines, or at least by that wing of it which believed middle-class support for a popular front might hasten victory. Here was a great outpouring of those "middle forces," as they were known in party jargon, whose support had been withheld from the struggle against the "Marcos–U.S. Dictatorship." These were people of money and influence whose admission to a common anti-Marcos front could add money and logistical support for a peasant army badly lacking in both. It was a chance to build a true popular front. The question became one of how, not whether, to build it.

The blueprint for that lay in a 1977 revision of the National Democratic Front's Ten-Point Program, the basic formula for appealing to non-communist sympathizers. The original Ten-Point program, issued in 1973, had been a sterile, almost useless document which stressed "armed revolution" as the only weapon against the dictatorship and rang with harsh jargon denouncing imperialism, feudalism and capitalism. As nourishment for the party faithful it was perhaps of help, but as an enticement to the non-Marxist middle class it was a flop. In the more sophisticated 1977 version, some old party jargon remained but most of the more jarring clichés had been stripped away. It called for building "a broad unity of patriotic and progressive classes, groups and individuals all for the purpose of overthrowing the U.S.-Marcos Dictatorship." But its most disarming message was aimed at those unradicalized "middle forces" who despised Marcos but feared just as much the prospects of a revolution from the left that would impose a socialist system on the Philippines. To ease their minds, the 1977 document introduced the notion of a "Democratic Coalition Government" open to those of many persuasions and pledged to diversity. The post-Marcos coalition government, it declared, "should recognize all the national and democratic forces that shall have caused the downfall of the fascist dictatorship and give them ample opportunity to participate in legal and peaceful political activities." The key provision promised:

There should be no monopoly of political power by any class, party or group. The degree of participation in the government by any political force should be based on its effective role and record in the revolutionary struggle and on the people's approbation. We always stand for the independence and initiative of the various political forces working for the overthrow of the fascist dictatorship.

The coalition government should allow the free interplay of national and democratic forces during and after elections. Thus, a truly democratic system of representation can develop and operate to the benefit of the people. Such a government should always be subject to the will of the people.[8]

In this 1977 version, the NDF program was the sort of manifesto bourgeois moderates could subscribe to: A sharing of power with no party dominant, independence of all within the coalition, and free participation in post-Marcos elections. Politics would be open to everyone. The new prescription even offered a sort of incentive program for non-communists whose influence in the new coalition would be measured by their prior efforts in bringing Marcos down. In short, join up now and reserve your seat in the new parliament.

Armed with this appeal, the NDF in 1985 contemplated a suitable structure for the new front. The NDF itself would not suffice, being still suspect as a party-controlled apparatus. The device sought was a new umbrella organization nominally untainted by party control, one that could be directed generally from the underground but still maintain a come-one-come-all facade. On all sides, impromptu protest groups springing up might be usable. The most formidable, at first, was "Justice for Aquino, Justice for All," or JAJA, led by José Diokno, a distinguished nationalist and civil libertarian but also a determined anti-communist. Soon there emerged a more militant group, "Coalition for the Realization of Democracy," or CORD, which staged spectacular protests and succeeded, in 1984, in paralyzing Davao City. Also on the left was the Nationalist Alliance for Justice, Freedom and Democracy, composed of militant ideologues and labor leaders and lent prestige by the presence of Lorenzo Tañada, the aging patriarch of Philippine nationalism and heir to Claro M. Recto's mantle. Gradually, the street protests grew more militant under the direction of such groups, their rhetoric less associated with Aquino's murder and more with the left's familiar assaults on imperialism and fascism. The streets, as Jaime Cardinal Sin observed to a friend, "are beginning to run Red." With the party's encouragement, the NDF at last tried to weld these street groups and "cause-oriented" organizations into the new front. It would require from the party sophistication and a good deal of flexibility, a willingness to make compromises. But at the crucial moment, the party's hardliners balked, demanding control of the movement and forcing moderates to flee once more.

The scene of this spectacular failure was the founding of the *Bagong Alyansang Makabayan,* or New Nationalist Alliance, known by its shortened Tagalog name of Bayan. Organized by the left to seize leadership of the protests, it initially included the names of celebrated nationalists and anti-Marcos figures such as Tañada and Diokno, the labor leader Roland Olalia, Butz Aquino, brother of the martyred hero, and Jaime Ongpin, a leading figure in the business community. Even a radical non-Marxist group known as the "SocDems" was willing to join. All seemed in place for a unified front until the factions gathered in May 1985, to discuss voting power on the national Bayan board of directors. At first, a power-sharing arrangement giving each of three major factions equal votes seemed acceptable. Suddenly the word came down to leftists known as "Nat-Dems" (for National Democrats, actually representing the NDF): Hold out for more votes. Exactly who was responsible for the sudden shift is still not known, but it most certainly reflected the view of CPP hardliners. The non-communist moderates— Aquino, Ongpin, Diokno—bolted and the coalition collapsed. For some, the CPP's attempt to manipulate total control of Bayan was conclusive evidence that no accommodation with the communists could ever work. Diokno later told me:

I had initially hoped to get all of the "cause groups" together, to end the fragmentation in the opposition [to Marcos]. It ended in a dispute over the percentage of seats in Bayan which each group would control. It was not entirely the left's fault, there was much mistrust on all sides. . . . But it showed that we can never deal with the underground left on a permanent basis. Until the underground learns how to work with the concept of shared powers, you cannot work with them.

The fiasco also brought into the open the deep division within the party over the popular front question. The hardliners wanted no alliances which they could not control. The more flexible, including many leaders of the NDF, were furious with the ideological purists who had wrecked the new front. Several NDF veterans talked openly of the party's failure. One of them, Victor, told me:

Bayan should have been a broader alliance. People were turned off by the hard-line posturing of some of the key people in our sectors. So they got out of Bayan at the national level. It shows the inexperience of our united front work. We still have a lot to learn about how to be flexible without giving up principles. We have been too rigid and hard line. We have been too rigid in both the line we took and in the method. Sometimes all it would mean is listening carefully to the other sides. The breakup of Bayan, especially the walkout of businessmen like Ongpin—it was not over big principles, but just over how many seats each group would get. It was not over the [U.S. military] bases, for example. Some of our people now realize the nature of this problem and will teach more flexibility. I think there is this lingering influence of the Chinese approach to the united front. I think eventually there will be a more realistic united front structure.

Bayan, minus its moderate constituency, did survive and became in 1985 part of the campaign to topple Marcos through street protests and labor strikes. Oddly, it became more popular and influential in the cities outside Manila. Its chapters in Negros, Cebu and Davao proved resilient, losing only a few of the middle-class troops. Its mission was to engage in "all forms of non-violent political actions" against the government. Within a year, Bayan claimed to represent more than a thousand local constituent groups with a membership exceeding two million people. The largest of these were the militant labor federation, *Kilusang Mayo Uno,* or the May First Movement, and a new farmers' association, *Kilusang Magbubukid ng Philipinas,* or the Movement of Farmers of the Philippines. There were also in its ranks thousands of teachers, businessmen, attorneys and students.

Bayan officially positioned itself on the political spectrum as a non-communist organization which both opposed Marcos and disparaged participation in elections which, it maintained, were useless. Its weapons were street protest and labor strikes. Zenaida Uy, a university professor and chairman of Bayan in

Cebu, called it "pressure politics" and saw in massive demonstrations an educational tool to teach the non-committed to seek change by manifesting defiance. A major hope was that through such exercises the Filipino who had been brought up to enjoy, even revere, elections could be shown their futility under Marcos. The tactic served brilliantly in 1984, when a national election was boycotted by hundreds of thousands. In late 1985, most Bayan leaders expected to repeat the performance in boycotting the "snap" presidential election Marcos was considering.

The NDF had secretly contrived in the founding of Bayan, with party approval, and its influence was strong, although not always determining. The government and many others considered Bayan a mere front adhering to the CPP line in all ways. I found the relationship more complex and curious. The NDF certainly considered it a front. Almost all Bayan members were aware of NDF manipulation but continued to work within it anyway. Bayan leaders in Bacolod, Negros Occidental, for example told me they disapproved of the NPA's armed struggle but endorsed massive street protests as a way of "dismantling the government." They believed, sincerely I felt, that they could control the revolutionary element in Bayan and maintain its direction as a non-communist, anti-government front.

What actually emerged from this odd assembly was a sort of two-tier front. In the underground below was the NDF, party-dominated but flexible and occasionally independent. Above was Bayan, officially non-communist but sharing many of NDF's goals and tactics, led by both communists and non-communists. There evolved a parallel structure of two interconnected organizations united by the common belief that at that stage of history, 1985 and early 1986, massive anti-government demonstrations could remove Marcos. "Bayan is a separate, legal group," said Victor, the NDF veteran. "They take great pains not to be linked with us. But lots of those in Bayan are linked organizationally or sympathetically with us." Jes, the Manila party organizer, described Bayan and NDF as separate but sympathetic groups. "When we organize mass actions here, we always coordinate with Bayan," he said. "There are some party members in Bayan. Sometimes we suggest actions to Bayan, sometimes Bayan makes its own suggestions."

225

This dual role placed a heavy burden on Bayan leaders, who were accused of following the CPP line. They were not dupes of the CPP. Most whom I interviewed in that period were aware of the party's efforts to manipulate them. They believed they could work with a party which espoused armed violence and military revolution without personally endorsing those weapons. Doing so, however, required much verbal agility. Several sought to dissociate themselves from the party. "We salute but do not necessarily support our brothers in the hills," said Zenaida Uy in Cebu City when asked about Bayan's arrangements with the communists. "We respect their option for violent revolution but do not endorse it. We are for non-violence."

It was the NDF's task, a difficult one, to define the kind of government which a successful communist revolution would install if it ever came to pass. Who would run the state? How would the economy be managed? Would traditional democratic rights be preserved? In the early years, little attention was paid to answering these questions. There was little time to think past next day's raid or propaganda session. The NDF then was preoccupied with teaching people why they should rebel, not what they should expect to follow in the wake of victory.

The prescription laid down by Sison and other young radicals strayed from classic Marxism in that it did not call for a dictatorship of the proletariat. It defined a peculiar variant in which the state would represent several classes of citizens. "Programme for a People's Democratic Revolution" said the existing government would be replaced with "the people's democratic state system which is the united front dictatorship of the proletariat, peasantry, petty bourgeoisie, national bourgeoisie and all other patriots." That document promised a "democratic bill of rights" to preserve freedoms of speech, religion and assembly. There would be democratic elections. But all organs of government would be subordinated to something called the People's Revolutionary Congress, whose composition and procedures were left undefined.

Economic policy would be more in line with socialist orthodoxy. All properties held by big landlords would be confiscated and distributed to poor peasants. In the industrial sphere, all monopolies would be confiscated and all production of basic resources and power would be operated by state agencies. There would be a "socialist character" to the economy, the "Programme" said. Private enterprise would not be totally excluded, but its role would be minor. The "national bourgeoisie"—businessmen not allied with foreign interests—could develop a limited capitalist production if it did not "dominate or hamper" the livelihood of Filipinos.

This post-revolution prescription satisfied the orthodox young radicals in the 1960s, vague though it was on the subject of political control. It was sufficient guidance for the already committed, but was not a platform with which to appeal to non-communists. Its intimations of monolithic state control of the economy frightened businessmen, large and small, and middle-class reformers would not risk their lives and freedom for a party which promised merely to replace one dictatorship with another. Modifying it so as to attract the "middle forces," that whole world of moderate non-communists fighting primarily against Marcos and martial law, became the NDF's duty.

The NDF performed this duty in a series of ten- and twelve-point programs which appeared periodically, beginning with its initial document in 1973 and continuing until a totally different version was circulating in January 1985. That latest draft, written at a time when NDF recruitment was swift, offered soothing answers to all of the questions the most bourgeois Filipino might ask. Nowhere did it mention socialism or dictatorship of any class or party. It promised fair, clean elections at all levels of government and guaranteed by name all of the traditional Western democratic freedoms. Agricultural plantations owned by foreign interests would be confiscated, but there was an enticing carrot for the landlord who had no foreign ties. Toward him the state would be "flexible" and his position would largely depend on what his attitude toward the revolution had been. Most significantly, "rich peasants" would be allowed to maintain their standard of living and even use surplus capital to pursue other money-making activities. The new democratic coalition government would nationalize "vital and strategic" industries such as banks, energy, telecommunications, and some sectors of the export-import trade. But private enterprise would be encouraged in many fields.

On paper, then, the new prescription of 1985 shaped up as a middle-ground social system, one which would be drastically

227

different from the old regime but not radically different from the other mixed economies in Asia. The phrase "on paper" is used advisedly, because it was never clear whether the considerable changes it embraced reflected the views of the Central Committee of the Communist Party of the Philippines. It was the NDF's claim, of course, that it was an independent organization and that the CPP was only one of its constituent members, along with certain farm and labor groups. Not many knowledgeable people believed in the NDF's independence. As one sophisticated Manilan put it, the NDF was perceived as the Communist party in alliance with itself. In early 1986, with a climactic presidential election approaching, it was effectively demonstrated that the party line controlled, that the NDF, with the chips down, could only obey. How much of the new moderate program represented a real change in party doctrine and how much of it was merely candy-coating for the uncommitted is not known.

There are, however, fragments of evidence that a genuine disagreement exists over policy between the NDF and the CPP Central Committee and that a tug-of-war has been underway for years over the shape of a social system that would follow a victory by insurgents. In 1986, NDF officials became quite explicit about the differences. In a remarkable magazine interview, the NDF's highest-ranking public spokesman, Satur Ocampo, defined the schism. The Communist party, he said, "is a party with a socialist perspective.

That is, ultimately, the CPP intends to establish a socialist form of government and a society along a Marxist-Leninist concept, with, of course, corresponding adjustments based on the specific characteristics of the national situation in the Philippines.[9]

On the other hand, Ocampo explained, the NDF program embraced non-Marxist elements and openly welcomed disparate groups, even big landlords who sympathized with the revolution. He thus drew a distinction between "national democrats" who believed in pluralism and the CPP which, he made clear, still hewed to the Marxist-Leninist line. One is left with the sense that a genuine ideological conflict over fundamentals was raging somewhere within the highest councils. One had no way of telling, however, which would prevail if it ever came to matter in the Philippines.

In the late 1970s, years before the Aquino assassination, Filipinos from all walks of life had become restless and angry at the continuation of martial law and gradually began to lift their voices in protest. Thousands of Manilans took to the streets in 1978, beating pots and pans and blaring automobile horns to protest a rigged election. There was a substantial boycott of the 1981 election, despite a government attempt to enforce mandatory voting as a show of support for Marcos. Labor strikes, although technically outlawed, grew in size and intensity and became more politicized, more designed for generalized protest than for specific economic gains. Throughout the archipelago there occurred countless small demonstrations: teachers' walkouts, student strikes, parades to military headquarters to protest brutality, transport strikes whose success was measured by the number of jeepney drivers who stayed off the streets. Finally, the assassination of Aquino drew millions into the streets in a national protest that endured for months. Some were communist-instigated, but most were the work of citizen groups committed only to the notion that Marcos should go.

The NDF had begun to note, even before the Aquino murder, that the protests had two favorable results. For one thing, they very quickly politicized many Filipinos who had been previously uninterested in causes. Attempts by the military to shut down the protests created instant converts. In this period, NDF membership grew rapidly, roughly doubling each year after 1980. The second result was the seeming chaos which the protests brought to city streets. Davao and several other cities in Mindanao and the Visayas (but not Manila) were virtually paralyzed and shut down, especially when taxi and jeepney drivers could be persuaded to join. It was a fascinating new development for the NDF, which previously had had little success in urban centers where large military detachments were located.

Out of these initially spontaneous and casually organized protests, the NDF fashioned what came to be called the *welgang bayan,* or people's strike. Students of communist history noted their resemblance to that weapon of past reliability, the general strike, which had been used by European communist-led unions to foment disorder in the streets as a prelude to bringing down governments. The model required large concentrations of industrial workers, a condition which did not fit Philippine urban areas. But the people's strike—involving large numbers of squatters, clerks, transport drivers and the newly militant middle class—produced much the same result. The first deliberately organized *welgang bayan* was staged in Davao on November 27, 1984, by the local "Coalition for Realizing Democracy," many of whose members were with the NDF. It was a success. Workers stayed home, shops closed down, drivers left the streets, and squatters in the slums threw up barricades to block any traffic daring to move.

Welgang bayans spread to other cities. Some were successes, others not. They seemed to work best in municipalities where the NPA presence was strong and police already intimidated. Bacolod, in Negros Occidental, was paralyzed totally by coordinated marches of thousands of out-of-work sugar workers. In Cebu City, where the NPA presence was slight, a projected *welgang bayan* failed utterly when jeepney and taxi drivers refused to join. The underground left's direction and manipulation of these strikes was gradually handed over to Bayan chapters set up after the organization was founded in May 1985. Some Bayan leaders maintain the *welgang bayan* was their organization's own invention. Actually, it was the NDF which first learned to coordinate and discipline them. Victor, the veteran Mindanao NDF leader and party member, said:

The *welgang bayan* came from the NDF. We had studied the models of urban struggle in other countries and decided to devise a Philippine variety. And we saw in it a model to be used in urban insurrection. In western countries, a general strike is carried out totally by industrial workers to shut down major industries. But there was not enough industrial development in the Philippines to make this work here. You had to get support from the other sectors—drivers, students, the urban poor and the like. It was the NDF which put this together.

As the strikes multiplied, some of their more experienced organizers in the NDF began to see in them not merely an organ of protest but an entirely new revolutionary theory, a new formula for bringing final victory. The party's official doctrine, of course, disparaged urban guerilla warfare and insisted that triumph could come only through battlefield victory in the countryside. Urban NDF cadres, by the mid-1980s, saw a different way out of the tunnel. The *welgang bayan* could be fine-tuned and disciplined to produce in cities throughout the Philippines a day of insurrection when the government forces would be simply immobilized. The "insurrectionists," as this faction came to be called, grew in number and pressed their arguments firmly, to the point that by late 1985 a full-scale party debate had begun over substituting an urban strategy for the old concept of rural conquest.

Many NDF leaders whom I interviewed accepted the insurrection thesis, believing the example of the Sandinist victory over the Somoza regime in Nicaragua gave it credence. Their scenario went like this: On the given day, people's strikes would be mounted in every major city. Masses would clog the streets, occupy public buildings and paralyze local branches of government. In the turmoil, power lines would be cut and the military's line of march would be blocked by sheer numbers of people. Outwardly the result would be chaos, but in fact the communist local committees would be in command. They would seize control of broadcasting stations, proclaim the formation of a provisional government, and assume control of the country. George, a Visayan NDF leader and one of the insurrection theory's enthusiasts, described the intended scenario most vividly:

Our initial discussions call not for destroying the symbols of government but simply forcing the government to stop functioning. We would force government officials just to resign and go away. It would be like what happened in Nicaragua. There would be barricades and attacks by the people using stones, bolos, slingshots and homemade bombs. The people would run into the streets when they heard of the confrontations on the radio. Our NPA would deal with the military. In many cities we are close to this stage of mass uprisings already [in late 1985]; 1986 and 1987 are the years to watch.

The training ground for such uprisings was, of course, the *welgang bayan.* "From the first," said Victor, another NDF leader, "we saw the *welgang bayan* as the tactic preparing people for insurrection."

This scenario never replaced victory in the countryside as the party's primary strategy. The party's old guard and top ranks of the NPA resisted it. What had emerged, by early 1986, was something of an informal compromise in which armed struggle and insurrection would go hand in hand at the proper time. Satur Ocampo told me that the idea of abandoning armed units in the countryside was never the issue. The party had, he said, recognized that the rapid politicization of urban dwellers and their willingness to protest had added a new dimension. But it was never regarded as the key to victory. "A review was undertaken with a view that it might be possible to have a combination of military action, both in the countryside and in urban protest for the final, total victory. It was to be a combination of those things, instead of just concentrating on armed struggle in the countryside."

In late 1985, the party's front work had become extraordinarily successful. NDF organizers were active in at least one fifth of the country's *barangays* (one-fourth, Ocampo thought) and in hundreds of them NDF Barrio Committees were the actual governments. The penetration of labor unions and other non-communist organizations was proceeding swiftly, even in Manila where grassroots work had been traditionally slow. Perhaps most significantly, the party had in place the semblance of a true popular front in Bayan, especially in the cities of Mindanao and the Visayas where prominent citizens and middle-class organizations remained loyal despite the national leadership fiasco in Manila earlier in the year. The front's own strategy of promoting people's strikes as the first stages of a national insurrection was becoming more and more popular. Everywhere one went in those days, NDF leaders confidently predicted that in perhaps three more years the revolutionary forces would move on to the second phase of their struggle, to the "strategic stalemate," when they would be an even match for the government.

They were, too, much encouraged by the apparent weakening of President Marcos's control and popularity, and by the growing signs that the United States was at last losing patience with his rule. Many took as proof of his diminishing power Marcos's own vague suggestions that he might hold an unprecedented "snap" election to demonstrate that he still held the reins. The party and, at first, many in the NDF looked forward to this. A national election provided them with the opportunity of mounting a massive boycott—and election boycotts had proved effective weapons for building the national front in 1981 and 1984. They guessed that another boycott would prove to even the most anti-communist of the centrist politicians that playing Marcos's game in yet another rigged election was futile and that the result would be to lift the NDF to a higher peak of popularity. It was to be the party's worst misjudgment.

13

★★☆

His final appearance is awkward yet unforgettable. Ferdinand E. Marcos, looking tired but at first determined, stands on a balcony of Malacañang Palace one last time, looking down at several hundred supporters who cheer and wave small Philippine flags. Most have been bussed to the palace to form the backdrop for what would be, although few sensed it, the president's final television appeal. The setting had been used often with success: Ferdinand and Imelda, smiling and exuding regal confidence. It is not unlike those pleasant scenes of the Queen gazing fondly down from the balcony of Buckingham Palace.

On this day, February 25, 1986, Marcos rambles more than usual, tossing off a careless speech full of vague promises and threats and pleas for perseverance. The little flags wave hesitantly, their bearers unsure of the timing. Marcos waves back, an arm raised in a gesture that in the past had signified defiance. Suddenly, his fist moves to his left eye and appears to wipe away a tear. A frowning Imelda, noticing this, peers over his shoulder. Inexplicably, both begin to sing a patriotic tune in Tagalog. Ferdinand, looking confused, mumbles into the microphone. Perhaps to erase this clumsy moment, the government television camera pans again to the sea of little Philippine flags, but it, too, errs. In one corner of the picture a palace information aide is caught anxiously pumping his arms skyward to draw more applause, pleading for a crescendo. Quickly, the camera moves back to the balcony. Marcos turns slowly to enter the palace. He grasps the edge of a door to steady himself and then disappears inside.

The instant historians said in chorus that the fall of Marcos was foreordained, that the tides of history and an inevitable popular uprising had swept him out. I think they were wrong. Marcos simply blundered. In calling for the "snap election" of February 1986, he made an uncharacteristic and colossal error. It polarized the forces against him at the moment when he was least able to resist. Corazon Aquino's people's revolt, which flowed from that violent and fraud-ridden election, would never have taken place had Marcos not proclaimed that final test of his will and ingenuity.

Why he did it remains a mystery. Marcos was one of modern history's shrewder tyrants, a man not merely gifted in manipulation but favored with genius in balancing forces in his favor. He had not imposed martial law on an unwilling people, but had shaped opinion so that enough Filipinos would accept it to make it work. He feared two powerful forces more than any other: the United States and the Philippine Catholic church. He had displeased both but had also made both see that his rule was in their interests, at least until the final days.

The Americans and the church had put enormous pressure on Marcos to reform after the brutal assassination in 1983 of his arch-rival, Benigno Aquino, Jr. Neither necessarily wanted him to step down because the alternative to him was unclear, but both insisted that his rule become more humane and palatable to the opposition. Both, too, feared revolution from the left and thought that the frightening growth of the communists could be arrested only if Marcos liberalized his reign. I doubt that Marcos himself believed that. But I believe that he felt called upon to prove once again to Washington and the Catholic church that his power was intact, his abilities undiminished, and his popularity sufficient to make the old balancing act work. To prove this, he put his honor and ego on the line in an unnecessary election he thought he would win in the usual way. José Diokno, the opposition leader who despised him said it simply and best: "His *macho* was at stake and he just decided to bull it through."

The signs that Marcos had made a dreadful error, and that he realized it, were everywhere apparent in the months preceding the election. The president behaved like a man acting against his own better judgment, and the result was a series of uncharacteristic false starts and reversals. Interviewed by one American television correspondent, he insisted that there would be no snap election. Interviewed a week later by another American television correspondent, he announced there would in fact be an election, but only for the office of president. Then he declared both the presidency and vice presidency at stake. The surest proof of his indecision was known to few Filipinos. Secretly, Marcos attempted to manipulate the Supreme Court into declaring the special election invalid. The court refused, leaving him to face the judgment he had mistakenly sought.

Another signal that Marcos was losing control of events lay in the unexpected agreement by opposition parties to unite behind a single candidate for president, Corazon Aquino. Conventional wisdom held that the traditional parties and splinter groups could never overcome their separate aspirations to form a single bloc. And division meant defeat, because the Marcos party, the New Society Movement, retained enough muscle in the towns and cities to win any three-way contest. For nearly a year, a loose and fractious grouping of anit-Marcos factions attempted to form a unity slate in the event the president risked a special election. In the end, Marcos's old fear that the church might stand against him proved justified. Jaime Cardinal Sin, next to Marcos himself the smartest of Philippine politicians, employed his great prestige to construct the slate of Aquino for president and Salvador Laurel for vice president. From the moment Aquino reluctantly accepted the cardinal's choice, the election was transformed into something beyond politics. It became a fairy-tale event—the simple, brave widow challenging the wicked but failing king to avenge her martyred husband. Although ill and given to mistakes of judgment, Marcos might have triumphed in the sort of election to which, before martial law, Filipinos had become accustomed. He might have survived the customary battle in which fraud and violence were common on both sides and in which victory went to the side with the most money and guns. But this was a national morality tale, summoning up all of the hatreds and passions of the past twenty years, a great melodrama which did not end when, as everyone expected, Marcos's Commission on Elections proclaimed him the winner. Aquino, secure in the church's endorsement, simply ignored the official results, proclaimed herself the victor, and took her crusade into the streets.

The end came as the Marcos government collapsed on international television. Defense Minister Juan Ponce Enrile, the canny architect of martial law in 1972, defected, apparently fearing he would be arrested, and so did Gen. Fidel Ramos, chief of staff. Thousands of Filipinos, encouraged by Catholic church radio broadcasts, rushed to protect them in their isolated encampment at Camp Crame. From February 22 to 25, the standoff continued, with Marcos's military either unwilling or unable to break through the human wall. Gradually, field commanders obeyed Ramos's call to defect, the crowds at Camp Crame swelled, and Marcos gave a final fateful command barring the use of heavy firepower to dislodge the traitors. On the twenty-fifth, Marcos arranged to have himself inaugurated as president in a nearly private ceremony at Malacañang, and then he and Imelda stepped onto the balcony for the last performance. A few hours later he was flown out of the country to exile.

The melodrama had enlisted Filipinos from almost every walk of life. Farmers had trooped by the hundreds of thousands to Aquino rallies. Nuns and priests became poll-watchers. Ordinary people roped themselves to ballot boxes to protect their votes for the widow. Government computer clerks refused to tally ballots fraudulently compiled. Businessmen, bureaucrats, taxi drivers and housewives faced down the tanks sent to end

237

the military holdout at Camp Crame. In all of this outpouring, there was one conspicuous absence, that of the Communist Party of the Philippines.

In the months before the election, the CPP found itself in a mood of extreme self-confidence bordering on euphoria. Never had its prospects seemed so brilliant. The early 1980s had been a period of rapid growth and it seemed, after the years of trial and error and near extinction, that destiny favored it at last. The NPA armed soldiers numbered more than 20,000 and they were increasingly massed in larger units, often in full battalion strength. Only Mindanao's Muslim provinces remained untouched by the NPA. The party's political gains were even more impressive. More than 30,000 Filipinos had been admitted to party membership and the latest recruits had come predominantly from the ranks of peasants and workers, not the universities. The most striking achievement, however, was the rapid pace of political organization in the barrios. The party believed, in early 1986, that about one fourth of the nation's 41,600 barrios were infiltrated and influenced by local cadres. In a growing number of them, NDF underground committees were the de facto government.

Party officials acknowledged that a number of external factors contributed to their success. The most obvious was a deteriorating Philippine economy that failed to create meaningful new jobs and which actually reduced, in real terms, the income received by even those steadily employed. The military's abuses had grown more widespread, touching almost every community where government troops were garrisoned and producing a new crop of NPA candidates with each turn of the screw. And at every stage, the Marcos government seemed committed to some blundering callousness which diminished its mastery of events and even its claims to legitimacy. The crude slaying of Benigno Aquino was not simply a mark of brutality. It revealed a regime struck suddenly by panic.

But to the cocky cadres of late 1985, good fortune did not flow merely from such "objective conditions" as these. It was in large part a credit to their own ingenuity that events were running so favorably in their direction, they believed. They meant by this not merely their own skill in organizing the masses or the novel tactics developed in hundreds of raids, ambushes and occupations of city halls. They believed their grand strategy of armed struggle had worked, that it had, in the strictly political sense, positioned the party to be the beneficiary of all the damage those external factors had wrought. Economic disintegration, military abuses, the indifference and brutishness of the Marcos government had served to polarize the country in their favor. People of all classes were compelled to choose, to become either pro- or anti-Marcos, and those who chose the latter path increasingly had to turn to the CPP. There was no realistic alternative. The traditional opposition, that wavering, hapless agglomeration of out-of-power politicians, was not a serious option. It could talk but not act. Power did in fact grow from the barrel of a gun and when all the hairs were split and all of the brave talk exhausted, only the party had the gun. It was this hard fact which in the polarization of the 1980s caused so many to turn to the Communist party, or so the party's leaders maintained. "We were in place," one middle-level cadre observed late in 1985:

I mean that if we had not been there as an organization all of those other things would not have mattered. You have got to understand that no matter how much people turned against Marcos then, none of that would have made any difference if we had not been there to take advantage of it. And to make it mean something. That's really it. We were in place.

In this heady atmosphere, party members began to speak of a timetable for victory. Officially, the struggle was then still in the first stage—the strategic defensive—of the three stages through which a Maoist revolution must pass. In late 1985, it was confidently predicted that within three to five years the second stage, strategic stalemate, would be reached. In that phase, the revolutionary forces would attain a rough parity with those of the government and become unbeatable in the battlefield. That stage would be a brief one. Rather quickly, the struggle would advance into the third and final stage, the strategic offensive, when the cities would fall, the government would collapse, and the red flag would hang over Malacañang. It was with this certitude that the party turned to the matter at hand, Marcos's special election, and made the biggest political blunder of its seventeen-year history.

Marcos's plan to reelect himself for another six years at first posed no particular problem for the CPP. It regarded all elections as irrelevant sideshows arranged by the president periodically to give his regime the facade of a democratic government. Its policy was to boycott them, and in both 1981 and 1984 it induced many supporters to stay away from the polls. In 1984, it had gone beyond a passive boycott to sanction obstruction. Ballot boxes were carried away by NPA squads and campaign posters were defaced. The boycott became a positive political act. Street marches and demonstrations to protest rigged elections polarized people against the government and underscored the party's role as the only meaningful alternative to the tyrant's rule. "The 1981 boycott and demonstrations were a key development for us," one NDF official recalled. "By our count, about a half-million people at 47 different places joined in the boycott demonstrations in 1981 and they were even bigger in 1984. These were the first nationally organized movements against Marcos."

The party saw no reason to abandon its boycott policy for the 1986 election, even though it recognized the emotional appeal which Corazon Aquino would bring to the contest. Its initial judgment of her was unflattering. She had no program of government and she vacillated on the most important issues, declared *Ang Bayan*. An editorial noted that early in 1985 she had signed a pledge with other opposition leaders calling for the removal of United States military bases. But then she changed her mind. Moreover, the editorial warned, Aquino herself came from a "comprador-landlord class background" and among her advisers were "pro-imperialist big compradors" from the Makati business community and a group of conservative churchmen the party labelled "clerico-fascist." Finally, she was evidently hostile to the NPA. In an interview with *Time* magazine, Aquino declared herself opposed to armed violence and said that if elected she would insist that the guerillas lay down their arms and seek amnesty from her government.[1]

240

A month later, in January 1986, with Aquino's popularity growing, the party softened its rhetoric without relaxing its fundamental opposition. She had been "carrying on a vigorous anti-fascist campaign, thus making valuable contributions to the people's overall anti-fascist struggles," said a new editorial. "For this she has generated tremendous support from large segments of the population." But she remained indecisive, vague about social programs, and critical of the left. "All these indicate that, well-meaning though she may be, she is politically naive or that she has not transcended her own comprador-landlord class background even as she counterposes herself as Marcos's 'exact opposite.' "[2]

Regardless of Aquino's strengths and faults, the communists asserted, the election itself was no different from Marcos's "past bogus elections" and it had "the makings of being the biggest political swindle ever attempted by the U.S.-Marcos clique upon our people since the imposition of martial law in 1972." The American influence in promoting the election was obvious, despite Washington's "feigned neutrality." The United States had grown fearful of Marcos's declining power, *Ang Bayan* said, and was encouraging the election merely to serve its interests by fostering more stability within the elite, both pro- and anti-Marcos.

Imperialism wants to gradually moderate the conflicts among the local reactionary classes, reconcile them, and consolidate their ranks within the framework of puppet fascist rule. It wants to broaden the political base of such rule and lay the ground for the orderly transfer of power when Marcos dies or when it finally wants to get rid of him.

Boycott was the only proper role; participation was merely a diversion.[3]

There was a further motive in promoting the 1986 boycott: It would hasten polarization and contribute to that insurrectionary mood which many party cadres saw as the real key to victory. A large number of NDF partisans had become convinced that the official policy of armed struggle and rural guerilla warfare would never succeed. Instead, they looked to simultaneous insurrections in the towns and cities, culminating in a governmental collapse, as the more likely formula. The

241

"insurrection scenario" required large and continuous demonstrations of the sort engineered in the *welgang bayans* of the past year. An election boycott would be the perfect mechanism for polarizing people to that high level of protest. The middle class, fooled into participating once more in a rigged election, would finally see the light and in their fury turn to the left and its radical program. Nilo, an underground organizer, explained to a New York *Times* correspondent:

What we foresee is that moderates will be pushed more and more to align themselves with the progressive left—businessmen, professionals, students and, even more so, the people in the countryside. For us that's very favorable. That ripens the conditions for a popular uprising.[4]

Almost from the beginning, the boycott policy had been questioned by some in the NDF who sensed that its effect might be the reverse of that intended. It might, they suggested, alienate rather than attract those middle-class elements determined to support Aquino and give electoral politics one last try. Local cadres were approached by ordinary peasants who wanted to vote for Aquino and refused to boycott. In the cities, the party was accused by its fringe supporters of opting out of a climactic struggle and detracting from Aquino's potential vote. Bayan, which had obediently followed the CPP boycott line, began to suffer defections among its large following of non-communist anti-Marcos activists who felt obligated out of sympathy for Aquino's widow to take part in her campaign. Even Lorenzo Tañada, the revered nationalist who nominally headed Bayan, announced that he would vacate his position to support Aquino.

As the campaign proceeded and Aquino's crowds grew to massive proportions, the level of NDF dissidence also increased. Relatively high-ranking cadres, in lengthy memoranda addressed to the Executive Committee of the CPP Central Committee, warned that the boycott would boomerang, leaving the party more isolated from middle-class factions than before. In interviews during January 1986, I was struck by the openness of the criticism and, too, by the fact that it extended to issues other than the election boycott. The Executive Committee, it

242

was said, was behaving in an undemocratic fashion, ignoring the voices of the rank and file. The committee had become stubborn and insensitive. The most serious charge contended that the Executive Committee had abandoned the cardinal party rule of "democratic centralism," under which major decisions were to be made only after extensive internal discussion. It was said that the committee had, in its aloofness, even refused to submit the boycott issue to the politburo.

In the end, the boycott position laid down by Rodolfo Salas, the party chairman, and Rafael Baylosis, the secretary general, prevailed. Their only compromise was to authorize a so-called "soft boycott," which meant the NPA would not steal ballot boxes or deface campaign posters. The final *Ang Bayan* editorial before the February 7 voting rebuked those dissenters who thought the boycott a passive and "defeatist" act. On the contrary, the paper said, a boycott "exposes and spotlights the election's spuriousness and futility." It would demonstrate with finality that armed revolution was the only path, and in the process would build the party's strength for the final struggle. "For all its meaninglessness as a means of overthrowing the hated U.S.-Marcos dictatorship, the snap election will teach many more among our people a most valuable political lesson: that revolution, not a rigged election, is the correct path to change."[5]

The optimism was quickly proven misplaced. With the entire country gripped in election fever, the appeal to boycott was either ignored or denounced by Aquino partisans. Bayan steadily lost the middle-class support it was designed to appeal to. Its street protests attracted only the committed radicals, and they were dwarfed by the size of Aquino's huge and emotional crowds. When Bayan foolishly produced a 15-point program which Aquino was to accept if she wanted that organization's support, it was coolly and quickly rejected. The radical left was suffering the worst of fates at a revolutionary moment in Philippine history. It was beginning to appear irrelevant.

Party dissidents who had warned of just such a fate grimly followed the boycott line, accepting party discipline without agreeing with party policy, and cheering themselves with the notion that when the election was over and Marcos was once again inaugurated their foresight would be recognized and

Aquino's frustrated partisans would join the radical left. "History will vindicate us," a political organizer with KMU, the radical labor federation, predicted. "After the election, it will still be Marcos in power and then the line will be drawn between the dictator and the anti-dictator forces." A high-ranking party cadre who had authored one of the most critical dissents rejected by party leaders confided one week before the election that talks had already been opened with Aquino's people on a post-election reconciliation. The left's plan was to engage them in anti-Marcos protests, initially moderate in tone but rising in both intensity and radical content until they exceeded even those spontaneous outpourings that had followed Benigno Aquino's assassination. "We expect to pick up great support from among Cory's people," he told me. "They will be the most frustrated when she loses and Marcos wins. A significant portion of them will be so radicalized they will be open to the armed struggle."

Nothing of the sort happened. Huge street demonstrations did follow Marcos's claim of victory, but they were led by Aquino, not the left. The climactic scene at Camp Crame which brought Marcos down was filled with irony for the communist side, for it resembled in so many ways that dream of insurrection conceived by the NDF. Thousands and thousands of angry people massed in the streets. The government was virtually immobilized. At a crucial moment, key elements of the military defected to the mass movement. And finally the regime simply collapsed, replaced by a provisional government waving a "freedom constitution." Victory went not to the CPP but to a housewife-turned-politician of centrist views and upper-class instincts who held the left in contempt. "It was all so ironic," observed one of the NDF's leaders. "The left was so conscious of being in the vanguard. It ended up being at the tail end of the movement."

The "boycott blunder," as it was called, was the party's worst tactical error and it raised two large and divisive questions. The first was about the character of the party itself. Since the earliest days when it threw off the habits of acquired Maoism and began to find its own way, the Communist Party of the Philip-

244

pines had taken pride in its flexibility. Dogma bowed to experience, errors were candidly dissected, and new tactics sprang from the debates over old ones which had failed. The boycott debacle revealed another side of the CPP, one which was rigid and dogmatic, unable to gauge political change, hostile to internal dissent. The party leaders had confused a climactic emotional crusade in 1986 with the election protests of 1981 and 1984 and coldly ignored those who recognized the difference. Had the CPP become embalmed in its own dogma after all?

The second question was aimed at the future of the communist movement in the new post-Marcos era. Could it survive without its favorite enemy? Non-communists had long claimed that the CPP flourished only as an antidote to Marcos's New Society, that Marcos himself was the NPA's best recruiter, that communist ideology meant little to the peasant converts. Would it now disintegrate? Salvador Laurel, the experienced professional politician who was now the country's vice president, predicted confidently that with Marcos gone ninety percent of the guerillas would troop down from the hills, surrender, and rejoin the mainstream of Philippine society. Was he right?

To this second question, the party's searching assessment that followed Aquino's victory produced an answer that was optimistic, self-serving, and it seemed to me, flawed. It held that although a certain amount of support had been lost among peripheral supporters, the mass base remained solid and little longterm damage was done. In an interview eighteen weeks after Aquino's accession, Satur Ocampo, put it this way:

We have not noticed any reduction in the mass base, among the farmers and workers. But there is a weakening among the middle-forces, especially in Metro Manila. They used to be very supportive in logistics and in participating alongside the mass movement. Now we see them still supporting us on such issues as the nuclear power plant [on Bataan] and [the removal of] the American bases.

But there has been no loss in the mass base that I am aware of. The peasant masses do not see any change in their social, political and economic positions. They can see that Cory is not like Marcos. But the military presence is still the same. The PC and the CHDF are still the same in areas where they operate against the NPA. Cory keeps defining the role of the soldiers and trying to control the abuses. But she has no effective control over the armed forces.

This assessment was valid so far as it went. NDF organizers in Davao and Negros echoed Ocampo's view that few defected from the mass base. It was also true that few NPA guerillas surrendered, disproving Laurel's forecast. But the loss of middle-class support was extensive and costly for it set back the party's popular front campaign just when it seemed at last to be succeeding. Noel, the radical priest in Davao, conceded that his efforts to attract left-leaning priests into the Christians for National Liberation stalled completely after Aquino took office. Other front organizers described similar reversals. The disappearance of Marcos and the much publicized reform of the Philippine military, one of them said, had satisfied a surprising number of fringe supporters and left them disinterested in the CPP:

We have found that some whom we thought we had convinced to rationally understand the structural problems were in fact only anti-Marcos and anti-military. We had tried to teach them that the problems were not caused by evil men but by an unjust system. Some obviously did not understand. . . . To that extent the victory of Cory is a real dilemma for us.

There were, too, practical effects of the boycott blunder and Aquino's accession which, it seemed to me, the communists underestimated. In the struggle for public opinion and popular acceptance they could not afford any longer to be perceived as anti-Aquino. The practical consequences of this fact were far-reaching. They could not, for example, mount large public demonstrations against her government, not even against the military. In a speech at the Philippine Military Academy, Aquino had referred to the cadets as "my soldiers." The perception that the military was now *her* military precluded protests of the sort that were common before Marcos fell. In the months after the February revolt, Bayan and the NDF were unable to approach the level of the old *welgang bayan* uprisings.

For the same reason, the NPA was forced to scale down its

military operations. It cancelled a series of planned seizures of municipal halls and concentrated its assaults on popular enemies not identified with the Aquino government—the paramilitary "fanatic" organizations which harrassed citizens and the most hated landlords who maintained large private armies. The party could not afford to ignore the new president's appeal for a ceasefire and it agreed to enter preliminary peace talks although it dreaded the confusion and dissension this would cause within the NPA. "We have to do a lot of explaining to the ordinary fighters," Ocampo admitted.[6] Guerillas who had risked capture and death for nearly two decades resented the suggestion that their gains might be negotiated away. Their fears were ultimately soothed but not without some rebelliousness. In Panay, a party district leader was approached by a solemn delegation of veteran guerillas who had heard radio reports of a military ceasefire. "They asked us to turn over our guns to them when we arranged the ceasefire," the cadre said. "They made it clear they were prepared to go on alone without us."

The final cost of the boycott was a wrenching intra-party split, the most serious one, ideologically and personally, since Sison led his small band out of the old Communist party in 1968. Few details of this collision of wills have leaked out, but it is known that for months after the February revolt the party's top leadership was locked in a major "rectification," the term used for crucial internal debates. On the defensive were Salas and Baylosis, the two top leaders who had assumed control after Sison was imprisoned in 1977. The boycott was the focal point but the argument carried over to broader issues: the leadership's inflexibility, its disdain for dissent, its dogmatic insistence on the old theme of armed victory in the battlefield. The divisive issue of how far to bend doctrine in order to form alliances with middle-class non-communists also was raised. It was as much a settling of accounts on long-standing grievances as it was a debate on the boycott, a collision between the doctrinally pure lodged in the party leadership and the risk-taking experimenters concentrated in the NDF. A veteran leader of the NDF told me in those months that it reflected not a struggle between separate factions but a more fluid contest between "tendencies" which had long existed:

Within the movement, there are many cadres who want to stick with the standard Marxist-Leninist dictum just so that they can never be considered wrong. They are hardline and very timid. They only want to be doctrinally correct. Then there is the more open tendency. These people are willing to take risks and in particular they are willing to make compromises with the middle forces. Those in the first tendency had slowed us down for years—they always stuck to the known facts and the old ways of doing things.

In the end, Salas, Baylosis, and the rest of the old guard lost. The terms of their defeat were stated in a blistering criticism of the boycott policy contained in the May 1986, issue of *Ang Bayan*. It disclosed that the politburo had characterized the boycott as a "major political blunder" occasioned by a total misreading of the anti-Marcos mood:

Where the people saw in the February 7 snap election a chance to deliver a crippling blow on the Marcos regime, a memorandum by the Executive Committee saw it merely as "a noisy and empty political battle" among factions in the ruling classes.

And when the aroused and militant moved spontaneously but resolutely to oust the hated regime last February 22–25, the party and its forces were not there to lead them. In large measure the party and its forces were on the sidelines, unable to lead or influence the hundreds of thousands of people who moved with amazing speed and decisiveness to overthrow the regime.

Had the executive committee's error been merely a political misjudgment, it might have been passed over lightly with a reprimand. But it had resulted from a breakdown in established procedure, specifically a failure by the committee to thrash out the differing views before rendering a decision to boycott. It had erred, said the *Ang Bayan* editorial, "in its understanding and application of the Marxist-Leninist organizational principle of democratic centralism." This was perhaps the most serious charge that could be made by one Philippine communist against another, for "democratic centralism" had been a revered principle. Cadres had long boasted that majority rule and the toleration of dissent distinguished the CPP from rigidly orthodox and authoritarian parties in other countries. Accusing

248

the Executive Committee of violating it was like charging treason.

It was the rainy season in July when the explanation of these events trickled down to the farmers in Iloilo Province on the Visayan island of Panay. The barrio in the steeply sloped foothills etched with terraced rice fields had been safe NPA territory for years, the government's CHDF detachment long since driven away. But the mass base of peasants and independent farmers was restless and confused by the epic turnabout in Manila, the flight of Marcos, the accession of Aquino's widow. Many felt the NPA, which was their term for all forms of the communist movement, had been on the wrong side. They had ignored the party's boycott and voted for Aquino. On that day in late July 1986, the party was to atone and explain. About a hundred people from the mass base—grizzled farmers, old women, young mothers with babies in arms—gathered in the rustic bamboo chapel which alternated as church and communist propaganda hall. At the blackboard, eager to begin before the afternoon rains pounded on the tin roof, was that local hero of the movement, Javier.

Javier began with the boycott, formally extending the party's apology for misreading events and the mood of people like those present. "We accept the fact that we had our weaknesses in the past," he said in the local Ilonggo dialect. "We failed to feel the pulse of the masses who wanted to participate in the election for the sake of change." A few in the audience nodded silently, and Javier moved on to the present. Mrs. Aquino's government displayed many progressive instincts but it was shaky because she shared power with two Marcos holdovers, Defense Minister Enrile and General Ramos. The people should be alert to those military leaders' moves and be prepared if they launched a coup to topple President Aquino. If that happened, the people must respond with massive protests to defend the President and if they did the NPA would protect them. The local *barangay* captain raised his hand: Only with American imperialists' support, he said, would Enrile and Ramos attempt to remove Aquino. There were more assenting nods. Javier moved on to the pressing issue, the approaching local elections. There would be a new political party which would understand the needs of the masses, he said, and the people would have plenty of opportunity to vote this time around.

Such scenes were common throughout the communist fronts in those summer months as the CPP rallied from its worst political defeat. Gradually, through such "consolidation" meetings, the party seemed to recover its poise and a semblance of its old resiliency. The great post-Marcos "rectification" was winding down. Rumors of vast purges were denied. It was not clear then whether the old guard's leaders, Salas and Baylosis, had been forced from office, but their authority was clearly dwindling. Ocampo, the NDF leader whose star had risen in the party as theirs had fallen, proclaimed that a new "democratization" was taking place to assure dissenters a voice. "There was a lack of democracy in the adoption of the [boycott] policy," he said. And so " . . . then we had to see to it that in the formulation of major policies on major questions, a free debate—as extensive and as wide as possible—should be encouraged."[7]

The party was still very much on the defensive in the new political environment, uncertain how to treat the Aquino government. It was impossible to oppose Aquino frontally. She was enormously popular and, after all, she had released from prison two revered CPP leaders, Sison and Dante, and many other political prisoners. In truth, the party doubted she would be long in office. They anticipated an Enrile coup or a gradual eclipse of her appeal as poor Filipinos found no fundamental change in their daily lives. But so long as Corazon Aquino retained her Goddesslike stature as savior of the nation, the CPP was stymied. The armed guerillas were instructed to avoid major encounters and the *welgang bayan* abandoned as a weapon. Thus, the two scenarios for potential victory that had once contended for party acceptance—control of the battlefield and urban insurrection—were equally incompatible in the new reality. Either would have brought the party into a no-win confrontation with a popular Philippine president.

Although those revolutionary avenues were closed, the CPP found that in the post-Marcos era new ones were suddenly opened. A curious phrase, "Democratic space," became popular. It meant, roughly, that there was room to maneuver in a number of "legal" arenas that would have been shut off under Marcos's reign. It was the Aquino government's position, defined by the several human rights attorneys in its ranks, that radical political activity was legal so long as it did not provoke revolutionary acts. The government had also succeeded, precariously, in imposing some restrictions on the military. They were not always observed, but the rule that radical suspects could not be punished without trial and that salvagings should cease did reduce the worst military abuses. The effect was to provide the CPP and especially the national front with "space" for more propaganda and politicization in the barrios. Political organizers were assigned to new areas that had been too dangerous before and instructed to expand influence in those which had been only lightly infiltrated. Indeed, the military's own surveys disclosed that during the entire period of the election campaign, the "people power" revolt in Manila, and the confused aftermath, the communist penetration of local villages increased significantly. It calculated that 14 percent of the country's 41,600 *barangays* were affected to some extent by the CPP at the end of 1985. This had increased to 18 percent by mid-1986.[8]

Other new vistas opened, too. Aquino's Constitutional Commission, assigned to write a new fundamental law, was closed to the party, but a number of its members represented either party front groups or other radical organizations, and the commission's debates became a forum for pressing the party's position on key issues, especially the removal of U.S. bases and a sweeping land reform program. The government's offer to open "ceasefire" talks initially put the party on the defensive; but it also gave communists recognition as a force to be dealt with. Finally, the party was swathed in a new respectability bestowed by the news media. Newspapers treated the NDF, surprisingly, as a legitimate political force whose views deserved public airing. This was an immense gain for the popular-front movement. Never before had it been able to routinely put its opinions before the public. In some areas where communist influence was widespread, radio stations, eager to expand

251

broadcast audiences, actively solicited the party's statements. In Iloilo City, for example, three stations regularly broadcast taped messages submitted by the NDF.

By necessity and invention, then, the CPP was drifting into new fields. These moves had two things in common: They were legal endeavors, and they were political, in the broad sense of the word. There was nothing official about the new move. The party's charter still prescribed armed revolution as the path to victory and a great many cadres still looked fondly on a scenario of victory through urban insurrection. The new avenue of political struggle had opened more by chance than by design. There was much doubt that the new government would leave that avenue open. A coup from the right, many cadres warned, would promptly close off the new "space." But despite the doubts and reservations, the CPP neared its eighteenth birthday with a strange new cut to its clothing. It was beginning to look, to the dismay of some and the delight of others, like a conventional political party.

A glimpse of what this departure might accomplish was offered one day in a peasant's home in the hills of Panay where some of the CPP's ranking cadres were taking a week's retreat to evaluate the new politics. They were excited at the prospects. Sison had recently announced formation of a new party which would be masked as an independent party but would in fact serve the CPP's purposes. Local elections would be held soon, the first of the post-Marcos period.

Nene, a member of the CPP district committee on Panay, talked of the communists' hopes for seizing local offices throughout the island. NDF front organizations were solidly entrenched in about one third of the 98 towns, she said, and their candidates could easily win control under the banner of Sison's new party. In another third of the towns, the communists were strong but not dominant and would be forced to work in coalition with established parties, like the old Liberal Party or a new grouping, the PDP-Laban. They would be weak in the final third where towns were controlled by conservative planters.

The notion of winning power by ballots instead of bullets intrigued Nene. She was a vivacious woman in her late thirties, a Manilan who had abandoned a comfortable home and her university to serve the party many years earlier. She had fought in the mountains and borne a son who was by then sixteen, himself a prospective guerilla. It had been a grueling life, fighting and hiding, and only recently had Nene been promoted to a party political job and allowed to live in a city on Panay. Playing politics in the conventional sense, she thought, was a wise move under the new circumstances. "It might hasten things a bit," she said. She smiled, and then suddenly bent over in a comic imitation of an aging woman. "Some of us are getting on in years."

14

★★★

On November 27, 1986, the government of President Corazon Aquino and the National Democratic Front signed formal agreements which prepared the way for a sixty-day cease-fire, beginning on December 10. For the first time in eighteen years, the New People's Army laid aside its guns, and a mood of reconciliation settled on the country. In Manila and many villages, the soldiers of the NPA were received with a startling warmth. Troops of the rebels' central front in Negros descended from Mount Canlaon and were embraced in Bacolod in a festival of peace. On the Bataan peninsula, Satur Ocampo and other leaders of the NDF marched in a procession of armed rebels from the underground. Most remarkable was the reception in Manila, where Ocampo, Antonio Zumel, and other members of the NDF negotiating team were accorded the status of instant celebrities. They gave lectures, appeared on television talk shows, and held news conferences in the manner of mainstream politicians. Their sudden respectability, wrote a prominent columnist, was not a mere propaganda coup. They had "planted their official presence in the city without disturbing anyone's slumber or causing undue alarm."[1]

This achievement was, of course, due less to the communists' bargaining skill than to President Aquino's patient insistence on national reconciliation, a goal she pursued with near religious zeal, and to her considerable political attainments. Within less than a year after taking office, she had caused a new constitution to be drafted, arranged a truce with Muslims in Mindanao, and brought the Philippine military under the control of moderate officers. In her most celebrated victory, the president faced down Defense Secretary Enrile and dismissed him after a clique of his officers sought to destabilize her government by spreading rumors of a coup. She had made triumphal tours to the United States and Japan as a symbol of renascent democracy. It is true that she had reneged or failed to follow through on a number of important campaign promises—very little was heard in 1986 of her land-reform pledges, for example—and there were many complaints of her governments' everyday inefficiencies. But the successes and the aura of selflessness and humility that still clung to her months after the defeat of Marcos sustained her popularity and made her the most admired national leader since Ramon Magsaysay in the 1950s. The power that flowed from those successes made possible her opening to the left and the cease-fire with the communists.

Leading the communists into the cease-fire and to the bargaining table in December was no minor achievement for Ocampo and that faction of the CPP which had opposed the election boycott and argued for the appearance of conciliation with the Aquino government. Although elevated to party prominence when their anti-boycott position proved correct, Ocampo and his colleagues still faced criticism when they espoused a policy of critical collaboration with the new government. Ocampo told me that local NPA commanders, in particular, felt bitter about proposals for a cease-fire, believing that they were falling into a trap. Ocampo argued that a refusal to accept the cease-fire offer would cast the NDF as an obstructionist force and cause it to lose even more of its middle-class support.

255

It was a mixture of motives which finally brought the communists to the bargaining table and the signing of the cease-fire agreements. Some in the party seem to have seriously believed that the time had come to stop fighting and start talking because the possibility of military victory seemed to them remote. The nondoctrinaire in NDF had long hoped for a political settlement. For others it was a mere tactical diversion, a time-buying option which offered opportunities to strengthen the NPA, acquire more weapons, and prepare for an intense military conflict. It is impossible to determine which of these views was more decisive in the party's deliberations leading up to the cease-fire. But the final result on the whole suggested that the party had adopted a sophisticated and realistic approach to the new circumstances created by Corazon Aquino. Nearly isolated by its foolish decision to boycott her election campaign, the party had recognized its political misjudgment and recaptured much of the ground lost in the contest for public support.

Moreover, agreeing to the cease-fire brought the communists two distinct practical advantages. The first was an extension of what the political cadres called "space"—the freedom to organize grass-roots groups as legal political organizations that could participate in elections. The new party founded by Sison and others, *Partido ng Bayan,* grew swiftly in the period preceding and during the cease-fire, its membership drawn largely from the labor and peasant groups formed originally as clandestine underground organizations to support the NPA. The new political party's strategy was to make maximum gains in the local and parliamentary elections scheduled for May of 1987. It was assumed by Sison and other *Partido ng Bayan* leaders that they could win between twenty and twenty-five percent of these contests, either by fielding their own candidates or joining coalitions with other parties. If the strategy worked, a new party of the left, one strongly influenced by the CPP, would be an especially strong force in the new national legislature. The cease-fire and the period of relative calm which preceded it provided valuable time for the organization of this new political network.

The second advantage was inherent in the mere signing of the cease-fire documents, which set forth the rules under which the NDF could participate and even permitted it to open a coordinating office in Manila. The event created an appearance of parity, as though the government and the communists were equal parties in a legal undertaking. It was not as dramatic an achievement as the CPP originally hoped. Ocampo had told me, in August, that the party wanted to be granted official status as belligerents, thus conferring on it certain rights recognized under international law. Aquino's negotiators rejected this demand and Ocampo had not pressed it. But the widely publicized signing of the cease-fire ground rules went far toward a kind of formal recognition of the NDF as a legitimate political and legal force in the Philippines. Conservatives were horrified at the connotations of such a privilege. Many communists believed it to be the crowning achievement of the post-Marcos period. Sison, who for reasons that were not clear attached little importance to the cease-fire, believed that the semblance of parity which the signing conferred was the only attainment of value. "We have the signature of the government and that is the single most important gain," he said during an interview in December. "The National Democratic Front is recognized as a co-equal party in the contract. This is the only advantage for the left."

Despite the superficial signs of amity, neither the government nor the NDF believed that negotiations during the cease-fire would produce an agreement leading to lasting peace. As the talks began in December 1986, the NDF insisted that it should share power with the Aquino government under some arrangement. This was a revival of the NDF program's position on "coalition government," and in the party's traditional interpretation "coalition" was merely the first stage in forming the national democratic state. Aquino could not possibly accept a power-sharing arrangement with a communist dominated front. On this ground alone, there seemed no room for compromise.

The cease-fire was achieved and the peace talks begun because neither side wished to surrender that elusive quality, moral superiority. For seventeen years under President Marcos, the CPP had enjoyed the position of "good guys" in the struggle against authoritarianism. The Robin Hood role is an extremely compelling one in Philippine lore, drawn as it is from the romantic rebellions waged by bandit gangs against the

Spanish and by the resistance movements which fought both the Americans and Japanese. To break off the peace talks and begin an armed struggle in the hills was to risk losing that moral high ground when the enemy was a popular president. The Aquino government faced a similar dilemma. Defeating the communists militarily would require a long, exhausting, and bloody civil war, the success of which would turn on the support of millions of poor farmers and workers. Deeply suspicious of the NDF line, warned by the powerful church to avoid concessions on basic issues, Aquino nevertheless felt that she, too, had to preserve moral authority. A precipitate breaking off of the peace talks could cost her much of the high ground she had won. And so the talks went on.

This book must end at a point of maximum uncertainty, with the government and the communist movement talking peace but planning more war, with both the AFP and the NPA training for combat in their respective camps. Any one of several outcomes seems possible, including total civil war, extended negotiations, and a combination of the two, a talk-and-fight scenario lasting for months. There was, too, the possibility that if the cease-fire was prolonged indefinitely, the conflict might resolve into an electoral struggle with the communist movement, through its new front party which included many non-communists, concentrating on the first elections of the post-Marcos era. It was useless to speculate on the possibilities. The calm at the end of 1986 offered a better opportunity to look back and examine the forces and events which had produced such a fateful moment.

The Philippine rebellion contained the three ingredients common to most Third World revolutions of our times. There was the popular base of impoverished peasants and farm workers who for centuries had been an impotent mass of passive victims. There was the middle-class intelligentsia to ignite them, in this case that gifted corps of nationalists and reformers who drifted in the current of their times into radicalism. And finally there was the ideology of Marxism which fused and cemented them into a single force and sustained them through many reverses. These were the elements combined in the formula which had brought victory to Mao in China, Ho Chi Minh in Vietnam, Castro in Cuba, and the Sandinistas in Nicaragua.

The Philippine experience proved that this combination does not always form an irrepressible tide sweeping inevitably toward victory. What the Communist Party of the Philippines had accomplished by late 1986 was formidable but not overwhelming. The NPA was a hit-and-run army of perhaps 25,000 inadequately armed guerillas lacking sanctuary and foreign support and pitted against government forces perhaps six to eight times its size. The NDF held footholds, some solid and some precarious, in perhaps one-fourth of the country. Sison's communist party had come far in eighteen years but it was not yet the overpowering force capable of toppling a popular government.

The CPP's progress had occurred in a period historically most favorable to communist insurgency. The Marcos era was a Marxist's paradise. A corrupt, authoritarian ruler backed by an abusive military machine and an impotent civil government is a well-worn formula for communist success, and for most of its eighteen years the CPP had enjoyed the role of leadership against that kind of regime. It grew most swiftly in the early 1980s when it could claim a superiority over other groups opposing Marcos, when it could point to those noisy factions and declare: "They talk, we act." They presented the hard and familiar choice which has faced so many caught in the middle of events in our times: Not to choose the communist way was itself a choice, one in favor of continued autocracy.

The Aquino government, whatever its strengths and faults, for at least a time removed the necessity for such a choice. The fall of Marcos cost the communists considerable support among the educated middle class and the clergy, those who had been tempted before to side with the party. Aquino's accession changed the moral equation overnight in the Philippines because those seeking a commitment to right old wrongs no longer had only the choice offered by the communists. They could rally around her, restrain the military, and begin that vast restructuring of Philippine society that was needed to bring peaceful social change. In truth, I found few Filipinos of any persuasion in that winter of 1986 who believed that this would happen. But the new choice was at least available. And Corazon

259

Aquino's will and resourcefulness had already proved surprisingly productive.

But the communist movement which she faced was also resourceful, possessed of several strengths and, I concluded, underestimated by a great many Philippine leaders. Indeed, with a few notable exceptions, the Philippine establishment which replaced Marcos's reign seemed to me to be as uninformed about the CPP and the leftist movement as its predecessor. There was the same inclination not to take that movement seriously, to regard the events of the past eighteen years as the curious pastime of some misguided intellectuals fond of playing at revolution. For months after Aquino's accession, prominent leaders in her government still clung to the belief that the renegades would at any moment come down from the hills to seek amnesty and that their peasant army would exchange their weapons for a few hectares of government supplied land. This displaced optimism, or, as some would have it, this willing suspension of disbelief, on the part of Philippine leaders, survived long after it became clear that the communist movement would not fade away.

The Philippine movement is versatile and flexible and has avoided so far that ideological rigidity which seems to have afflicted some others like it in the Third World. Its beginnings owed much to Mao, but it had jettisoned the more restrictive parts of Maoism as soon as they proved impractical. It has made room for all kinds of pragmatic changes, ranging from tactical reforms on the battlefield to strategic reversals of sweeping import. Born of disgust with the tepid "parliamentary struggle" of the old communist party, for example, the CPP had by 1986 embraced electoral politics as a possible key to national victory. A doctrinaire party might have fought the Catholic Church. The CPP used the church and sought to bend it to the movement's service, preaching all the while that there was no essential conflict in being both communist and Catholic. Dogmatic exclusivity might have restricted a movement in a country as varied as the Philippines. The CPP and the NDF, instead, reached out to every identifiable group and class—to Catholic priests, Muslims, middle-class intellectuals, former bandit gangs, and even the most backward native tribes.

A second important strength was the evolution of a collective leadership which seemed to replace itself after each reversal. The capture in the mid-1970s of its principal theorist (Sison) and its most formidable field tactician (Dante) might have decimated a tightly structured organization run from the top by charismatic generalissimos. Instead, they were replaced by relatively unknown figures who prepared the party and its army for the years of greatest growth. Perhaps there were instances in which the capture or death of a local commander affected the NPA's effectiveness, but I heard of none, not even from the Philippine military, whose very competent intelligence network seemed always aware of the NPA leaders down to the squad level. The collegial leadership in the CPP Central Committee's executive committee and in the regional bodies, I suspect, was a major reason why the movement thrived and did not fade away.

The absence of foreign communist support—money, guns and ammunition—was the main restraint on the growth of the NPA. But it was also a movement strength. For one thing, it enabled party front organizers to portray the movement, accurately, as a totally indigenous one unsullied by foreign intervention. It also freed the party leadership to act on its own instincts, without having to consult with foreign advisers or to worry that some ideological deviance might result in their supply lines being cut. The former, I thought, was especially important in recruiting middle-class supporters and non-ideological liberals who might have spurned a party linked to Moscow or Beijing. As the remarks of Ocampo (Chapter 1) and others show, the CPP's disdain for foreign assistance has faded and offers from the Soviet Union or some Third World revolutionary government would now be welcomed. It remains to be seen whether the about-face would stain the respect garnered from years as a nationalist and indigenous radical movement.

Finally, the movement has been strengthened, especially in its most recent years, by the recruitment of a new young leadership drawn directly from the peasant base. No longer is it an organization of the poor and uneducated led by an estranged elite from the universities. In the communities and villages which I visited, the leadership positions were increasingly being filled by men and women who had little formal education, whose young adulthood had been spent fighting or organizing

261

for the local front groups and the NPA. The view from Manila of the communist movement is still largely one of the University of the Philippines drop-out hustling an assortment of dumb peasants. At the local level, that is an increasingly unrealistic view. It is true that many in the higher echelons of party and army are from middle-class and university backgrounds, the martial-law babies grown up, so to speak. But their numbers and influence are diminishing. It is more common now to find local positions being filled by the likes of Javier, the Panay NDF leader who turned radical because he could not afford high school, or of Dina, the brassy squatter's daughter who rose to party leadership in Punta Dumalag. These examples suggest two thoughts. One is that the movement's roots go deeper than most outsiders have suspected. The other is that these new-comers will shortly be in command and in a position to take the party where they want it to go. I suspect, too, that they will be more militant than many of their predecessors and less likely to seek the sort of political solutions to which the older college crowd now seems open. They have made the communist movement a part of the everyday life of thousands of communities in the Philippines and have tasted the pleasures of many local military victories. It is difficult to imagine the Javiers and the Dinas of that country giving up their struggles and melting once more into the background.

The *carabao* is the Philippine farmer's most valuable posses-sion, his means of earning a livelihood. It is a large ponderous animal which plods unhurriedly through its chores—hauling wagons, plowing fields, churning mud in the rice paddies. The *carabao* has also been transformed in popular culture into a national symbol, its rather unromantic traits made to represent the best in the nature of the common man. It is said that, like the *carabao,* the Filipino is patient to a fault and slow to anger but when once aroused fights tenaciously and ferociously. The metaphor seems appropriate in view of the life of the Philippine revolution. The *carabao* has been aroused.

Acknowledgments
★★★

The primary sources of information for this book were interviews with members of the Communist Party of the Philippines and farmers, workers, priests and others who were associated with the National Democratic Front and the New People's Army. A large proportion of the interviews were conducted among party members and sympathizers at the local level, especially in Negros, Panay, Cebu and Davao.

The interviews took place between December 1984, and December 1986, most of them before that period of leniency when members of the underground could surface without fear of arrest. For that reason, almost all of them insisted on using their underground, or party, names, and they are so identified in the text.

In arranging the interviews, I enjoyed the assistance of several intermediaries. Among them I would like especially to thank two friends who are known by their party names of Anaya and Juana Claros.

Outside the Left, I interviewed a large number of persons—businessmen, farmers, journalists, politicians and professional and military people—who were on the sidelines of the revolution and had watched it unfold from positions of detachment. Many were especially helpful in verifying or challenging the versions of events received initially from the CPP, NDF and NPA. The responsibility for deciding what to believe and what not to believe is mine.

I am also grateful to many other knowledgeable Filipinos who agreed to discuss the communist movement and Philippine affairs in general. Among those particularly helpful, I would like to thank F. Sionil José, Francisco Nemenzo, Bishops Francisco Claver and Antonio Fortich, Fathers Ireneo Gordoncillo and Romeo Empestan, Felix Bautista, Abby Tan, José Diokno, J. V. Bautista, Leto Villar, Ricardo Arnaldo, Laurente Ilagan, Zafiro Respicio, Cesar Europa, Zenaida Uy and Paul Rodriguez. At the Ministry of National Defense, I was fortunate to have the cooperation of Silvestre C. Afable, Jr., assistant secretary of defense for public affairs, Brig. Gen. Eduardo Ermita, deputy chief of staff, and Navy Captain Rex Robles.

Two excellent books on Philippine agrarian revolt were of immense help in understanding the background out of which the present communist movement emerged. They are *The Huk Rebellion: A Study of Peasant Revolt in The Philippines,* by Benedict J. Kerkvliet (Berkeley: University of California Press, 1977) and *Huk: Philippine Agrarian Society In Revolt,* by Eduardo Lachica (Manila: Solidaridad Publishing House, 1971).

Among books not directly related to the present communist movement, the following were helpful:

Bernstein, David. *The Philippine Story.* New York: Farrar, Strauss, 1947.

Buss, Claude A. *The Arc of Crisis.* Garden City: Doubleday, 1961.

Constantino, Renato and Letizia. *The Philippines: The Continuing Past.* Manila: Foundation For Nationalist Studies, 1978.

Friend, Theodore. *Between Two Empires.* New Haven: Yale University Press, 1965.

Golay, Frank H. *The Philippines: Public Policy and National Economic Development.* Ithaca: Cornell University Press, 1961.

Grunder, Garel A., and William E. Livezey. *The Philippines and the United States.* Norman: University of Oklahoma Press, 1951.

Jenkins, Shirley. *American Economic Policy toward the Philippines.* Stanford: Stanford University Press, 1954.

Kirk, Grayson L. *Philippine Independence: Motives, Problems and Prospects.* New York: Farrar and Rinehart, 1936.

Lansdale, Edward G. *In the Midst of Wars* (New York: Harper and Row, 1972).

Lichauco, Alejandro. *The Lichauco Papers: Imperialism in the Philippines.* New York: Monthly Review Press, 1973.

Mijares, Primitivo. *The Conjugal Dictatorship of Ferdinand and Imelda Marcos.* San Francisco: Union Square Publications, 1976.

Nemenzo, Francisco, ed. *The Philippines after Marcos.* Sydney: Croom Helm Ltd., 1985.

Rosenberg, David A., ed. *Marcos and Martial Law in the Philippines.* Ithaca: Cornell University Press, 1979.

Saulo, Alfred B. *Communism in the Philippines: An Introduction.* Manila: Ateneo de Manila Publications, 1969.

Shalom, Stephen. *The United States and the Philippines: A Study of New Colonialism.* Philadelphia: Institute For the Study of Human Issues, 1981.

Stanley, Peter W. *A Nation in the Making: The Philippines and the United States, 1899–1921.* Cambridge: Harvard University Press, 1974.

Steinberg, David J. *Philippine Collaboration in World War II.* Ann Arbor: University of Michigan Press, 1967.

Sturtevant, David R. *Popular Uprisings in the Philippines, 1840–1940.* Ithaca: Cornell University Press, 1976.

Taruc, Luis. *He Who Rides The Tiger* (New York: Praeger, 1967).

Taylor, George E. *The Philippines and the United States: Problems of Partnership.* New York: Praeger, 1964.

Notes
☆☆☆

Chapter 1

[1] Armitage, testimony before House Foreign Affairs Committee, Subcommittee on Asian and Pacific Affairs, October 4, 1984.

[2] "The Philippines: A Situation Report," Staff Report to the Senate Select Committee on Intelligence, October 31, 1985, page 2.

[3] Department of State, "United States Policy toward the Philippines," executive summary, page 2.

[4] "The Philippines: A Situation Report," page 17.

Chapter 2

[1] The New York *Times,* July 4, 1946.

[2] Ibid.

[3] Roxas, Inaugural Address, July 4, 1946.

[4] Finley Peter Dunne, *Mr. Dooley In Peace And War,* (Boston: Small, Maynard, 1898), p. 45.

[5] Quoted in Teodoro A. Agoncillo, *A Short History of The Philippines* (Mentor Edition, New American Library, 1975), p. 162.

[6] Quezon's equivocations are discussed in Peter W. Stanley, *A Nation in the Making, The Philippines and the United States, 1899–1921* (Cambridge: Harvard University Press, 1974), pp. 169–170, and 182.

[7] Taft, speech in Montpelier, Vermont, August 26, 1904.

8 Manuel L. Quezon, *The Good Fight* (New York: Appleton-Century, 1946), pp. 107–108.

9 Grayson L. Kirk, *Philippine Independence: Motives, Problems and Prospects* (New York: Farrar and Rinehart, 1936), pp. 94 and 136.

10 Congress passed the Hawes-Cutting Act for Philippine independence over President Hoover's veto in January 1933. In Manila, Quezon engineered its rejection by the Philippine legislature for several reasons, one of them being its insistence on retaining U.S. army bases in the country after independence. The Tydings-McDuffie Act was enacted in 1934, leaving the bases issue obscure, and was accepted by the Philippine government. It provided for a ten-year transitional period beginning in 1935 to be followed by complete independence.

11 Tydings, Hearings before House Ways and Means Committee on the Philippine Trade Act, 1946. Cited in Shirley Jenkins, *American Economic Policy Toward The Philippines* (Stanford: Stanford University Press, 1954), p. 56.

12 From Stephen R. Shalom, *The United States and the Philippines: A Study of Neocolonialism* (Quezon City: New Day Publishers, 1986), p. 61.

13 Agoncillo, *A Short History of the Philippines,* p. 285.

14 Recto, cited in Renato Constantino, *The Making of a Filipino: A Story of Philippine Colonial Politics* (Quezon City: Malaya Books, 1969), p. 105.

15 Ibid., p. 119.

16 Recto, address at Arellano University, Manila, April 9, 1949.

17 Recto, address at the University of the Philippines, April 17, 1951.

18 Ibid. His reference to "unequal treaties" was to those forced on China and Japan by Western nations in the past. These included one-sided commercial agreements and extraterritorial rights. The latter sometimes provided that foreigners who committed crimes would not be subjected to arrest and trial by authorities in those countries.

19 Ibid.

20 Quoted in Agoncillo, *Filipino Nationalism, 1872–1970* (Quezon City: Garcia, 1974), p. 300.

21 Quoted in Agoncillo, *Filipino Nationalism 1872–1970,* op. cit., pp. 72–73.

22 Quoted in Renato and Letizia R. Constantino, *The Philippines: The Continuing Past* (Manila: Foundation for Nationalist Studies, 1978), p. 276.

23 Joseph Burkholder Smith, *Portrait of a Cold Warrior* (New York: Putnam, 1976), p. 280.

24 Quoted in Claude A. Buss, *The United States and the Philippines: Background for Policy* (Washington: American Enterprise Institute For Public Policy Research, 1977), p. 37.

25 From a newspaper column by Carmen Guerrero-Nakpil, undated, cited in Claude A. Buss, *Arc of Crisis* (Garden City: Doubleday, 1961), p. 155.

26 Cited in Buss, *The United States and the Philippines: Background for Policy,* p. 38.

27 Nemenzo, Francisco, "Divergence And Consensus: Trends in Philippine Communism," p. 9 of paper presented at Seminar on Armed Communism in

Southeast Asia, Institute of Southeast Asian Studies, Singapore, November 17, 1982.

[28] From author's interview with a former student who requested anonymity. The reference to Filipinos being killed referred to several shootings by American military base guards of natives who were caught scavenging for waste metal. The United States held criminal jurisdiction over such offenses and the guilty servicemen were frequently transferred out of the country to avoid trial.

[29] From author's interview with Francisco Nemenzo.

[30] From author's interview with Sison.

Chapter 3

[1] The exposition of the Huk revolt draws heavily on the brilliant study by Benedict J. Kerkvliet of the University of Hawaii. See *The Huk Rebellion: A Study of Peasant Revolt in the Philippines* (Quezon City: New Day Publishers, 1979).

[2] Kerkvliet, p. 41.

[3] Ibid., p. 43.

[4] Taruc, Luis, *Born of the People* (New York: International Publishers, 1953), p. 56.

[5] Kerkvliet, op. cit., p. 99.

[6] From an interview with Alejandrino in *Solidarity,* No. 102 (1985): 67.

[7] Cited in Eduardo Lachica, *Huk: Philippine Agrarian Society In Revolt* (Manila: Solidaridad Publishing House, 1971), pp. 113–14.

[8] Kerkvliet, p. 146. This study contains several first-hand accounts of the repression.

[9] Jesus Lava, From an interview with Lava in *Solidarity,* no. 102 (1985): 83.

[10] Kerkvliet, p. 233.

[11] William Pomeroy, *The Forest* (New York: International Publishers, 1963), p. 157.

[12] Events in the final years of the old Huk movement are drawn from Lachica, p. 156–63; *Sunday* Magazine (Manila) (April 6, 1986): 3–8; and Francisco Nemenzo, "Philippine Communism after the Huk Rebellion," a paper presented at a meeting of the Asian Studies Association of Australia, Adelaide University, May 13–19, 1984.

Chapter 4

[1] Interviewee requested anonymity.

[2] Nemenzo, interview.

[3] Rodriguez, José, "Our Idle Millions, A Potential Powder-keg," *Weekly Graphic,* Manila (July 13, 1966): 22. (Cited in Justus M. van der Kroef, "Communist Fronts In The Philippines," from *Problems of Communism* (March–April, 1967): 74).

[4] Nemenzo, Francisco, "Philippine Communism after the Huk Rebellion," p. 8.

[5] Cited in Lachica, *Huk: Philippine Agrarian Society in Revolt,* p. 178.

[6] Sison, interview.

268

7 Nemenzo, "Rectification Process in the Philippine Communist Movement," from *Armed Insurgencies In Southeast Asia* (New York: St. Martin's Press, 1984), p. 75.

8 Sison, interview.

9 Nemenzo, "Rectification Process in the Philippine Communist Movement," op. cit. p. 80.

10 Sison, interview.

11 These accounts are drawn from interviews with the Sisons and military records cited in Lachica, op. cit.

12 Lachica, op. cit. p. 192.

13 Interviewee requested anonymity.

Chapter 5

1 Smith, *Portrait of a Cold Warrior,* op. cit. p. 137.

2 *Between Two Empires* (Manila: Solidaridad Publishing House, 1969) p. 29.

3 Arnold Abrams, "Kings For A Day," from *Far Eastern Economic Review* (December 4, 1969).

4 Benedict J. Kerkvliet, ed., *Political Change in the Philippines: Studies of Local Politics Preceding Martial Law* (Honolulu: University of Hawaii Press, 1974), p. 20.

5 "Society Without Purpose," from *Graphic,* (January 17, 1968). Reprinted in Constantino, *Dissent and Counterconsciousness* (Manila: Erewhon, 1970), p. 13.

6 From "MAN's Goal: The Democratic Filipino Society," adopted March 15–16, 1969. Mimeograph.

7 Marcos, Inaugural Address, 1966.

8 Benigno S. Aquino, "What's Wrong with the Philippines?" reprinted in *Solidarity,* No. 102 (1985): 12.

9 Cited in Lachica, *Philippine Agrarian Society in Revolt* p. 193–194.

10 Harvey A. Averch, John E. Koehler, and Frank H. Denton, *The Matrix of Policy in the Philippines* (Princeton: Princeton University Press, 1971).

11 Enrile disclosed in 1986 that the "attack" on his limousine had been faked. For accounts of phony bombings and other incidents, see Primitivo Mijares, *The Conjugal Dictatorship of Ferdinand and Imelda Marcos* (San Francisco: Union Square Publications, 1976), p. 33, et. seq. Mijares was a news reporter close to Marcos and later his "media czar." He disappeared shortly after publication of the book.

12 From an interview entitled "Asia Philippine Leader" (April 1, 1971), cited in David Wurfel, "Martial Law In The Philippines," *Pacific Affairs* (Spring, 1977).

13 A striking number of the party cadres whom I interviewed also recalled their parents enduring financial setbacks and loss of social status. Julie Sison once said that her husband had come from a "declining landlord family."

Chapter 6

1 Details of the raid at Isabela were provided by Francisco, who led the NPA contingent, and by Raymondo Espiritu, who was appointed officer-in-charge, or temporary mayor, of the town in 1985.

[2] From a captured NPA document, cited in Lachica op. cit., p. 313.

[3] "Specific Characteristics of Our People's War," in *Philippine Society and Revolution* (Reprinted by International Association of Filipino Patriots, Oakland, Calif., 1979), p. 188.

[4] Ibid., p. 184.

[5] Armitage, "Situation in the Philippines and Implications for U.S. Policy," statement submitted to the Subcommittee on Asian and Pacific Affairs, House Foreign Affairs Committee, October 1, 1984, p. 6.

[6] This version of the assassination was supplied by a Bacolod citizen sympathetic to the NPA. It matches official police accounts.

Chapter 7

[1] *Ang Bayan,* April 1984, p. 10.

[2] The *New York Times,* August 11, 1985, p. 1.

[3] From a memorandum by Bernard Wideman, May 21, 1979. Wideman, an American journalist, reported on the Philippines for the *Far Eastern Economic Review* and the *Washington Post.*

[4] *Ang Bayan,* February 1984, p. 8.

[5] This version of the Karingal killing was supplied by a communist party official in Manila. A KMU labor leader gave an identical version and proclaimed it a victory for the union.

[6] From "Our Urgent Tasks," in *Philippine Society and Revolution,* p. 231.

[7] Interviewee requested anonymity.

[8] Interview with Luni in Davao.

[9] Quoted in Henry W. Bragdon, and Samuel P. McCutchen, *History Of A Free People* (New York: MacMillan, 1960).

[10] *Ang Bayan,* November 1984.

[11] *Ang Bayan,* November 1985.

Chapter 8

[1] Interviewee requested anonymity.

[2] The *New York Times,* March 4, 1986.

[3] *Far Eastern Economic Review,* January 2, 1986, p. 15.

Chapter 9

[1] The story of "Baby" Aquino is drawn from personal interviews and accounts in the *Asian Wall Street Journal,* February 12, 1985, and the *Washington Post,* June 5, 1986.

[2] The *Washington Post,* August 15, 1984.

[3] "Programme for a People's Democratic Revolution," in Lachica, op. cit., p. 298.

[4] *Philippine Society and Revolution,* p. 298.

[5] From *Philippine Society and Revolution,* p. 185.

[6] "Our Urgent Tasks," from *Philippine Society and Revolution,* p. 255.

[7] The *New York Times,* May 13, 1985.

[8] "Rectification Process in the Philippine Communist Movement," a paper delivered at seminar on Armed Communism in Southeast Asia, Institute of Southeast Asia Studies, Singapore, November 17–19, 1982.

Chapter 10

[1] Cited in United States Department of State, Report on Human Rights, 1983.
[2] Hearings, Subcommittee on Asian and Pacific Affairs, U.S. House of Representatives Committee on Foreign Affairs, June 17, 1983.
[3] Hearings, United States Senate Committee on Foreign Relations, October 30, 1985.
[4] "The Situation in the Philippines," staff report prepared for the Committee on Foreign Relations, U.S. Senate, October 1984.
[5] Hearings, U.S. House of Representatives Committee on Foreign Affairs, subcommittee on Human Rights and International Organizations, September 22, 1983.
[6] The official asked for anonymity.
[7] An account of the AFP soldier's privations is found in Michael Richardson, *International Herald Tribune,* July 5–6, 1986.

Chapter 11

[1] José Rizal, *Noli Me Tangere,* translated by Leon Ma. Guerrero (London: Longman Group Ltd., 1961), p. 98.
[2] Cited in Garel A. Grunder, and William E. Livezey, *The Philippines and the United States* (Norman: University of Oklahoma Press, 1951), p. 126.
[3] *Veritas,* April 9, 1984, p. 12.
[4] "Liberation Praxis and the Christian Faith," in *Frontiers of Theology in Latin America,* Rosini Gibellini, ed. (Maryknoll, N.Y.: Orbis Books, 1979), p. 7.
[5] Account given by Father Romeo Empestan, author interview, December 1985.
[6] Earl Martin, "The Philippine Church Amidst Revolution," from *Peace Section Newsletter,* Vol. XII, No. 5 (September–October 1982), published by the Mennonite Central Committee, Akron, Pa. Martin had been a missionary in Bukidnon.
[7] Col. Galileo C. Kintanan, "Contemporary Religious Radicalism in the Philippines," from the *Quarterly National Security Review of the National Defense College of the Philippines* (mimeograph, undated).
[8] "The BCC-CO Program: An Orientation." Special issue of May 1983, published in Manila by the BCC-CO secretariat (mimeograph).
[9] From an untitled BCC-CO manual widely circulated in the Visayas.
[10] Ibid.
[11] Christians for National Liberation, Second National Congress, undated documents. The papers were provided to the author by a member of CNL.
[12] Ibid.
[13] CPP documents cited in Dennis Shoesmith, "The Church," from *The Philippines After Marcos,* R. J. May, and Francisco Nemenzo, eds. (Kent: Croom Helm Ltd., 1985) p. 84.

271

[14] Quoted in *Yearbook of International Communism,* Stanford University, 1978, p. 284.

[15] "The Role Of The Church Under Martial Law," a national survey by the Major Religious Superiors of the Philippines, November 26, 1973 (mimeograph).

[16] Abby Tan, the *Washington Post,* July 5, 1979. Quoted in memo to author.

[17] Address to the Manila Rotary Club, October 21, 1982.

[18] *Asian Wall Street Journal,* September 23–24, 1983.

[19] Address, September 4, 1984.

Chapter 12

[1] "Programme for a People's Democratic Revolution," in Lachica, p. 287 (emphasis added).

[2] "The People's Revolutionary Struggle and the National Democratic Front in Mindanao, 1985." The memorandum was given to author by a party member in Mindanao.

[3] "Program of the National Democratic Front of the Philippines," revised draft, January 1985, p. 11.

[4] "Onward with the Struggle for National Democracy," published by the National Alliance for Justice, Freedom and Democracy, November 1984, p. 13.

[5] Nemenzo, "Rectification Movement in the Philippine Communist Movement," p. 89.

[6] "Programme for a People's Democratic Revolution," Lachica, p. 300.

[7] Ibid., p. 300.

[8] Preparatory Commission, National Democratic Front, November 12, 1977, p. 1 (mimeograph).

[9] Interview in *Midweek* (Manila) (July 23, 1986): 3.

Chapter 13

[1] *Time,* December 16, 1985.

[2] *Ang Bayan,* January 15, 1986.

[3] Ibid.

[4] *International Herald Tribune,* December 30, 1985.

[5] *Ang Bayan,* January 15, 1986.

[6] *Midweek* (Manila) (July 23, 1986): 9.

[7] *Midweek* (Manila) (July 23, 1986): 16.

[8] Interview with Brig. Gen. Eduardo Ermita, deputy chief of staff, New Armed Forces of the Philippines, July 30, 1986.

Chapter 14

[1] Francisco Tatad, in *Business Day* (Manila), cited in dispatch by the Associated Press, December 11, 1986.

Index

★ ★ ★

273

279

284

287